# You Run the Show
# or the Show Runs You

**Professor Harold W. Rood**

# You Run the Show
# or the Show Runs You

*Capturing Professor Harold W. Rood's*
*Strategic Thought for a New Generation*

## J. D. Crouch II and Patrick J. Garrity

ROWMAN & LITTLEFIELD
Lanham • Boulder • New York • London

Published by Rowman & Littlefield
A wholly owned subsidiary of The Rowman & Littlefield Publishing Group, Inc.
4501 Forbes Boulevard, Suite 200, Lanham, Maryland 20706
www.rowman.com

Unit A, Whitacre Mews, 26-34 Stannary Street, London SE11 4AB, United Kingdom

British Library Cataloguing in Publication Information Available

**Library of Congress Cataloging-in-Publication Data Available**

Crouch II, J. D., and Garrity, Patrick J.
You run the show or the show runs you : Capturing Professor Harold W. Rood's strategic thought for
a new generation / by J. D. Crouch II and Patrick J. Garrity.
p. cm.
Includes bibliographical references and index.
ISBN 978-1-4422-4473-3 (cloth : alk. paper) -- ISBN 978-1-4422-4474-0 (electronic)
1. 2. 3. I. II. Title.

♾™ The paper used in this publication meets the minimum requirements of American
National Standard for Information Sciences Permanence of Paper for Printed Library
Materials, ANSI/NISO Z39.48-1992.

This book is dedicated to the men and women of America's armed forces for their sacrifice on behalf of their fellow citizens in the preservation of our liberty, and alongside whom Professor Rood fought.

# Contents

# Acknowledgments

We must begin, of course, by acknowledging our personal and intellectual debt to Professor Harold W. Rood, scholar, gentleman, and patriot. Professor Rood's family kindly allowed us to quote and cite many of his published and unpublished writings. Those of us who studied with Dr. Rood, even if we never ventured to his northern California rural abode, were well aware of how important those writings were to him.

We thank the Claremont Institute for allowing us to draw on the writings he published for it over the years, including those in the *Claremont Review of Books*, and the U.S. Naval Institute *Proceedings* for permission to cite from Professor Rood's article, "Distant Rampart" (Copyright © 1967 U.S. Naval Institute/www.usni.org). Donavan Chau and Christopher Harmon generously allowed us access to letters and writings of Dr. Rood that were in their possession.

We deeply appreciate the time and trouble taken by Daniel Palm, Kevin Smith, Christopher Flannery, Stephen Cambone, and the late William R. Van Cleave, to review various drafts of the manuscript.

The members of the extended Rood community, too numerous to thank individually, have done much to perpetuate his memory and teachings. We note especially the assistance of the Claremont Institute (Brian Kennedy, Ryan Williams, John Kienker, and Ben Judge); the Henry Salvatori Center at Claremont McKenna College (Charles Kesler and Mark Blitz); the Ashbrook Center at Ashland University (Peter Schramm, Roger Beckett, David Tucker, Ben Kunkel, and Lisa Ormiston); Hillsdale College (Larry P. Arnn, Mickey Craig, Matthew Spalding, and R. J. Pestritto); and the Missouri State University Department of Defense and Strategic Studies (Keith Payne and John Rose). Colleen Sheehan and her most capable colleagues and students (William B. Allen, Brenda Hafera, and Alexios Alexander) at the Ryan Center, Villanova University, played a critical role in the preparation of the manuscript. The Miller Center at the University of Virginia, as always, provided a welcome home for Dr. Garrity's research (Andrew Chauncey, Marc Selverstone, and David Coleman).

The most able editorial staff at Rowman & Littlefield, in particular Jon Sisk, Elaine McGarraugh, and Benjamin Verdi, ensured that the manuscript received all the help it needed.

The Earhart Foundation, which supported Professor Rood and his students over many years, once again came to the aid of a good cause, through a grant to assist the book's completion and promotion.

We are sure that we are leaving someone out who should have been recognized, as is perhaps inevitable when one rushes to complete another impossible Rood assignment at the last moment, and for that we apologize sincerely. Professor Rood would never have forgotten any of his students, of that we are sure. We hope he will grade this paper indulgently, with lots of useful marginal comments. And then off to breakfast at Walter's or dinner at La Paloma.

# Introduction

Professor Harold W. (Bill) Rood (1922–2011) taught courses in International Relations, Diplomacy and Military Power, American Foreign Policy, Constitutional Development in the West, and Politics and Technology, at Claremont McKenna (Men's) College and Claremont Graduate School, and in the Defense and Strategic Studies programs at the University of Southern California and Missouri State University. He influenced his students profoundly, even those who disagreed with all or part of his teachings, but he published comparatively little. What he did write is scattered about. His one major work, *Kingdoms of the Blind: How the Great Democracies Have Resumed the Follies That So Nearly Cost Them Their Life* (1980), is out of print and difficult to find. He pointedly avoided the traditional means of promoting himself and his works. He showed no interest in assuming policy responsibilities. As a result, he was not well known outside his circle of students and friends, all of whom agreed that he and his ideas should be much better known.

In this book, we attempt to document and synthesize Professor Rood's core teachings to preserve them as best we can, and to stimulate new thinking in his intellectual spirit. We have tried to reconstruct the approaches, arguments, and views of Professor Rood in a fair and accurate rendering. Throughout this work we present his views, not ours. It is not our goal either to endorse or renounce them, but to reveal their substance, depth, and inner logic to the students of international politics who will never have the opportunity to experience his teaching.

It is impossible to convey fairly the force—and the charm—of his manner of teaching. You really had to be there. Yet as we opened our files and boxes to compose this text, we reminded ourselves of how remarkably rich, thoughtful, and provocative his arguments were then, and still remain today. We think they are well worth exploring with a new generation of students and friends in new times which, as Rood would be the first to tell us, are perhaps not so new after all.

Our presentation of his thought is necessarily uneven, as Rood did not flesh out in writing all of his many ideas and arguments. Doubtless, while we have tried to be faithful to our understanding of these teachings, some may say we "got it wrong." If that is the case, we ask your indulgence for whatever errors this volume may contain, but we will have achieved one of our objectives at least: to stimulate a rethinking of the applicability of the views and approaches he presented on international politics.

We base this text on his writings, published and in manuscript, our lecture notes, his classroom study guides, and the collective memories of his students. We have organized his thoughts into what strikes us as a logical framework, using his own words as much as possible (even if they are not directly quoted). This involved a certain degree of repetition of some of his arguments. We have kept our own interpolations to a minimum and attempted to make it clear when we have intervened.[1]

This book is meant to be, so far as that is possible, a presentation of Rood's views for use by students and practitioners as they consider the validity and implications of his dictum that in international relations "you run the show or the show runs you." Rood wanted, above all, to instruct his students in the hard logic of power, especially as that logic played out in international politics. He was concerned with dispelling what he thought to be the comforting illusions that often plague democracies and Western intellectuals on that score, particularly as they confronted totalitarianism and its ideological defenders.[2] If you want to know what is really going on, he would say, "ask a truck driver." He wanted to educate the future leaders of the country in the hopes that they might apply the lessons learned in their studies: "In a world that can promise neither peace nor safety to sovereign nations, it is the burden of statesmanship to look ahead to distant dangers that are today obscured by more immediate concerns, only visible, perhaps to the informed, thoughtful and far-sighted."[3] Above all, he wanted to educate ordinary citizens in their duties, especially for the time when they (or their children) might have to put their lives, fortunes, and sacred honor on the line in defense of the Republic. They deserved to know what the fight was all about, and how and why it was worth fighting.

Rood's teaching style was as distinctive as many of his teachings. He did not use the standard academic texts in his courses, even forgoing Hans Morgenthau's *Politics among Nations*, then the bible for academic realists. Nor did he typically assign historical classics such as Clausewitz (Sun Tzu, interestingly, was the exception). Instead he insisted that his students, as he put it, should figure things out for themselves. He sought to aid them in this process by giving them seemingly impossible research assignments—long before the days of Google—that tested their character as well as their ingenuity (to say nothing of the patience of the librarians, upon whom his students would descend with a list of one hundred obscure terms to define). When a student was ready to read about strategy, Rood believed that no one could consider himself truly educated without, say, having worked through the entire fifty-some volumes of the *United States Army in World War II* series (the Green Books), along with other official military histories, those of the Royal Navy in particular, and of the Prussian Army in the Franco-Prussian War.

To broaden the students' horizons, he recommended unusual sources such as Edward Spears' s*Liaison, 1914* and *Assignment to Catastrophe*, Nicholas Spykman's *America's Strategy in World Politics*, F. E. Adcock's *The Greek and Macedonian Art of War*, J. A. R. Marriott's *The Eastern Question*, the works of John W. Wheeler-Bennett, including *Brest-Litovsk: The Forgotten Peace*, and novels such as *The Cruel Sea* and *The Thirty-Nine Steps*. He believed that, once the students developed their own independent understanding of how the world worked, they would naturally be drawn to the classics without becoming slaves to them—much less be sucked in by the "mostly nonsense" he believed passed for cutting-edge scholarship. Rood pointed to texts that summarized the operation of international politics, as opposed to texts of theory about international relations. He developed his own theories, if you can call them that, from a deep understanding of the enduring principles of those operations.[4] As he told one student: "You're trying to become a political scientist, which according to Aristotle, means that you need to know everything—and that's going to take a while."[5]

Rood's engaging style of teaching entertained but was not meant as entertainment; his lessons were often hard, not only in the sense of challenging to grasp, but also sometimes difficult to accept. He typically made his arguments in the most provocative fashion, to stimulate independent thinking. He took positions contrary to the received wisdom of the day. He was, for instance, an indefatigable supporter of the war in Vietnam, long after the establishment had turned against it. He went beyond being merely unconventional, often turning the world upside down for his students. He was prepared, for example, to make the case that the Cuban missile crisis was a victory for the Soviet Union, and that Yugoslavia was not truly non-aligned.

Suffice it to say that his approach of understanding the world around you *before* purporting to explain it was—in an academy filled with international relations theorizing—quite different, to say the least. "All those ponderous words and phrases like 'sufficiency,' 'deterrence,' 'qualitative superiority,' 'essential equivalence,' 'mutual assured destruction' and the rest are obscure in meaning and even when explained, leave the ordinary sensible mind with the impression of flim-flam," Rood told his students. "To be tempted into asking some simple question like, 'who's going to win if there's a war' is to brand oneself pitifully naïve at best, or at worst, a throwback to some earlier days when wars were won by the side that was strongest and best prepared to wage war."[6] Whatever view one took of Rood's particular arguments, he never left the impression of flim-flam to the ordinary sensible mind. His teaching exemplified the old adage that "an education is what you have after you forget all the facts."[7]

Rood's teachings about power were hard, but they did not abstract morality from the equation—he was hardly a conventional "realist." Although he often cited the famous formulation, from the Melian dialogue in Thucydides, that "the strong do what they will, while the weak suffer what they must," he found that an insufficient guide to what democratic strategy ought to be. "It is only the strong that can afford to be kind and only the strong that can protect the weak."[8]

## THE ORGANIZATION AND SUMMARY OF THE ARGUMENT

Professor Rood's teachings and scholarship challenged his students and colleagues to *think* for themselves. History and common sense should be their guide. Most of his writings that we use in this book were produced from the 1960s through the 1980s (although he had important and unconventional things to say about the wars with Iraq in 1990–1991 and 2003, and about China as late as 2011, as we shall see). If Rood's approach to the study of international politics—about the eternal qualities of strategic principles, rightly understood—has any validity, the dates of publication really should not matter. In fact, their distance from current events gives us some way to judge how well his teachings hold up, recalling Churchill's observation that "time is a long thing." It may still be too soon to tell.

In chapter 1, we summarize Rood's argument about the nature of political life. He argued that human beings are purposeful creatures, who naturally seek to control their environment and to provide themselves with a sense of order and community. They do this through politics—the organization and application of power to accomplish some purpose. Power is intrinsic to politics. Power is necessary to maintain domestic peace and establish justice, and to defend the community against outsiders who would impose their sense of order and justice. It is the responsibility of leaders of legitimate regimes, those that act in the interest of their citizens, to ensure that domestic disorder does not lead to foreign interference in internal affairs, and that war waged by foreigners does not bring about domestic disorder or worse. Peace, justice, and defense are complementary, not antagonistic, objectives.

Defense of the realm is necessary, Rood argued, because politics is at the heart of relationships among governments (chapter 2). There are clashes of will among nations just as there are clashes of will within nations. In international politics, war, according to Rood, is the means by which humans, to a first (if not final) order, determine who will organize things, and for what purpose they will be organized. The enduring factors of international politics include the constant competition of the great powers to organize the international system to their advantage, and the high probability that some great power, sooner or later, will resort to war—at a minimum, the threat of war—to that end. Other great powers, sooner or later, will resist that attempt. Rood thought that certain deeply rooted patterns of international politics, and the great powers' preparations for war, provide important clues as to who is trying to do what to whom, and thus who likely will be one's adversaries and allies. These deeply rooted patterns include the struggles over whether Germany (or China) will be divided or united; the desire of Russia to dominate the accesses to the open seas as well as to control the Eurasian heartland; and the search by the great powers for strategic advantages in the Middle East and the Caribbean Basin.

In this world of great power competition, Rood argued, "you run the show or the show runs you." Running the show is what strategy is all about. For Rood, the ultimate goal in strategy is to confront an enemy with such a preponderance of forces, and such superiority of strategic position from which to deploy those forces, that the enemy, however much he may resist, must ultimately conform to one's will. Chapter 3 describes some of Rood's key teachings about how a nation might seek to run the show and achieve a preponderance of forces—through prewar preparations or through the initial phases of war; by exploiting the complementarity (or unity) of diplomacy and military power; by recognizing the value and limitation of strategic surprise as a component of strategy; through the practice of deception and disinformation; and by creating the conditions for the successful deterrence of war.

Rood did not think that all regimes were equally adept at the practice of strategy. He paid particular attention to a problem that we characterize here as the "democratic strategy deficit" (chapter 4)—the inherent reluctance of democratic peoples to take the possibility of war seriously and thus to ignore preparations by others to wage war against them. Rood believed that both democratic idealists and so-called realists have a persistent blind spot in this regard. He contrasted this with totalitarian views on the nature of politics and war, which assume that politics is a continuation of war by other means, and vice versa. Rood concluded that, as a result, democracies are particularly susceptible to strategic and tactical surprise. He considered the ways in which democracies might overcome this strategic deficit, through strong and responsible executive leadership, and through a military establishment that takes seriously its responsibility to prepare for war.

For most of Rood's professional career, the most important strategic challenge was that of the Soviet (or Russian) Problem. Rood argued that the Soviet Union, and the group of powers that it led, had embarked on a worldwide struggle against the West over the issue of how the world should be organized. In chapter 5, we offer examples of Rood's extensive documentation of how the Soviets had patiently accumulated strategic advantages in Central Europe, the Mediterranean, the Middle East, Southeast Asia, Northeast Asia, and the Caribbean Basin, as well as in conventional and nuclear forces. Soviet tactics included a high degree of deception and disinformation about the nature of the communist world's strategy and objectives. To Rood, these accumulated strategic advantages suggested strongly that the Soviets were preparing to go beyond a Cold

War, to wage a hot one. By the late 1970s, he was convinced that global war was virtually certain unless the United States and its allies took immediate steps to remedy a situation of nascent Soviet strategic superiority. The West, in fact, did so, with apparent great success in the 1980s—but Rood warned that appearances could be deceiving; that the dissolution of the Soviet Union did not necessarily mean that the Russian Problem had been solved; and that in certain respects the problem might even become worse.

The ability of the United States to defend itself and secure its own interests amid the problems in the world—to run the show—depends on its appreciation of sound strategic principles, in the context of America's geographic position, historical experience, and the nature of its regime. In chapter 6, we summarize what Rood believed to be the enduring principles of American strategy: (1) America's wars with transoceanic powers should not be fought on America's soil; therefore (2) if the United States is forced on the strategic defensive at the outset of a war, it should transition, as rapidly as possible, to the strategic offensive; (3) American influence ought to be exerted so that strategic threats to the United States may be contained or canceled without recourse to full-scale or general war; therefore (4) if the United States wants to avoid fighting a big war, it must be prepared to fight a lot of little ones; (5) to execute this strategy, the United States must have allies abroad and bases from which to conduct military operations. Following these strategic principles, the United States must engage itself fully in and along the Eurasian periphery—the "Rimland"—to prevent hostile powers from successfully waging war to dominate the resources of Europe and Asia. He argued that the Vietnam War, rightly understood, should have been fought, and could have been won, on that basis.

Rood did not believe that these American strategic imperatives, and the enduring patterns and problems of international politics, ceased with the end of the Cold War. As we shall see in chapter 7, he maintained that Western efforts to cash in on the "peace dividend," such as the removal of most U.S. combat forces from Europe, tended to undermine the long-term defense of the Rimland and its marginal seas. He believed that the United States still faces challenges by a coalition of hostile powers seeking to reorganize the international system to their individual likings. That reorganization will require the removal of American military power and political influence from Eurasia. To counter this pressure, Rood argued, the United States must find ways to ensure for itself the necessary strategic depth and alliances, so that it can still decide the outcome of Eurasian wars when it finds it in its interest to do so. Based on that line of reasoning, he supported the U.S. war against Iraq in 2003, and the surge in 2007. He was of the opinion that the United States should take the occasion to remove a particularly dangerous dictator and disarm his regime, in order to anchor itself strategically in a key region (as it should have done in

Vietnam), while disrupting the hostile campaign by Iraq's de facto great power allies (Russia and China) to diminish the American presence in Eurasia.

As even this brief summary demonstrates, there is much here to challenge and provoke the reader. Rood's arguments do not fit into many of our comfortable assumptions about how the world works. One might therefore be tempted to dismiss his analysis as being that of a nostalgic member of the "Greatest Generation" or an unreconstructed Cold Warrior. Before doing so, however, one should take seriously his contention that history did not end in 1945 or 1989; that World War II and the U.S.–Soviet conflict were not aberrations but part of the deeper geopolitical grooves that still define the contours of human existence. There may not be another Pearl Harbor, D-Day, or Cuban missile crisis, but those events still hold their lessons, as do Napoleon's invasion of Egypt, the Franco-Prussian War, Japan's Twenty-One Demands, the Zimmerman telegram, and the breakup of the Ottoman Empire and reorganization of the Middle East following World War I.

Rood certainly was not anxious for another great war; quite the contrary. He was not a militarist or a warmonger. Nor was he an armchair general: he served in World War II and the Korea War, and for many years was an intelligence officer in the U.S. Army Reserve. His academic research and military experience led him to conclude that great wars are especially difficult and dangerous for democratic peoples to fight. If great wars are to be avoided without appeasement, Rood insisted, the United States and its allies must follow rigorously the imperatives of strategy—they must run the show. For Rood, the beginning of strategic wisdom is the recognition that wars, and defeat, are still possible.

## NOTES

1. In his writings, Rood provided copious primary and secondary documentation for his arguments, especially those dealing with foreign strategic activities. The authors decided not to overburden the reader of this book with such references, either to the sources that Rood used or to the standard authorities in the field (with the exception of certain texts to which he frequently referred his students). We felt that making Rood's argument as clear and accessible as possible was our primary task. Those interested in more details can consult Rood's original writings. The Claremont Institute's Center for American Grand Strategy (Claremont, CA) will serve as a repository for documents relating to Rood's career. We have also modernized and standardized certain spellings of names and places.

2. As one of his students, and later a colleague, observed: "I think that Dr. Rood worried that the appliances and innovations of modern life had over time blurred our contact with the realities of life and death, be they witnessing births and deaths at home, the slaughter of livestock for a family's sustenance, or the demands of the nation's security. Yet those challenges to the nation, he believed, would be repeated over and over again into the future, and it behooves us as citizens to steel ourselves for the sacrifices that at any time may come." Steve Maaranen, in *Memories of Professor Bill*

*Rood, Scholar and Gentleman, from his Students, Colleagues, and Friends*, ed. Patrick J. Garrity, Christopher Harmon, and Colleen Sheehan (unpublished manuscript, January 2012), Print, 54.

3. Harold W. Rood, "China's Strategical Geography and Its Consequences," in Vol. 1 of *China and International Security: History, Strategy, and 21st Century Policy*, ed. Donovan C. Chau and Thomas M. Kane (Santa Barbara, CA: Praeger, 2014), 1.

4. When a student once asked Dr. Rood whether he subscribed to the Realist Paradigm, he responded by indicating the wall. "That wall is real. If you don't believe me, try walking through it. Now here—" At this, he waved his hands in empty air. "This is a paradigm. Try walking through that, and see how different it feels." Thomas M. Kane, in Garrity et al., *Memories of Professor Bill Rood*, 43.

5. Terry Hallmark, in Garrity et al., *Memories of Professor Bill Rood*, 33.

6. Harold W. Rood, *Kingdoms of the Blind: How the Great Democracies Have Resumed the Follies that So Nearly Cost Them Their Life* (Durham: Carolina Academic Press, 1980), 81–82. "Students of politics, in addition to reading political science journals, should read to find out what's going on in the world." Jeff Hanson, "A Collection of Prof. Harold W. Rood's Quotations," in Garrity et al., *Memories of Professor Bill Rood*, 36.

7. "Meticulous research, the ability to see importance in what might otherwise seem to be unrelated or unimportant events, precision in thinking and writing were expected. Above all, Bill taught us to never stop searching, researching, and learning. Bill's principle was that knowledge and intelligence are what we continually seek and not necessarily what we have." William Van Cleave, in Garrity et al., *Memories of Professor Bill Rood*, 77.

8. Harold W. Rood, "Forty Years On: A Soldier Reflects" (Claremont, CA: Public Research, Syndicated, October 30, 1985), 3. "Only in a very safe environment can you afford to be civilized. . . . One has to be very strong to be kind." Hanson, "A Collection of Prof. Harold W. Rood's Quotations," in Garrity et al., *Memories of Professor Bill Rood*, 34.

# ONE

# The Nature of Politics

## The Inherent Logic of Events

*Professor Rood was not a theorist of international politics in the classic sense. Yet in his teaching of strategy he postulated a number of basic principles related to how politics work and how they operate in the international sphere. This chapter lays out Rood's principles and what he regarded as the important factors and ideas that shape the behavior of states.*

*Those students already steeped in international theory will find in Rood an unconventional approach to this subject, yet one most closely tied to classical realism. Needless to say, there exists an expansive literature with alternative approaches to the subject. Students unfamiliar with international relations theory might consult a survey or two on I.R. theory.*[1]

*Rood's approach was distinguished by his focus on what he regarded as the most immutable aspects of international politics: human nature, the impact of geography and physical constraints, the "constitutional arrangements" through which men seek to control and govern their environment, and the inner logic of historical themes as they interact with others in the sphere of politics. A student or practitioner of international politics should contrast Rood's theory with those of others and ask: "Which seem better aligned with political affairs?"*

In the introductory lectures to his classes, after demonstrating the proper technique to employ a bayonet or the regulation of an old M1A1 carbine or Lee Enfield rifle ("this is International Relations!"), Professor Rood typically laid down the basic assumptions that he thought should inform one's view of the world.

Political events, he told his students, do not as a rule occur at random but instead follow an orderly progression from cause to consequences—"nothing happens for no good reason," as he liked to say. In strategic matters and in the conduct of successful war, there is an inherent and discernible logic. Events connected with such matters may be reasoned through as rigorously as any of the correct proofs of Euclid's propositions. That is because strategy and war deal with physical objects and material events in time and space. And the physical universe has its own inherent and immutable logic that is subject neither to human preference nor to sentiment.[2] "Rather than being subject to sentimentality, strategy is concerned with the laws of the universe—and there are great penalties when they are ignored."[3]

Stated this bluntly, it might appear that Rood was a determinist or a materialist, that he removed individual human agency, as well accident and chance, from the realm of politics and strategy. That was not the case, however—at least not simply so. Human agency, he noted, is not always predictable. Whether men and women actually grasp the inherent logic of strategy as they act politically is a function of their awareness of their own motives and of their grasp of reality, for to suggest that men and women act logically is not to suggest that they will not act on what they prefer to believe rather than on that which can be demonstrated. In societies where public actions can be freely discussed, even those things that can be demonstrated remain the subject of debate, especially if they are the kinds of things that would require a substantial response by all who share in the political community.[4]

Moreover, Rood argued, in the political as in other spheres of human endeavor, appeals to emotion and sentiment are most often disguised as appeals to reason. In its way, this demonstrates the importance that men and women attribute to reason as the right basis of public action. It does not, however, automatically follow that the inherent logic of events in the world will dictate responses appropriate to the nature of the events. Based on observation, logic, and reasoning, it is possible to discern the relationship between events, to grasp the significance of the relationship, and to understand where a chain of events can lead. Yet it is not possible to demonstrate what will happen until after it has happened, when it may be too late to avoid the penalty of inaction or wrong action.[5]

This raises the question of the role and importance of statesmanship and generalship in strategy. Rood did not place particular emphasis on great statesmen or commanders. He focused instead on the deeply rooted elements of international politics and the verities of strategy.[6] For instance, "a small, well-equipped force, gallant and determined, was sure to be defeated by a large, well-equipped, equally determined force."[7] In the realms of accident and chance, the rain falls on the just and unjust alike.

What perhaps elevates enlightened statesmen and great commanders is their clear grasp of the elemental forces and strategic verities, and their ability to use that understanding to shape and execute strategy. They understand what they can accomplish within the limits permitted by physical objects and material events in time and space. Rood could certainly be eloquent in his appreciation of the importance of, say, Winston Churchill, to the defense of Western civilization.

> If Churchill was a politician and office holder he was something more than a sunshine patriot. His country he would have prosper and endure and remain the center of a world-wide empire actuated by love of liberty and based on the rule of law. His affection for the United States came not just with his mother's blood but with his conviction that the English-speaking people had a shared interest and common cause in the preservation and progress of Western civilization. . . . Churchill and Britain were household words to be spoken in a single breath wherever men and women preferred freedom to safety.[8]

For Rood, strategy involved an appreciation of human agency in the broadest sense, that of a fixed and understandable human nature (something that modern social science is at such great pains to deny). One of the most essential facts about human nature is that human beings are purposeful creatures, who naturally seek to organize their environment to provide a sense of control and order. As a political scientist, Rood was not especially interested in how governments were formally organized. More significant, he taught, was the "small c" constitution, what they actually did and how they did it—levied taxes, minted coinage, built roads, established courts, monopolized violence, and defended and extended the security perimeter. All governments worthy of the name did the same. The better of them served the interests and needs of their people.[9] Even during the so-called Dark Ages, Rood said, men and women did not sit about reflecting sadly about how dim the light had become, while waiting for the Renaissance to occur. In the seeming worst of times, they still went about their business, building roads, issuing coins, preparing for war, and the like.[10]

Organization and control are present even in what seem to be the most chaotic and violent of circumstances. There was purpose and organization behind the urban riots in America in the 1960s and in the mass genocides in Africa of the 1990s. After all, Rood observed archly, someone has to staff spontaneous political uprisings and to provide the buses and the sandwiches and protest signs. Human organization, in fact, is not spontaneous—it requires work. For Rood, this is *politics*: "the organization and application of power to accomplish purpose. Power is the capacity to do work, to accomplish physical changes in the world, to exert force, whether on people or on things."[11] Power is intrinsic to politics, something that intellectuals often forget.[12]

> Politics is the organization and application of power for the accomplishments of the purposes of the political community. Power is the capability to alter, move, or destroy physical objects in the universe. Where human beings are the object of the application of power, power

lends the ability to inflict pain, injure, and kill, and therefore to govern, influence, and coerce human beings. Politics deals in conflict and the resolution of conflict.[13]

Politics, then, is at the heart of how groups of human beings arrange themselves or are arranged to achieve some order and predictability in their lives—whether those beings are fortunate enough to govern themselves or must submit to being governed by a special designated few. (Rood taught that technology was the other means besides politics that humans use to organize themselves and to accomplish purpose; but he clearly thought that that technology, in the end, was subordinate to politics.) Those who by right govern themselves, do so most usually through representatives, freely chosen, whose actions take place within arenas of conflict, that is, politics, which reflects the differences of view and purpose existing among those being represented. Where an elite group governs with slight reference to those governed, the arena of conflict, politics, exists within the elite that acts to suppress opposition while promoting a consensus that secures the freedom of the elite to act as it sees fit.[14]

A free people expect the power of government to be exerted on their behalf to suit their interests and protect the rights they possess in nature, not from the edict of kings or the decisions of government. But even among a free people politics is always at work. That there is accommodation, compromise, and even appeasement only demonstrates politics to be conflict, whether resolved in a civil fashion or by exertion of force.[15] "Politics is not a soft art," Rood told his students, "because important things transpire in politics. . . . In politics, if it's possible and fruitful, it's likely to be tried."[16]

## PEACE, JUSTICE, DEFENSE

Rood characterized the basic political purposes of the political community and the paramount obligations of lawful government as those of "peace," "justice," and "defense." Those purposes and obligations are not a matter of whim or preference. Those things simply arise, everywhere and always, out of the necessity for an orderly, civil society. The maintenance of community depends on the provision, by those who rule, on prescriptions for the preservation of domestic peace, the maintenance of justice among the citizenry, and the safety of the community from outside interference.[17] These obligations exist irrespective of the nature of the regime and whether its constitution is written or unwritten. For Rood, constitutional (small c) development in the West is the story of the way in which various societies succeeded, or did not succeed, in meeting the tripartite imperatives of lawful government.

Rood cited Thomas Aquinas, in his *De Regimine Principum*: "The objective of a ruler should be to procure the welfare of that which he undertakes to rule. . . . Now the good and welfare of the associated multitude is the preservation of its unity, which is called peace, without which the utility of social life perishes. . . . Justice and domestic peace march hand in hand."[18] Henry de Bracton, writing in the thirteenth century, "Concerning the Laws and Customs of England," spoke of "For What the King has created and of his Ordinary Jurisdiction:"

> Moreover, the king was created and chosen for this: that he should make justice for all . . . because if there were not one to make justice peace could be wiped out, and it would be vain to establish laws and do justice if there were no one to protect laws.[19]

The relationship between peace and justice is evident when one considers the importance of each to the preservation of the community. Rood cited Stephen Langton, Archbishop of Canterbury in the time of King John and the Magna Carta, to the effect that without peace there can be no justice and that without justice there could be no peace. Rood put it this way: "Where there is no justice—when men cannot get that which is due to them according to law, those who are strong tend to take by force that which they think to be their due, while those who are weak are beset for they must either submit to the strong or lose their lives."[20] The preservation of the community—maintaining peace in the realm, which requires the enforcement of justice—is the sole justification for the existence of the ruler and the government in a lawful, or free, society.

Not all regimes are legitimate or lawful. Some rulers seek domestic peace through coercion and the denial of justice. Rood drew a fundamental distinction between the position of the tyrant and that of the lawful prince. As John of Salisbury, Policraticus, wrote circa 1160:

> The tyrant is one who oppresses the people by violent and despotic rule, even as the prince governs by the laws. Moreover, the law is the gift of God, the model of equity, the pattern of justice, the image of the divine will, the guardian of security, the force unifying and consolidating the people, the rule of conduct for officials, the exclusion and extermination of vices, the penalty for violence and all wrongdoing. . . . The prince fights for the laws and the liberty of the people; the tyrant reckons that naught has been accomplished unless he has made the laws of no effect and enticed the people into servitude.[21]

Strong rule per se is not inconsistent with justice and peace, however. On the contrary, it is a precondition for them. Rood noted accounts of the great anarchy in England during the reign of King Stephan, which began in 1135. A weak king meant weak law and eventually lawlessness, and the growth of factions where those who were strong collected about themselves those weaker than themselves. The weak in turn sought the protection of powerful men, because neither the king nor the laws could protect them. The powerful men pursued their own ends, preferring to support one faction or the other rather than see orderly government in the realm. The root of the disorder was the rivalry for the Crown of England and the consequence of King Stephan's failure to suppress, as he had the obligation to do, those who would remove him, despite the fact he was anointed king. By contrast, Stephan's successor, Henry II, received contemporary praise for his recovery of the strength of the monarch and the order of the realm.

The great Elizabeth I nearly failed this test when she remained reluctant to execute the law against a kinswoman and fellow queen, Mary, despite the overwhelming evidence of the conspiracies against her and the nation of England. So long as Mary lived to lend hope to the cause of those who saw profit in her support, so long would England be faced with the threat of civil war and the inevitable foreign interventions that would have been the consequence of such a contest. The refusal of a monarch to fulfill his or her obligation to preserve the constitution and, therefore, the community—whether through laxity or carelessness—raised the question of the monarch's right to continue to rule.

Rood argued that this basic test of legitimate rule had obvious implications for the third imperative of lawful government—the defense of the realm. It is the nature of politics and the human condition that justice, peace, and defense of community require, from time to time, the application of force.[22] If a nation has no domestic peace because it lacks justice and therefore is divided and weak, it cannot be expected to protect its borders or otherwise take steps to ensure its security against external threats.[23] As the case of Elizabeth and Mary illustrated, the external threat will tend to combine with the internal threat; foreigners will intrigue with and support domestic political factions, or with parties in a civil war. The nation will soon cease to enjoy its own peace and justice; that will be imposed upon it by those who have the power and will to destroy the community. When the weak, faction-ridden French government and people failed to defend France in 1940, there was no justice in France, save for that dictated by the occupying authorities. France was ruled at the pleasure and for the convenience of the Nazi German government. The lives and property of Frenchmen were no longer protected by French law. France ceased being a Republic, or even a nation.[24]

To be sure, we no longer live in a time when monarchs ruled "by the grace of God," when they and their councilors could be held accountable by God when they failed in their obligation to secure the liberties of their subjects and preserve the community. Rood certainly did not propose to return to this world; he was a democrat by conviction. But the obligation did not cease when free societies came to believe that the just powers of government derived from the consent of the governed. The obligation to peace, justice, and defense came to be shared between those who governed in the name of the people and the people themselves.

Rood observed that the Declaration of Independence justified the creation of a new nation as a necessary means to secure safety and happiness. The Preamble to the Constitution of the United States elaborated on the goal of good government: "We, the people of the United States, in order to form a more perfect Union, establish Justice, insure domestic Tranquility, provide for the common defense, promote the general Welfare, and secure the Blessings of Liberty to ourselves and our Posterity, do ordain and establish this Constitution for the United States of America." Rood observed:

> What needs doing to preserve the Republic inside is a matter for politics among Americans. We cannot have peace without justice any more than the English could in the time of King John. It cannot escape notice that the chief controversies of our time, here at home, have to do with how justice shall be done. It can be no less clear, however, that there can be neither peace nor justice if the nation is not defended from whatever threatens it abroad.[25]

The transition from lawful and free, but non-democratic regimes to those of, by, and for the people created peculiar challenges for those concerned with national defense. As we shall see in chapter 4, Rood believed that liberal democratic regimes face particular difficulties in this respect, because they tend to regard the three legs of the stool of lawful government to be of unequal length, or to be in tension if not opposition. Liberal regimes typically assume that the needs of domestic peace and justice are somehow compromised by efforts to defend the nation—that more guns means less butter and that more security means less freedom. Rood thought this misconception to be a problem, especially when liberal democracies are confronted with the existential threat posed by tyrants and lawless states in their modern guise of totalitarianism.

## NOTES

1. A good starting place is James E. Dougherty and Robert L. Pfaltzgraff Jr., *Contending Theories of International Relations: A Comprehensive Survey*, 5th ed. (New York: Longman, 2001)

2. Harold W. Rood, "Soviet Strategy and the Defense of the West," *Global Affairs* 2 (Summer 1987): 17–18. See also Harold W. Rood, "Early Warning, Part II," *Grand Strategy: Countercurrents*, February 1, 1983, 5.

3. Jeff Hanson, "A Collection of Prof. Harold W. Rood's Quotations," in *Memories of Professor Bill Rood, Scholar and Gentleman, from his Students, Colleagues, and Friends*, ed. Patrick J. Garrity, Christopher Harmon, and Colleen Sheehan (unpublished manuscript, January 2012), Print, 35.

4. The argument in the following three paragraphs is taken from Rood, "Early Warning, Part II," 5.

5. Therein lies the difficulty in solving the problem of early warning to avoid political, strategic, or tactical surprise, and in dealing with the consequences that may flow from such surprise (see chapter 3).

6. Deng Xiaoping was a veteran of the Long March who outlasted many purges and became the paramount leader of China for a decade and a half. His many titles included "Chairman of the Central Military Commission." In a telephone call in 1991, Christopher C. Harmon asked Rood about Deng's significance. "What will happen

when the old man dies?" Harmon asked. Rood instantly replied: "They'll find a younger old man."

7. Harold W. Rood, "Strategy Out of Silence: American Military Policy and the Preparations for War, 1919–1940" (PhD diss., University of California, 1960), 196.

8. On Churchill, see Harold W. Rood, "The Sinews of Peace and the River of Time" (unpublished manuscript, May 19, 1992), Print, 2. See also Rood, "Soviet Strategy and the Defense of the West," 18.

9. Steve Cambone, in Garrity et al., *Memories of Professor Bill Rood*, 9.

10. This was a major theme of Rood's course at Claremont McKenna College on Constitutional Development in the West.

11. Harold W. Rood, "Commentary on Books and Other Works Useful in the Study of International Relations," *Classics of Strategy and Diplomacy*, Ashbrook Center, accessed November 12, 2012, http://www.classicsofstrategy.com/strategyanddiplomacy/rood.pdf, 1.

12. Harold W. Rood, *Kingdoms of the Blind: How the Great Democracies Have Resumed the Follies that So Nearly Cost Them Their Life* (Durham: Carolina Academic Press, 1980), 280.

13. Rood, "Soviet Strategy and the Defense of the West," 1. Formulated differently: "Power is the ability to manipulate and inflict pain on others." Hanson, "A Collection of Prof. Harold W. Rood's Quotations," in Garrity et al., *Memories of Professor Bill Rood*, 34. In saying this, Rood meant more than the capacity to inflict physical injury or death, although that was certainly the bottom line of political power. He referred often to the ability to inflict psychological pain, such as that which one spouse could cause another, or a child could cause a parent (or vice versa), in order to manipulate human relationships. In the larger realm, nations threatening war do the same by conjuring up the image of death and destruction in order to create fears and by playing upon others' feelings of guilt to obtain their ends.

14. Rood, "Commentary on Books," 1.

15. Ibid., 1.

16. Hanson, "A Collection of Prof. Harold W. Rood's Quotations," in Garrity et al., *Memories of Professor Bill Rood*, 34.

17. The following section, unless otherwise indicated, is taken from Harold W. Rood, "A Free Society in an Unfree World: Peace, Justice and Defense" (unpublished manuscript), Print.

18. Quoted in ibid., 11–12.

19. Quoted in ibid., 13.

20. Quoted in ibid., 14–15.

21. Quoted in ibid., 14.

22. Ibid., 42.

23. "To weaken a country you demonstrate that it is unable to defend its borders." Hanson, "A Collection of Prof. Harold W. Rood's Quotations," in Garrity et al., *Memories of Professor Bill Rood*, 34.

24. Harold W. Rood, "The Strategy of Freedom," *Grand Strategy: Countercurrents*, July 1, 1981, 15–17.

25. Rood, "A Free Society in an Unfree World," 51.

# TWO

## The Nature of International Politics

### *There Is Going to be a War*

*This chapter examines Professor Rood's approach to the subject of war and the use of force. His view of international politics is one of constant conflict, in which states fight to promote their objectives and even to maintain their very existence. His analysis was not mechanistic or deterministic. His approach was never outside a larger set of historical themes and enduring "problems" of internation-al politics that, while they do not repeat themselves per se, constitute a set of more or less continuous conditions under which states operate.*

*The problems presented here are by no means a comprehensive set of such issues in international politics, but they represent what we believe are the most important among Rood's examples of "strategy at work." They invite the reader to consider what other problems of international politics are in continuous opera-tion. And, of course, Rood's often unconventional interpretations, such as his treatment of the origins of the twentieth-century wars with Germany or his examination of the nature of conflict in the Middle East, invite challenge, debate, and alternative appraisals. A rich literature exists in all of these areas and, in the endnotes, we have tried to point to those texts that influenced his thinking.[1]*

*Rood contends that strategy is in operation at all times; that is, the leaders of states are constantly looking for ways to advance and defend their interests, and they act when they see those opportunities. With that in mind, he taught that one should identify and attempt to explain the "objective conditions" political leaders confront (and seek to create), and explore the apparent anomalies in the behavior of states that fly in the face of conventional explanations. Such an approach can be a rich and valuable tool when applied to the examination of contemporary problems.*

Rood observed that if politics is at the heart of governments, it is also at the heart of relationships among governments. "International relations is an arena where politics is exercised by nations and other entities to accomplish goals and secure interests."[2] There are clashes of will between nations or communities of nations just as there are clashes of will within nations. In the international sphere, clashes of will arising from profound differences in outlook and purpose lead to conflicts that are irreconcilable short of war. Nations that would overset the status quo to establish a new order in the world will resort to force if it is within their capability to do so. Violence and force are intrinsic to revolution, even as they are to good order. A nation determined to achieve some important purpose in the international sphere, the accomplishment of which will likely require the exertion of great military power, is most apt to consider war to be a mere extension of foreign policy by other means.[3]

Rood disagreed with the conception that war is a pathological phenomenon that can somehow be cured. Such an argument, although promoted sincerely by the well-meaning, "serves well the interests of regimes that understand the terms 'war' and 'politics' to be distinctions of degree and not of kind."[4] War is the political means by which humans, to a first (if not final) order, determine who will organize things, and for what purpose they will be organized. The adoption of the U.S. Constitution may have been an act of reflection and choice by the citizens of the Union, but it was only made possible by successfully winning a war for independence. The Constitution and Union had to be defended in a great civil war. American democracy as we know it probably would not have survived defeat in the great conflicts of the twentieth century.

One of the bedrock certainties of international politics, therefore, according to Rood, is that there is going to be a war, somewhere, sooner or later, and probably sooner rather than later. "Those who predict war have statistics on their side; those who predict peace everlasting are always wrong."[5] The statesman and strategist must keep this fact foremost in mind at all times. Rood taught as if there is no true "peacetime" or "postwar" period. There is either war, or the preparation for war. The outcome of any war—including the relative costs paid by the winners and losers—is substantially determined by which side has prepared the best. To be unprepared is an almost certain recipe for defeat. Even if the war is somehow won, it will entail costs far beyond what were necessary and will leave the victor less able to secure domestic peace and justice— and thus in a weaker position for the next round of conflict. Even if a particular war does not immediately involve the United States, it is bound to have consequences for our global power and for the likelihood of a future war in which we will be engaged.[6]

We must stress that Rood was not a warmonger or militarist. He believed that he reached these conclusions about war objectively, as a political scientist. For a professor of international relations to pretend that the world was something other than it was, in the name of academic fashion or to avoid frightening his students, would be a true disservice. Rood certainly did not advocate rushing off to war willy-nilly; quite the opposite. When it came to policy making, Rood admired those whom he called "hard heads," such as Harry Truman and Dean Acheson. As we shall see, Rood thought that such a hardheaded view of the nature of international politics allowed policy makers and military planners the best opportunity to prevent war—especially general war, the sort of conflict that placed democracies at the greatest risk. That same hardheaded view informed Rood that the avoidance of war is not always our choice. The first order assumption—"there's going to be a war"—serves to clarify one's thinking about real choices in the real world, such as the kind of war we might have to fight and the purposes for which it should be fought.

One might object that war is no longer a rational means of deciding human organization, certainly not among the great powers, because—fill in the blank—nuclear weapons have made it too destructive, the globalized economy has created too great a stake in peace, conquests no longer pay for themselves, or liberal ideals have spread too widely. To this, Rood would point to previous predictions of the end of war, such as those by Norman Angell, which have proven premature, to say the least.[7] As to the most common objection to the possibility of war among the great powers, Rood wrote: "Nuclear weapons have not made war impossible, they have only changed the conditions under which wars will be fought. They have in no manner reduced the importance of strategy nor the inherent advantage of military superiority over military weakness."[8]

Rood thought it essential to understand the corollary to the certainty that there will be a war: there will be winners and losers, and the winners will have the opportunity to organize the "peace" at the expense of the losers. The winners will be able to impose their own notion of domestic justice on the vanquished. He often cited Alistair Horne's *To Lose a Battle, France 1940* to drive this point home. Rood recognized, to be sure, that there may be Pyrrhic victories, where the winner suffers as much as the loser; and that wars often involve limited aims, such as the resolution of border issues.[9] Nevertheless, Rood believed that the bottom line of war—who rules in whose land—should never be ignored. Wars for limited aims easily expand. Regime change may be relatively benign, as in the case of the American occupation of Japan after World War II; but the hard fact was that a U.S. proconsul dictated a new Japanese constitution that prohibited (among other things) an independent means of national defense.

The typical outcome of war is much harsher than that between the United States and Japan. "The cost of defeat is reckoned not just in the losses suffered by the armed forces in killed, wounded, and captured, nor in the equipment destroyed or seized by the victorious enemy," Rood commented. "A far heavier cost is exacted from those for whom the defense has failed: the people of the defeated nation. They lose the right to rule themselves."

> Recall the fate of the Third French Republic. On May 10, 1940, France was a free, democratic nation. Barely two months later, its armies defeated in the field by the German *Wehrmacht*, France ceased to be a nation. The French Republic became the French State, ruled to suit the pleasure and convenience of the Third Reich. Three-fifths of France was under the direct rule of the German Army, the Gestapo and the SS. The remainder of France was ruled from Vichy by a government suitable to the German authorities. All that France had so often fought for and for so long cherished was lost. In that part of France ruled from Vichy, Frenchmen were subject to laws more repressive than any that had been imagined even in the days before the French Revolution. . . . Those who had governed France under the Republic had lost their right to rule—not by the democratically-expressed wishes of the French people, but by the fiat of a foreign government. [10]

For any student who might find such questions of justice to be abstract, Rood offered concrete examples of the consequences of losing the right to rule. When a German naval midshipman was murdered in Paris, German officials ordered the seizure of one hundred French hostages. Fifty of the hostages were to be readied for immediate execution with their bodies to be exposed in the Place de la Concorde. In order to prevent these executions, the French government had to convene an Extraordinary French Tribunal that was instructed to condemn to death, under a law passed retroactively, six communists already in prison before the midshipman was murdered. The Vichy government had either to accept the execution of innocent hostages, or conduct sham trials and condemn men who were themselves innocent of the death of the German midshipman. All six were executed.

Rood asked the students also to consider the German occupation's economic cost to France. "I have already said that the payment of the debts contracted by the war presents no problem," Hitler ruminated one evening at dinner. "In the first place, the territories [they were no longer nations] conquered by force of arms represent an increase in national wealth which far exceeds the cost of the war." [11] Frenchmen paid for their defeat in goods, money, and labor, as did the citizens of Poland, Denmark, Norway, the Netherlands, Belgium, Luxembourg, Yugoslavia, and Greece. By 1943, over six hundred thousand French civilians were laboring in Germany. A year later, 57 percent of French male laborers (nearly four million men) were employed, directly or indirectly, in both France and Germany, in support of the German economy and the German war effort. The Germans even charged the costs of their occupation to the French: a total of 536 billion francs.

Because democracies find it difficult to imagine the possibility of war, they often neglect to consider the logical implications of having to fight a war for which they are not prepared—that of defeat. "Those who would remain free must pay a price to do so," Rood wrote. "Not the least of that price is the burden of defense, which itself seems to impinge on the very freedom that is to be defended. Yet the price of freedom is nothing compared with the cost of defeat." [12] Rood made this argument not merely in a quaint, historical sense, relevant only to times when men were less civilized, but as a lesson for the future.

Did Rood believe that the United States itself could be defeated, such that the American people would lose the right to rule themselves? Would Soviet troops actually land on Venice Beach, with Soviet tanks tooling down the Los Angeles freeways and a Soviet commissar setting up shop in the Los Angeles City Hall (or, for that matter, in the White House)? Rood did not use such images but when they were conjured up by his students and public audiences, they seemed far-fetched or amusing—the stuff of Hollywood movies like *Red Dawn*.

Rood would offer this basic rejoinder, more subtle but not less consequential in its applications. Suppose, for example, that the Soviet Union successfully invaded Western Europe and imprisoned hundreds of thousands of U.S. troops and their dependents, and otherwise held hostage those who had been friends of the United States. What price would Americans pay to see that they were safe? Would they perhaps assure the Kremlin that "anti-Soviet" elements would be removed from the U.S. government and prosecuted by a "people's court"? Would this not be a loss of our right to rule ourselves as we saw fit? [13]

## THE PATTERNS OF INTERNATIONAL POLITICS

For Rood, the study of politics constitutes a study of history; it is something made possible and useful because human nature exists and is unchanging.

> What has happened, how it came to happen with its consequences [is] therefore a guide to what can happen. The 20th Century so recently passed, provides vivid illustrations and experience of the exercise of politics whose consequences were monumental and painful and sometimes so decisive as to seem irreversible, or nearly so. Yet the great clashes of will that characterized the 20th Century did not originate the day before the century began but years and centuries before. What happened yesterday, is happening now and is about to happen can be better understood through the study of history. [14]

Rood oriented his study of strategy around the objectives and actions of the great powers—those nation-states or empires with the ability and desire to influence matters on a continental or global scale. The great powers often work directly or indirectly through smaller nations and nonstate actors. Great power conflict is the engine that drives international politics. Rood had no brief for interdependence theory or the argument that nonstate actors are coming to supplant nation-states. No doubt one could learn lessons of war and strategy by studying the actions and conflicts of lesser powers. These matter in the grand scheme of things, however, only so far as their actions enter the province of the great powers. For example, in Rood's judgment, the threat of terrorism, qua terrorism, is largely a matter for police action unless the terrorists are directed, sponsored, or utilized by the great powers in their conflicts with each other.[15]

According to Rood, the particular aims and strategies of the great powers are affected in decisive ways by the enduring facts of geography. He approved the quote of former British Defense Minister Denis Healy: "If a warship has to sail from the Mediterranean to the Black Sea, it must pass through the Dardanelles whether the government in Moscow is Czarist or Communist."[16] Rood placed particular emphasis on the writings of Yale University social scientist Nicholas Spykman: "Geography does not argue. It simply is."[17]

> In such a world, the geographic area of the state is the territorial base from which it operates in time of war and the strategic position which it occupies during the temporary armistice called peace. It is the most fundamentally conditioning factor in the formulation of national policy because it is the most permanent. . . . Because the geographic characteristics of states are relatively unchanging and unchangeable, the geographic demands of those states will remain the same for centuries, and because the world has not yet reached that happy state where the wants of no man conflict with those of another, those demands will cause friction. Thus at the door of geography may be laid the blame for many of the age-long struggles which run persistently through history while governments and dynasties rise and fall.[18]

Geography, to be sure, is a conditioning rather than a determining factor. But "size affects the relative strength of a state in the struggle for power," Spykman explained.

> Natural resources influence population density and economic structure, which in themselves are factors in the formulation of policy. Location with reference to the equator and to oceans and land masses determines nearness to centers of power, areas of conflict, and established routes of communication, and location with reference to immediate neighbors defines position in regard to potential enemies, thereby determining the basic problems of territorial security.

Geography, according to Spykman, is not to be understood narrowly; it includes topography and climate. "Topography affects strength because of its influence on unity and internal coherence. Climate, affecting transportation and setting limits to the possibility of agricultural production, conditions the economic structure of the state, and thus, indirectly but unmistakably, foreign policy."[19]

Geography conditions the distribution and configuration of the great powers, as well as their natural enemies and friends. Rood also urged his students to take into account the state of civil and military technology, of which some peoples and nations take better advantage than others.

The study of history and geography reminds us to think in the very long term, even and perhaps especially to make sense of day-to-day events. Rood argued that international politics are characterized by certain persistent patterns of great power interactions and their associated wars, as the great powers seek to organize the world to their liking or to keep others from doing so. Great powers exhibit these well-defined patterns of behavior despite apparent changes in political regimes. Certain "problems" in international politics have persisted for decades and centuries. Identifying and understanding these problems permit the student of strategy to understand better what is going on in the world—they constitute something of a set of rules and score card of regional and global conflicts. These problems are not immutable but their "resolution" generally requires absolute and convincing victory (or defeat) of one of the parties.

Problems in international politics often turn on the question of whether nations are to be unified or dismembered. We tend to think of borders drawn on maps as immutable, yet in our own time we have seen the creation of new nations and the fragmentation of others. Rood recommended that his students follow the emergence of the Union of the South Slavs into the Kingdom of Yugoslavia after the Great War of 1914–1918 in J. A. R. Marriott's *The Eastern Question* and Robert Lee Wolff's *The Balkans in Our Time*. Yugoslavia later fragmented as the government of the Soviet Union disestablished itself, creating a small war in Europe, which had been at peace since 1945. Czechoslovakia was created out of the elements of the defeated Austrian Empire in 1918; disappeared in 1940 as part of the evolution of the German Problem; emerged again in 1945, only to be submerged in what might be termed the "Russian Problem"; became once again free in 1989, only to see the break-off of Slovakia. The division of Korea continues to be a problem on the edge of international politics in Asia. The unification of Vietnam, brought on after the dissolution of the coalition defending South Vietnam, was accomplished by the force of arms applied from the North.[20]

Rood concluded that because nuclear weapons did not make war impossible, their impact on international politics could best be understood in the context of these long-standing patterns and problems. Writing in the mid-1960s, he and William R. Van Cleave concluded that "the spread of national nuclear forces seems to be a real possibility in the near future" and that one should not "overestimate the durability of inhibitions against the development of national nuclear forces."[21] India's interest in nuclear weapons, for instance, had increased greatly by China's first atomic test. The development of an Indian national nuclear force would likely intensify Pakistan's inclination to do the same. The resulting pro-liferation "chain reaction" could be predicted based on a consideration of the regional effects of the emergence of particular "Nth countries." Indo-nesia, Japan, Australia, and New Zealand would regard such nuclear developments in South Asia with alarm, creating incentives for those nations to consider becoming nuclear weapons states. The result might also be a regional alliance against the PRC's advance toward the Middle East, permitting the Indians to exercise responsibility for defense of the Indian Ocean area. For Rood, this assessment—written nearly fifty years ago—reflected the larger set of problems surrounding the security of Asia (considered below).[22]

Further, according to Rood, the problems of various regions tend to overlap and affect each other. For instance, the Imperial Japanese govern-ment, intent on solving its military difficulties on the Chinese mainland, took advantage of the defeat of France by Germany in 1940 to move into the French colony of Indochina. This provided Japan with air bases that could be used to assault the rest of Southeast Asia, including Malaysia and Singapore, in an effort to close off critical Western supply lines to China.[23]

Rood was particularly intrigued with the way in which the Soviet Union appeared to view the strategic interrelationships among various regions. Before the June 1967 Arab-Israeli War, for instance, the Soviet fleet had established bases on the Red Sea coast and at Berbera, in Somal-ia. Within a month of the Egyptian defeat in the Sinai, on July 10, 1967, a dozen Soviet warships steamed into Alexandria and Port Said. From that time onward, it seemed that the Soviet navy was ubiquitous in the east-ern Mediterranean and the Red Sea, offering a direct challenge to what had been Western naval supremacy in those seas. Coincident with the increase of Soviet naval activity in the Mediterranean and the Middle East was the increase in the Soviet presence in the Caribbean and the Gulf of Mexico. The Soviet fleet began making what appeared to be regular calls into Cuban ports in 1969. Soviet Tu-95 bombers began making visits to Cuban air bases by at least April 1970.[24]

Only in retrospect, Rood wrote, could one come to suppose that these Soviet naval deployments were intended to inhibit the United States in the Middle East as well as in the Caribbean and the Gulf. The dispatch of Soviet forces into the Gulf of Mexico and the Caribbean, in 1969 and 1970, led to the reaffirmation of the U.S. pledge made by President Kennedy during the Cuban missile crisis of 1962, which was not to invade Cuba so long as no "offensive weapons" were put there. The Soviet ships and aircraft in Cuba gave weight to Soviet guarantees of Cuban defense. By deploying its own forces into Cuba and the waters around the island, Rood argued, the Soviet Union made it evident that any future confrontation with the United States elsewhere would not provide Washington with the opportunity to deal with Cuba—unless the United States was willing to risk general war with the Soviet Union. Such a confrontation came during the Middle East War in October 1973.

Of course, one can point to an infinite number of problems and issues in international politics, especially if they are viewed from multiple perspectives (Germany has a French Problem, the French have a German Problem, and so on). Rood's writings and classroom lectures were grouped around a limited number of enduring topics that transcended the relationship between particular nations and that went directly to the vital question of how a particular continent (or the world) was to be organized. Rood's problem set, considered below, involved (1) the German Problem; (2) the Problems of Asia; (3) the Middle Eastern Question; and (4) the Caribbean-Cuban Salient. We summarize below Rood's presentation of each of these problems—in sufficient depth, we hope, to allow the reader to appreciate the thrust of his arguments, each of which would merit a book on its own. We treat the Russian Problem as a special case, in chapter 5.

## THE GERMAN PROBLEM

From roughly the time of the Reformation until the middle of the nineteenth century, Rood observed, the politics of central Europe was dominated by what might be called the "German Problem."[25] The notion of a German Problem in European history was hardly original to Rood, but as usual he followed his own distinctive line of analysis.

The German lands during this period were not ruled by a single power but by a bewildering collection of kingdoms, bishoprics, and the like. France, meanwhile, had become increasingly unified and coherent in power. Over all these centuries, the German Problem for France had one solution: to prevent the unification of Germany under centralized leadership, where the full power of Germany could be concentrated to accomplish purposes antithetical to the security and interests of France. If Germany were to be unified with centralized command over finances, resources, and armed forces, France would be imperiled. French interference in the affairs of Germany ensured that Germany would be unable to act on its own behalf. Since the time of the Capetians and of Philip Augustus, anything was better for France than a united Germany. Happily for France, the Peace of Westphalia, which ended the Thirty Years' War, left Germany divided with over three hundred separate political entities, each free to make treaties with foreign powers. France was then free to exploit the divisions to suit the demands of French security.[26]

Rood offered the following brief historical sketch of the modern evolution of the German Problem. The first major milestone in the unification of Germany occurred during the Seven Years' War, 1756–1763 (which had started in the Ohio Valley of North America, where the man who would become the first president of the United States was involved in the fighting). That great conflict included the Third Silesian War, where Prussia received Silesia in the settlement. Silesia in Prussian hands opened, a hundred years later, the way for the Prussian Army to win a decisive victory over the Austrian Army at Königgrätz (Sadowa).

The Austro-Prussian War of 1866 lasted six weeks and appeared to have broken out over unsettled differences between the two countries that emerged from the Austro-Prussian war against Denmark (1864) for the possession of the Duchies of Schleswig and Holstein. The Prussian General Staff's history of the Austro-Prussian War, *Campaign of 1866 in Germany*, explained that the Austro-Prussian war was even more far-reaching than this—it "was a necessity of the history of the world; it must sooner or later have broken out. The German nation could not forever exist in the political weakness into which it had sunk between the Latin West and the Slavonian East since the age of Germanic Emperors. . . . Prussia would not give up her Germanic situation without being annihilated. . . . Austria had an existence foreign from Germany." [27] Austria was to be eliminated as an arbiter of affairs in the German lands, which was a second major step in the domination of those lands, and central Europe, by a Prussia-dominated German state.

On June 6, 1866, while the Prussian Army concentrated on the border of Silesia opposite Bohemia, Prussian forces in Schleswig concentrated on the border with Austrian-occupied Holstein to move against the weak Austrian garrison that held that duchy. But there remained to be dealt with those armies of the German states, such as Bavaria, that were allied with Austria. These were subdued even as the Battle for Königgrätz unfolded. The Prussian Army halted at Pressburg, within sight of the towers of Vienna. The French Emperor interceded with an offer to mediate the quarrel between Prussia and Austria. The German states that had been aligned with Austria were in their submission, accorded the honors of war by the Prussian king. Austrian troops withdrew from Venetia, which was ceded to France, and by France to the new state of Italy. Prussia had gained 1,300 square (German) miles of territory and four million inhabitants.

The defeat of Austria occurred, Rood concluded, because the Prussian Army in 1866 was ready for war, while the Austrian Army was ill prepared. The Austrian Army had been considered one of the best in Europe, second only to that of France. But the Prussian Army ranged across Germany using the almost fifteen thousand kilometers of railroads that had been constructed there since 1835. The swift defeat of Austria's allies within Germany and the quick Prussian concentration against Austria enabled Prussia to win the war before the other European powers could bring themselves to intervene. The Prussians established a North German

Confederation as a way station en route to complete unification (excluding Austria).

The defeat of Austria in 1866 was a disaster for France. By the time Napoleon III chose to declare war against Prussia four years later, Prussian diplomacy, military training, and equipment had brought what had been the pro-Austrian German states into the Prussian fold, even if they were not part of the North German Confederation, and prepared them for war against France, whenever that should come.

The French military staff, having reviewed the experience of the French Army during its war in Italy in 1859 and the Prussian campaign against Austria, decided upon a reorganization of the army, which was to be completed by 1874. But the French emperor felt compelled to declare war on Prussia and to launch an offensive into the German lands four years before then. The declaration of war against Prussia was delivered in Berlin on July 19, 1870. But no French Army had yet been collected. French mobilization had not yet been completed. The *Garde Mobile* was called up on July 15, but that force was only at half its authorized strength and was not yet entirely equipped for war. Reserves were called out the same day to bring French Army units up to their war strength, but they had to find their way to their mobilization stations along railways overcrowded with elements of the army moving to the frontier, and then try to find the units to which they had been assigned.

By contrast, members of the Prussian Army, with elements of the other states in the North German Confederation, were deployed in their war stations by July 31, according to the defense plans drawn up in the winter of 1868–1869. The object of the armies was "to see the enemy's main force and to attack it."[28] While the French were still concentrating their armies on the frontier with the object of advancing toward Mainz and Coblenz, the Germans were concentrated and ready to strike into France to prevent the French invasion. On August 4, the Prussian Third Army attacked across the French frontier to seize the fortified city of Weissenburg, which it did by the end of the day.

Ironically, the assault on Weissenburg was carried out by the Bavarian First Infantry Division, part of the First Bavarian Army Corps, now operating as part of the Prussian Third Army. It was ironic because France's strategic intention had been to take the offensive to cut off southern Germany from Prussia, and to neutralize the armies of those states like Bavaria that had fought against Prussia in the Austro-Prussian War. But Prussia had, after the defeat of Austria, raised its standard of training and equipment to that of the Prussian Army and incorporated them into the campaign against France. The Bavarian success at Weissenburg manifested the wisdom of Prussian statecraft. The Third Army followed its victory at Weissenburg with those at Wörth and at Spicheren on August 6 and Mars La Tour on August 18.

By August 31, the French Army of Châlons was based on the fortress of Sedan and was forced to surrender. The Emperor Napoleon III, who commanded the army, was taken prisoner, as was his army. Paris was invested and besieged by September 19. By the New Year, all the important places in France had been occupied by the Germans. Peace was concluded in May 1871 at the Palace of Versailles, where the German Empire was proclaimed. Once again, Rood pointed out, a nation prepared for war and holding clear strategic objectives had triumphed over a nation that had neither.[29]

As the war began, the two rival monarchs both sought to explain the war in terms of the German Problem. On July 25, 1870, before the king of Prussia moved with his military headquarters to Mainz, he issued a proclamation to the German people: "Love for a common Fatherland, the unanimous rising of the German races and their princes . . . united as never before . . . the seed sown in blood . . . will bring a harvest of German freedom and unity."[30] The Emperor Napoleon had proclaimed to the French people on July 23, 1870: "We war not with Germany whose independence we esteem. . . . We wish that the nations forming the Great German nationality may freely dispose of their destinies. . . . We desire to gain a lasting peace."[31]

Thus was the German Problem seen by Napoleon III, who would lose his throne in an attempt to solve it, while William I dealt with what for Germans had become the "French Problem," by unifying Germany under the Empire. French policy had failed in 1864 and again in 1866—the Schleswig-Holstein War and the Austro-Prussian War—for each was a step toward the unification of Germany. Had France taken the side of Austria in 1866 and had Prussia been defeated, Prussia and the proto-German confederation would have been dismantled. In 1870, French diplomacy did not obtain the aid of London, St. Petersburg, or Vienna before deciding upon war and before the French Army was prepared to carry out French strategy against Germany. Thus long-standing French policy failed under the thrust of Bismarck's strategy of using blood and iron to bring about German unification.

The next seventy-five years, through 1945, saw a new manifestation of the German Problem, according to Rood. When Germany was divided and weak, Europe had been unstable. Now, ironically, when Germany was united and strong, Europe again became unstable. The logic of strategy dictated that it would be in united Germany's interest to see that France was dismembered and removed from the ranks of European great powers. Otherwise, France would inevitably seek allies to encircle and redivide Germany. Rood suggested that instead of going too far in the war with France, by taking Alsace and Lorraine, Bismarck did not go far enough in executing this strategic imperative. Of course, Bismarck had to reckon with the possibility of intervention by the other great powers to stop this, but those powers were then unprepared for that sort of war.

Bismarck may have believed that it was possible for a satiated Germany to remain secure in Europe, through wise diplomacy (based on the isolation of France) and the dominance of the German Army. But even if Bismarck were operating on this premise, rather than preparing to dismember France at a later date, other factors were at work, which led to the Great War of 1914. Still, everything pivoted around the transformed German Problem.[32]

Most important was the intersection of the German Problem and the ongoing crisis of nationality in the Balkans created by the recession of Ottoman rule. World War I did not stem, as later conventional academic wisdom would have it, from a system of entangling, interlocking alliances in Europe, from which a Balkan quarrel of peripheral importance led unnecessarily into a general European war. The Franco-Russian alliance of 1894 was, in this standard account, the original sin from which all resulting evil flowed.[33] Rood argued, to the contrary, that the alliances were themselves symptoms of profound forces at work, forces that created conditions that were more than the European powers could cope with.

To begin with, Austria, now excluded from its once-pivotal role in German affairs, was beset by imperial problems so deep as to threaten its existence. These included the demands of peoples and national states in the Balkans, each of which was subject to its own internal conflicts. The emergence of Serbia, Romania, and Bulgaria out of the disintegration of the Ottoman Empire not only raised intractable conflicts among the powers that had helped create them, but also led to intra-Balkan competition, which could be resolved only through the intervention of the great powers. The slow disintegration of the Ottoman Empire, a direct result of its growing inability to administer the territory it held, created that problem called the "Eastern Question"; this commanded the attention of France, Great Britain, Russia, Austria, and ultimately Germany. The Eastern Question complicated the relations among those powers when it came to resolving other European problems.[34]

Then there were the problems created by European interests outside of Europe. Anglo-Russian competition in Afghanistan and Persia, Russo-Japanese competition in Manchuria and Korea, and Franco-British-German friction in Africa all exacerbated the relations among the powers in their efforts to bring about any kind of European settlement. Within months of the conclusion of the Franco-Russian Alliance, Japan would defeat China on land and at sea, marking Japan as a major power in the Far East while inviting the intervention of France, Germany, and Russia in the matter, each in an effort to turn the situation in favor of its own interests in China.

Furthermore, the nineteenth century was a time of major social revolution in Europe, not just one symbolized by the French Revolution and the revolutions of 1848, but one made material by the growth of technology and its application to the industrialization of Europe. The great concentration of industry that grew along the Ruhr itself represented a revolutionary development. The introduction of the steam engine for manufacturing and land and maritime transport, the electric telegraph, the widespread development of railways, and the manufacture on a great scale of industrial products such as cast steel, chemicals, high explosives, and nitro-cellulose propellants all conspired to alter the standards by which national power could be measured.

For Rood, if there was one particular catalyst for a general European war in 1914, it was German hostility to England, which made the German Problem one for London as well as for the continental powers. The German challenge to British naval supremacy, which had begun with the Naval Law of 1898 and continued through subsequent naval laws, the Kaiser's evident pleasure at British discomfiture in South Africa, and the German disregard for British interests in the Far East all helped to sour Anglo-German relations. In other circumstances, Britain might have sought an Anglo-German entente to counterbalance the Franco-Russian alliance, but such German statements and actions were seen in England as posing a direct threat to Great Britain itself.

It could hardly be suggested that those in power in Germany were unaware of the impact on Great Britain of German policy in Europe and elsewhere, Rood observed. General Helmuth von Moltke, chief of the German General Staff, wrote in February 1906 to Prince Bernhard von Bülow, the German chancellor, of British views of the consequence of a Franco-German war:

> The change in the distribution of political power which a victorious Germany would occasion in Europe would be so great a national danger for England, that she would be forced to relinquish the neutrality which she desires, and which is the intention of the government.
>
> If Germany were in possession of the Belgian Coast, Holland would be forced to join Germany unconditionally. . . .
>
> It is argued also that Germany, if fixed on the Belgian-Dutch coast, must mean a perpetual risk of invasion for England. . . .
>
> Also such a change in the conditions of continental power would make England unable to use her home army for the defense of India, which would become necessary eventually. . . .
>
> The fleet, however strong, could not help to remove these difficulties. . . . Thus sufficient forces could not be kept in home waters to guard against the danger of a German invasion. . . .
>
> Thus also, England's need of self-preservation demanded her taking part in a continental war to prevent any such predominance of Germany.[35]

Since before the time of the Spanish Armada, Rood noted, it had been understood in Britain that the security of the British Isles required English supremacy of the "narrow seas" and the exclusion of any other great power from the coast opposite the British Isles. British suspicions of German intentions were not just hidden within diplomatic correspondence, but were clearly expressed in public under one guise or another. *Jane's Fighting Ships, 1906/7* contained a review of a book used by the Navy League in Germany as part of its program to have every German consent "to contribute even one shilling a year more to the upkeep of the German Navy." If they did so, "victory, fame, colonies, and wealth would be theirs beyond dispute."[36] Erskine Childers's novel of sailing, *The Riddle of the Sands*, first published in England in 1903, recounts the discovery by two young British yachtsmen of the prepositioning of German supplies in the Frisians for some future invasion of England. In these and similar works, the fearful specter was raised of an armed descent on the British Isles. And that was a matter not only of the safety of England itself but also of the defense of the Empire abroad. The substance behind the specter was the German High Seas Fleet at Kiel and in the Jade.

Matters evolved in Europe, then, not on the basis of the success or failure of diplomacy, Rood argued, but upon the change in the relative power among the nations of Europe. The most important such change was the growth of German industrial, military, and naval power that was, in both scope and nature, nothing short of revolutionary. The German Problem now manifested itself as a hemispheric and even global problem. The German aims were set forth by Chancellor Theobald Bethmann von Hollweg in September 1914. The "general aim of the war" was, for him, "security for the German Reich in west and east for all imaginable time. For this purpose France must be so weakened as to make her revival as a great power impossible for all time. Russia must be thrust back as far as possible from Germany's eastern frontier and her domination over the non-Russian vassal peoples broken."[37] And indeed, the need for such a war to secure those objectives for the *Kaiserreich* had been well understood and accepted by a broad segment of the German elite since the weakening of Bismarck's system after 1878. It was all a matter of timing.[38]

The fierceness with which the war was fought by Germany gave some measure of the importance of the war to German policy. The extraordinary measures invoked to accomplish the defeat of the allies were a measure of the dimension of German aims. The initial German military offensive in the West (the Schlieffen Plan) aimed at the destruction of the French Army on French soil, during the process of which all of France would have been occupied. If defeated, therefore, France's fate would be at Germany's pleasure; it would not be the result of diplomatic negotiations between two powers of equal status. The behavior of the German Army during the invasion of Belgium in 1914—what Rood characterized as a reign of terror—was not the consequence of an oversight or of the behavior of ill-disciplined troops. In his view, German policy intended to destroy the morale and the will to fight of the Belgian and French armies by inflicting atrocities on the civilian population. The German war effort was aimed at recasting Europe to suit German purposes, which entailed the destruction of the constitutions of France, Belgium, Imperial Russia, the Netherlands, and Luxembourg.

The defeat of Imperial Germany in 1918 did not reset the German strategic agenda. Rood emphasized that German objectives after World War I remained the same as they had been at the beginning of the war. Grand Admiral Alfred von Tirpitz closed the first volume of his *Memoirs*, written in 1919, thus: "England's day of judgment will have its birth in this very success [victory over the Central Powers]."[39] German policy toward France remained constant despite the change of regime, first to the putatively democratic Weimar constitution, and then to that of National Socialist Germany. Mathias Erzberger, president of the German Armistice Commission in 1919, who was widely regarded as a German moderate, wrote a letter to *The Times* (London) in January 1920:

> Another war between Germany and the Anglo-Saxons is inevitable. France is their strongest outpost on the continent but she has been so thoroughly weakened she will never be able to recover. If Germany can undertake the restoration of Russia she will be ready in ten or fifteen years to bring France without difficulty into her power. The march to Paris will be easier than that in 1914.[40]

What made those plans to resume the march to Paris possible was the secret German rearmament carried on from the very close of World War I, under the Weimar government, aided by the cooperation of the Soviet Union. When the Nazis did come to power, they accelerated German rearmament, mobilized the German people, and embarked upon a "new order" in Europe, which once more included the occupation and dismemberment of France.[41]

The failure of France (and Britain) to appreciate and deal with the continuity of the German Problem between 1918 and 1939 is discussed in more detail in chapters 3 and 4. Suffice to observe here that France, in constructing its famous Maginot Line, took care to site the artillery *ouverages* so the guns could not fire into German territory. That way, Rood noted, the line could be classified as "defensive" as defined in the Geneva Disarmament Conference of 1933. Amidst the so-called phony war in December 1939, a day after the Soviet Air Force launched bombing attacks on the capital of Finland, the French premier informed the French parliament that the French Army would not engage in offensive warfare against Germany in order to spare blood and suffering. France, he said, was well prepared to defend itself while being frugal in the expenditure of the lives of its citizens.[42]

In retrospect, Rood observed archly, this French strategy did not seem adequate to deal with the German Problem, as manifested in *Mein Kampf*, which was the blueprint of the National Socialist policy for reordering Europe. Rood noted that Hitler, shortly after the invasion of the Soviet

Union begun in the summer of 1941, reiterated these objectives succinctly at a top secret conference. Hitler's remarks were prompted by an article in a newspaper published in Vichy France—the rump French state that existed at German sufferance—which asserted that the attack on communist Russia was Europe's war and therefore it should be conducted for Europe as a whole. Nonsense, Hitler said, according to notes of the meeting taken by Martin Bormann. "It was essential that we should not proclaim our aims before the whole world; also, this was not necessary, but the chief thing was that we ourselves should know what we wanted."[43]

And what was it that Nazi Germany wanted? Germany, Hitler explained, would never withdraw from those areas that it already vanquished and would yet conquer. Decisions about particular administrative arrangements and territories that would formally be incorporated into the greater Reich would be determined on a case-by-case basis. "In principle we have now to face the task of cutting up the giant cake according to our needs, in order to be able: first, to dominate it; second, to administer it; and third, to exploit it. . . . [W]e had to understand that the Europe of today was nothing but a geographical term; in reality Asia extended up to our frontiers."[44]

> Never again must it be possible to create a military power west of the Urals, even if we have to wage war for a hundred years in order to attain this goal. All successors of the Führer must know: Security for the Reich exists only if there are no foreign military forces west of the Urals; it is Germany who undertakes the protection of this area against all possible dangers. Our iron principle must be and must remain: *We must never permit anybody but the Germans to carry arms!*[45]

When Germany was defeated in 1945, the modern German Problem was apparently solved for France. Unfortunately, it was done so with only token support from the French themselves, who had been occupied and dismembered in the meantime. Germany was again divided between East and West and its regime changed, into democratic and communist variants. The East German regime existed only with the support and sufferance of the Soviet Union. The political system, economy, and security of the Federal Republic was deliberately interwoven so tightly with that of the Western alliance that it could not represent a threat to its neighbors or reunify with the East without the acquiescence of the great powers. The presence of the United States in Europe was essential to the resolution of the post-1871 German Problem. As the saying went, the purpose of the Western alliance (NATO) was "to keep the Americans in, the Russians out, and the Germans down."[46]

This pattern of international politics in Europe endured for over four decades. The pattern reflected in large part the emergence, or reemergence, of a Russian Problem (see chapter 5). The old German Problem did not disappear entirely, however. The Soviet Union insisted that its deployment of forces forward in the Warsaw Pact nations was meant to meet a German revanchist threat. The Soviets, Rood noted, were especially sensitive over the possibility of West German acquisition of nuclear weapons, whether arrived at independently or through some sort of arrangement within the NATO alliance.[47] Nor were the Soviets alone worried about German acquisition of nuclear weapons. For instance, Sweden and Switzerland made noises about going nuclear to maintain their neutrality and security if Germany became a nuclear power. Much of intra-NATO politics turned on the question of reassuring or cautioning Bonn about its nuclear-related security concerns. West Germany, after all, had seen how France had attempted to gain independence and greater influence within and outside NATO with its nuclear weapons program. Bonn might well have decided that the French course was its most promising policy alternative.[48]

When the question of German unification emerged unexpectedly in 1989, as Russian power seemingly receded from central Europe, it turned out that the German Problem still had to be resolved. Not only did Russia oppose reunification at first, but West Germany's putative major European democratic allies—one led by a conservative (Margaret Thatcher), the other by a Socialist (François Mitterrand)—were also reluctant adherents. The skeptics liked to quote the French writer François Mauriac's *bon mot*: "I love Germany so much that I hope there will always be two of them." Concerns with German power, if for now only economic and political in character, remain at the heart of the ongoing challenges facing the European Union and the EU's relations with Russia.

Reunification was brought about despite this opposition because the Germans, or at least the West German leaders, wanted it, as did the United States. In the context of the times and for their own distinct purposes, no great power was prepared to create a situation where the Germans might go their own way to achieve unification. The American presence in Europe served as a necessary catalyst to clarify the new great power alignment without war (which, as chapter 6 indicates, is one of the central purposes of U.S. forward-basing in Eurasia). Rood concluded, however, that things were not quite as they seemed to most commentators. He argued that the Soviet Union, soon again to be Russia, had decided that the risk of reviving the German Problem was an acceptable price to pay to improve its ability to deal with its "American Problem." For Moscow, as Rood saw it, German unification was necessary to weaken and eventually eliminate the U.S. presence from Europe (see chapters 5 and 7).[49]

## THE PROBLEMS OF ASIA

In Rood's judgment, the collective problems of Asia in the twentieth century were caused by the rise of Japan as a modern economic and military power, Russian (Soviet) expansion to the east, and the breakdown and recovery of a unified Chinese empire. Taken from the distance of over a century, Rood concluded, it appears that these problems are really a China Problem—whether China is to be divided or unified. If divided, which power or powers will exercise rule on the mainland? If united, what territory exactly would constitute China's boundaries and strategic perimeter—and with whom, if anyone, would China be allied? We offer below a brief summary of Rood's assessment of the problems of Asia, in order, from the standpoint of Japan, Russia, and China.

Rood thought that Alfred Thayer Mahan's collection of essays, *The Problem of Asia and its Effect on Modern Politics* (first published in 1900), had been especially prescient in this regard. Rood also recommended "a very useful work in international politics," Gregory Bienstock's *The Struggle for the Pacific* (published in 1936). This work recognized the historic Japanese inclination to secure north China and predicted that, after having done so, she would undoubtedly make herself mistress of the Western Pacific and perhaps even seek hegemony over all of Asia. The purpose of the author was to "prove to people living on either Atlantic coast that they are seriously affected by what happens in the Western Pacific."[50] Bienstock noted that the historical animosity between China and Japan dated from at least the time of the Chinese Emperor Kublai Khan in the thirteenth century, who twice attempted the conquest of Japan. Toya-toma Hide-yoshi (1536–1598) was, as Bienstock wrote, the first Japanese statesman to argue that Japan's geopolitical circumstances with respect to China required Japan to achieve absolute dominion in China and Korea.[51]

The modern manifestation of the problem of Sino-Japanese relations, according to Rood, began with the overthrow of the Shogunate in 1868, the elevation of the emperor to the pinnacle of society and government, and the adoption of a constitution that centralized power in the hands of the government in Tokyo. This came about at a time when China was not a going concern. It was nominally an empire, but had an administration powerless to maintain internal order or to command the country's resources to defend its territory, control its borders, secure its coastline, and prevent foreign intervention in its affairs. Japanese policy henceforth was to keep China weak, backward, and disunited. When the time came to solve the problem of China, Japan would do so as part of a strategy of seeking hegemony over Asia through the ejection of the Western colonial powers.[52]

The Japanese saw a unified China to be a threat to the independence of Japan, which lies only four hundred miles across the East China Sea.

Rood observed that this was not unlike the problem faced by France with respect to the German lands. If those lands were unified under a strong central government, France was in danger of losing itself and therefore unification must be blocked. If China became unified under a strong central government, Japan thought itself to be lost. To prevent that loss China must be fragmented and kept isolated from foreign powers that might come to its aid, because those powers would use China as a means of weakening Japan. (Ironically, a weak China in an age of foreign intervention was almost as dangerous to Japan as a strong one.) The constituent parts of the mainland were to be governed by pro-Japanese Chinese under the oversight of Japanese commanders, in the manner in which Manchuria came to be governed after 1932.

The Japanese strategy against China began openly with the Sino-Japanese War of 1894–1895, which drove China out of Korea and gave Japan Formosa. The Russo-Japanese War (1904–1905) left Japan in possession of Korea, which became part of the Japanese Empire in 1910. Korea, in turn, was the main route to Manchuria. Japanese policy was conducted with patience and advanced when the opportunity presented itself. One such opportunity was presented to Japan in the Great War (World War I), when Tokyo became an ally of Great Britain, France, and eventually the United States. Tokyo's "Twenty-One Demands" of May 1915, and the treaty embodying those demands, conceded to Japan rights to coal and iron ore deposits in China, while forbidding to China the right to cede its territory, coasts, or islands to any power other than Japan. These demands were not fully realized at the time, but in that same year, Great Britain agreed that Japan was to receive the former German island colonies north of the equator: the Marianas (save for Guam, a U.S. possession), Yap and the Pellews, the Carolines, and the Marshalls. These made ideal bases from which Japan could sever communications between the United States and the Philippines and isolate America from China. The peace conference that ended the war in Europe granted a League of Nations mandate to Japan over the island chains.

In the mid-1920s, Admiral Roger Keyes, Deputy Chief of the Naval Staff, warned Winston Churchill, then Chancellor of the Exchequer, that Japan intended to turn the Europeans out of China and eventually out of Asia. Churchill said he could not conceive of such a possibility unless there was a serious realignment of the powers in Europe: a German-Russo-Japanese alliance. Lord Curzon, the Foreign Secretary, said Japan wanted only intimate and cordial relations with Britain. The Japanese, meanwhile, used commercial enterprises to penetrate those places they would target later in wartime. These enterprises passed secret subsidies to various nationalist groups that sought independence from the colonial powers.

In 1931, the Japanese, or at least militarist elements in the government and the Army, accelerated their plans to dismember and control China

through the invasion of Manchuria. Japanese Foreign Minister Koki Hiro-
ta, in his address to the Imperial Diet in January 1936, laid out the
government's long-term program for China. This plan included the read-
justment of Chinese-Japanese relations to bring about the cessation by
China of all unfriendly acts and measures and to encourage an active and
effective collaboration with Japan. The Foreign Minister also expressed
his hope to aid in the progress of the newly established Commonwealth
of the Philippines. At the same time, the Commander in Chief of the
Imperial Combined Fleets indicated that Japan's future commercial expansion must be directed to the Southern Seas, requiring the quick expansion of the Japanese Navy's cruising radius to include New Guinea,
Borneo, and the Celebes. It was hardly difficult to suppose, Rood observed, that Japan aimed at establishing its own form of the Monroe
Doctrine over East Asia.

The Japanese would hardly settle for a benign form of hegemony,
however. In January 1937, Japan launched a full-scale invasion of China,
seizing Peking, and attacking by land, sea, and air the cities of Shanghai
and Nanking, inflicting enormous casualties. In the course of this campaign Japanese aircraft bombed and sank USS *Panay* and bombed HMS
*Ladybird*, which were on their lawful occasion as part of the Yangtze
Patrol. The ships had been engaged in evacuating diplomatic and other
foreigners from Nanking.

The Nationalist Army in China, after Japan had seized China's sea-
ports, depended upon the Port of Haiphong for delivery of military assistance from abroad. These goods were moved by railway from Indochina
to Kunming in Nationalist-controlled territory. For Japan, occupying
France's colonial possessions in northern Indochina after the French defeat by the Germans in June 1940 was a logical step to isolate China from
foreign intervention. But the movement of Japanese forces into southern
Indochina in the summer of 1941 was part of a more ambitious strategy.
Saigon and Cam Ranh Bay became Japanese naval bases, while the Japanese naval air force used air bases around Saigon, which were within
bombing range of Malaya and Singapore. Elements of the Japanese Army
were deployed on the borders of Siam. Indochina became an advanced
base for operations against Siam and Burma and support of future operations in Malaya, the Philippines, Borneo, and the Netherlands East Indies.

Rood noted that while the Japanese were going about their business in
attempting to dismember and conquer China, Russia (the Soviet Union)
seemed no less patient and opportunistic. Russia, however, supported a
unified China (save certain lands in the north) that would effectively
become a Soviet protectorate. While Imperial Japan used commercial enterprises to penetrate places of interest and to support nationalist movements in anticipation of fighting against the Western colonial powers, the
Soviet Union employed indigenous communist parties throughout the
region, which were recruited, organized, subsidized, and directed from

Moscow through the COMINTERN.[53] After the war, these communist parties provided a vector for the exercise of Soviet and Chinese foreign policies in the area, complementing formal diplomatic efforts in the same vein. These communist parties were inevitably hostile to the governments that were indigenous to the countries of the region as well as to the Western colonial powers. That hostility took the form of agitation and outright insurgency.[54]

Japan had to destroy the European empires in Asia in order to dismember China effectively. This suited the Soviet Union's long-term interests perfectly, Rood argued. Japan's campaign to destroy the European empires and the American possession of the Philippines would eventually open opportunities for the Kremlin to establish a new set of communist countries to be erected on the wreckage of the European empires. It was an exercise in economy of force to let Japan accomplish what it could in an Asian war.

The Soviet-Japanese Nonaggression Pact of March 1941 reduced the threat to the eastern part of the Soviet Union, freeing Soviet forces for the coming struggle with Germany, while permitting Japan to go southward. Whether Japan won or lost, the Soviets reasoned, its military operations would weaken the hold of the British, Dutch, and French on their empires, and expose those territories to the rise of nationalist movements that the Soviets were prepared to abet through indigenous communist parties. If the West won, the Soviet Union would join in the final defeat of Japan and claim its spoils there. Meanwhile, the Chinese Communist Party, with the arms, equipment, training, and money provided by the Soviet Union, would attempt to unify China.[55]

In all of this, Rood argued, the traditional anticolonialism of the United States also objectively served Soviet interests. The United States thought that the end of the war should see the loosening or severing of the imperial ties of Britain, France, and the Netherlands to their territories abroad, creating conditions for the movement toward independence. President Roosevelt, for instance, pressed Churchill hard on the matter of Indian independence. Such newly independent nations were susceptible to Soviet influence in a manner not possible when imperial control was being effectively exerted.[56]

By 1949, Rood argued, the Soviets had achieved many of these basic objectives. Japan had been defeated, China had been unified under communist rule (save Taiwan), and the European colonial powers had been or shortly would be removed from Asia. The Soviet Union and China, sometimes together, sometimes in opposition, then competed with the United States to organize the security of East Asia and the Pacific. In Rood's view, Japan's independence came to depend on the faithfulness of the American guarantee to Japan's defense, upon which the role of the United States as a Pacific power is itself dependent.[57]

In this context, the leaders of Communist China remembered the lessons of Chinese history, particularly the consequences of internal weakness and disunity. The future problems of Asia, it appeared to Rood, will be shaped by how China deals with overcoming a century and a half of weakness. Since 1949, Rood noted, the Chinese government has suppressed internal dissent, sought the unification of Chinese territory, and promoted loyalty to the regime in Beijing. This has made possible modernization, industrialization, and the creation of competent, well-equipped armed forces. Chinese leaders understand the importance of China's border regions and have taken steps to ensure that the subject peoples in those regions remain under the control of the central government. They have constructed highways and railways into the border regions to facilitate commerce and communications. Han Chinese, accompanied by Communist Party cadres, have been transferred to the outlying regions to "dilute" the local population, despite resistance from the indigenous peoples. The Chinese government has also recovered formal sovereignty over Hong Kong, now a Special Administrative Region of the PRC. Its return to China is one more piece in the building of unity of Chinese territory. It was the last foreign-controlled enclave of those that once dotted the Chinese coast and that symbolized China's weakness before the world.[58]

China, in short, has become a world power, with effective centralized administration and authority that reaches to the most remote corner of the country. But, Rood observed, the process of strategic restoration is not yet complete. China will be acutely interested in exerting effective, and in some cases sovereign, control over territories that, in the past, have been the gateway for Chinese influence over the greater region (and avenues by which barbarian powers have sought to influence developments within the Chinese imperial heartland). Those territories are Taiwan, Korea, Vietnam (Indochina), and Burma.

The strategic importance of Taiwan to the defense of China was ably illustrated by Japan when it embarked on the conquest of China. In 1879, Japan incorporated the Nansei Shoto, the Ryuku Islands, into its empire. That chain stretches from a few miles off the coast of Kyushu to within about one hundred miles off the west coast of Taiwan. As such, it lies across the boundary between the East China Sea and the North Pacific. Japan then acquired Formosa, or Taiwan, from imperial China as spoils from their war in 1894–1895. Taken together with Taiwan and Kyushu, a naval power can, in time of war, control traffic from or to Chinese ports. Japan used Taiwan and the islands in the Formosa Strait in 1939 as bases from which to seize the ports on the Fukien (Fujian) coast opposite Taiwan, closing those ports to any shipments of arms from abroad in aid of the Chinese armies defending China. (The Fukien coast had been part of the "Twenty-One Demands" that Japan had levied on China in 1915.) Taiwan, under its present regime, has a capable and well-equipped armed force and a virtual defensive alliance with the United States and with Japan.

The independence of Taiwan therefore will not be tolerated by Beijing. Rood argued that for the People's Republic, the return of Taiwan to the "Homeland" is only a matter of time and careful preparation. Chinese communist leaders and their intelligence and counterintelligence services have monitored the situation on the island closely for over six decades. Today China continues to conduct a thorough campaign to seduce Taiwan's political leaders, while exercising whatever other means it has available to subvert political parties, exploit ethnic differences, and corrupt the Taiwan regime. Internationally, Beijing seeks to reinforce the message that Taiwan is an internal matter for the Chinese to decide. The United States will be reminded constantly that it must not unnecessarily antagonize a rising great power, a viewpoint that is already prevalent in the West. Whatever works, Rood argued, for China will have Taiwan. [59]

Chinese sensitivity over Taiwan reinforces the point that the control and defense of China's maritime approaches are as important to Beijing as is the defense and control of China's land frontiers. Rood noted China's numerically impressive maritime forces and coastal defenses, including antisubmarine warfare assets, naval patrol aircraft, and elements of the People's Liberation Army (PLA) trained for amphibious warfare. He also observed that, although armed vessels of those maritime services operate chiefly within the sight of shore, they also operate increasingly off the coast of Taiwan and off Luzon in the Philippine Republic. For Rood, all of those things demonstrate that China is a maritime power as well as a great commercial power, possessing the fifth largest merchant marine in the world. Its economic interests are now worldwide. There is hardly an important commercial port in the world where Chinese-flagged ships cannot be seen. [60]

Rood observed that the Korean peninsula remains, as it has been historically, the bridge that connects China to the Japanese home islands (the nearest of which, Kyushu, lies one hundred nautical miles across the Korea Strait from Pusan, Korea). It is also the bridge that connects Japan to China. Korea, overrun by the Mongols who ruled China in the thirteenth century, was a base for two invasions of Japan, both of which the Japanese repulsed. Korea was the objective of a Japanese invasion in 1592. Korea was made a vassal state of the Chinese empire in the seventeenth century. Japan secured preeminence in Korea after China's defeat in the Sino-Japanese War of 1894–1895, the war that also secured Taiwan for Japan. The defeat of the Russian Empire by Japan in the Russo-Japanese War (1904–1905) secured Korea for Japan, which became part of the Japanese Empire in 1910. [61]

When Japan invaded Manchuria in 1931, the rail and highway networks constructed in Japanese-held Korea provided land routes into Manchuria. These land routes helped support the Japanese Kwantung

Army as it detached Manchuria from China to create the puppet-state of Manchukuo. Manchuria, detached and occupied by the Japanese Army, opened the way for that army to detach part of Inner Mongolia and attach it to Manchukuo. Japanese industrial development in Manchuria and the exploitation of its rich natural resources supported the Japanese war effort against China and the Western allies. The products of Japanese exploitation could be moved by land to Japan, except for the short sea-crossing between Pusan and Kyushu from Korean east coast ports. Thus the Japanese evaded the Allied naval blockade during World War II until June 1945.

In short, Korea, in the hands of a regime allied with a great power considered hostile by China, is capable of deploying elements of sea and air power that pose a serious threat to the Chinese coast along the Yellow and East China Seas. Land and air forces operating from Korea into Manchuria raise the threat of detaching Manchuria from China. On the other hand, a Korean regime pliant to Chinese interests would make the Yellow Sea and the northern portion of the East China Sea virtual inland seas for China, conserving Chinese naval and air forces for other purposes while providing a secure land boundary with Korea.

These enduring strategic facts, Rood contended, help to explain the Soviet and Chinese approval of Kim Il-Sung's attack on South Korea in 1950, and the subsequent intervention by Chinese "volunteers" (eventually amounting to 750,000 troops) to forestall an American-led counteroffensive. American ground and air forces had entered the peninsula through the port of Pusan, a reminder of the immutability of geography. Once the North Koreans failed to unify the peninsula, it was Chinese and Soviet policy to preserve North Korea as a communist regime. The continuing interest of China in North Korea is evidenced by the presence of Chinese weapons in North Korea's military inventory over the years, including the PRC's support for the North's missile program, as well as substantial economic assistance.[62]

The Chinese (and Russians), in Rood's opinion, have not given up on their project to unify Korea under a friendly regime. The Korean peninsula remains a zone of contention among the Problems of Asia, and the principal obstacle to unification on Chinese terms remains the presence of U.S. forces in support of South Korea.[63]

Chinese interests in Southeast Asia, and particularly in the territory of what is now the nation of Vietnam, have been long-standing, and China has occupied the north of Vietnam at various times in history. During the war with Japan during the 1930s, that region, even though it was in French hands, served Chinese interests as a transit route for supplies to the Chinese Nationalist armies from Great Britain, the United States, and France. The Japanese occupation of Indochina in 1940–1941 demonstrated its full importance to the strategic defense of China, for it showed how a hostile sea power using Indochinese ports and air bases in the country could deny China access to assistance from abroad, threaten Chinese provinces on the border with Indochina, and cut Chinese maritime communications through the South China Sea. Japanese occupation of Indochina was one more step toward the isolation of China, thus increasing Japanese freedom of action to subdue China and to end the war with China on terms favorable to Japan.[64]

In the struggle for control of Indochina, after the Japanese had been defeated by the Allied Powers, the newly installed communist regime in Beijing, despite its internal difficulties and its commitment to the war in Korea, managed to offer substantial support to the Viet Minh forces in their campaign against the French. Rood concluded that Chinese support for the Viet Minh aimed at the unification of what became, after 1954, North and South Vietnam, under a regime whose ties were to China and the Soviet Union rather than to any other power. The Vietnamese Communist Party directed the opening of the campaign "to re-unite the country" in 1959, before the National Liberation Front in South Vietnam had formally been set up. Communist arms and military supplies began to be inserted into the South long before 1965, when the first American troops landed in South Vietnam.[65]

The Vietnamese War of National Liberation, as it was presented in the West, was in fact a war for unification, Rood insisted. Throughout the war, in which American, New Zealand, Philippine, Australian, Thai, and South Korean forces fought alongside the South Vietnamese Army, Communist China, along with the rest of the communist world, supplied North Vietnam with arms, equipment, and advisers. Besides great quantities of arms, China maintained as many as ten thousand railway and construction troops in North Vietnam to keep logistical supply lines open, and deployed twelve rifle divisions across the border in China. The United States, fearing that the Chinese might intervene as they did in Korea in 1950, limited its military operations against the North to prevent escalation of that sort.

The withdrawal of U.S. and Allied forces from South Vietnam in 1973, which enabled the unification of the country, served Chinese strategic interests, Rood argued. U.S. air, ground, and naval forces, in defense of a non-communist South Vietnam, no longer posed a challenge to China's primacy in the South China Sea. After North Vietnam's conquest of the South, the Chinese attacked the North in 1979 to "rectify" the border between Vietnam and China, as a means to reassert Beijing's regional preeminence.

Over time, Moscow became the principal supplier of arms to Vietnam, and it continued to be such even after the demise of the USSR. Rood noted, however, that while American bases in Vietnam were unacceptable to the Chinese, the presence of Russian military personnel in Laos and Vietnam, and continued Russian support for the Vietnamese Armed Forces, seemed not to exercise Chinese strategic concerns. But, after all,

Rood reminded us, the Soviet Union had been the chief sponsor and helpmate in China's unification under the communists, and the Russian Federation continues to supply the military, naval, and air force equipment that China requires and that is currently beyond China's own capability to manufacture.[66]

In sum, the unification of Vietnam on China's southern flank, and the yet-to-be-accomplished unification of Korea under the communist north, remain essential aspects of Chinese security policy. Rood contended that neither regime, lying along the boundaries of the Chinese giant, dares to violate China's vital interests if they wish to remain in power. At the same time, as well-armed and equipped military powers, North Korea and Vietnam can deal with internal disorder and also defend themselves against a coup de main from outside that would again put China's unity in jeopardy.

Rood observed that Burma's location on the borders of the Indian subcontinent and on the boundary of western China south of Tibet, where there is a triple meeting point of Indian, Burmese, and Chinese territories, makes Burma a part of China's strategic sphere of interest. (Rood used the term Burma rather than Myanmar, the name given to the country by the ruling military junta in 1989.) Burma's location on the Andaman Sea, the Bay of Bengal, and therefore the Indian Ocean, places much of the Burmese coastline along the principal sea route from the northern Pacific through the South China Sea and the Straits of Malacca, into the Indian Ocean and beyond into the Middle East, Africa, and the South Atlantic. Burma's human and physical geography renders the country susceptible to foreign intervention by powers that seek advantage from Burma's location.[67]

In 1937, the Nationalist Chinese government began construction of a road between Kunming in Yunnan and Lashio in Burma. The "Burma Road" connected to the railhead at Lashio that ran from the Burmese port of Rangoon. Once the Japanese occupied northern Indochina and the port of Hanoi after the fall of France in 1940, the Burma Road was the only supply route with which the Western powers who opposed Japanese expansion could aid the Nationalists. The Japanese campaign to conquer Southeast Asia immediately after Pearl Harbor was designed, in part, to seal off this route permanently and facilitate Tokyo's effort to consolidate control over China. The United States and its allies, in contrast, had a clear interest in maintaining the Chinese Nationalists (and the Chinese Communists for that matter) in the field, to tie down as many Japanese forces as possible. Japan captured Rangoon in March 1942 and gained control of the Burma Road the following month, defeating British, Indian, and some Chinese Nationalist forces.

The U.S. Army Air Force (the Tenth Air Force) was established in India in May 1942 and began heavy bomber operations against Rangoon. The first elements of the Tenth Air Force reached Kunming in China in

June. The United States eventually established bomber bases in China to support aircraft capable of reaching the Japan home islands and created an air bridge—"the Hump"—to restore a supply route to the Chinese Nationalist Army. Before the land route was reopened in February 1945, over four hundred thousand tons of supplies were delivered to China by air and 46,000 tons of vehicle fuel were delivered via a pipeline constructed by the U.S. Army engineers from Myitkyina in Burma into Yunnan. From a strategic perspective, British, Indian, and U.S. operations into Burma, and the advance of those operations by what was a comparative handful of U.S. personnel in China proper, made manifest to Chinese leaders the importance of Burma and India to the defense of China's western frontier. Thus, Burma's political orientation will be of constant concern to Beijing.[68]

In describing China's concerns with Taiwan, Korea, Vietnam, and Burma in this fashion, Rood did not mean to argue that Chinese strategy was "defensive," or that Sino-American tensions might be resolved if the United States and its allies would simply accommodate long-standing Chinese anxieties about security. China, Rood noted, "is a one-party, totalitarian regime where international politics is seen to be an arena of unending struggle for a world order in which Chinese interests are respected and deferred to by other powers. Beyond that compromise and accommodation are diplomatic acts useful if they do not impair the progress of China in the world, wherever that progress is intended to lead."[69] Rood's analysis of China's strategic sensitivities pointed to some sort of understanding with Russia over Central Asia and their common borders, at least in the short and medium term. He concluded, however, that China's efforts to solve the problems of Asia are bound to threaten Japan, India, and other Asian powers—which means that the United States cannot avoid hard choices about whether and how it will preserve its own precarious security perimeter in the Asia-Pacific region.

## THE MIDDLE EASTERN QUESTION

The Middle East, Rood observed, has been an arena of conflict since the earliest times of history. Its location at the juncture of Europe, Asia, and Africa has left it exposed to outsiders seeking advantage within the region or moving across it as a bridge to elsewhere. But indigenous forces have been no less tumultuous at times, as potentates extended their territory in the face of resistance, to be subdued later by others more powerful and capable. The region since time immemorial has exerted its influence over peoples outside the region, while peoples outside the region have, with varying degrees of success, attempted to subdue, control, or exploit the conflicts within the region, as a matter of necessity or in hopes of gain. Rood concluded that when peace has reigned in the Middle East, it was the work of some power able to exert its authority in such a fashion that the discomforts engendered by religious differences were of small consequence when measured against the ruthless application of that authority.[70]

Given the central geographic location of the Middle East, the principal European powers at any particular time have pursued various interests in the region—strategic, imperial, commercial, or religious. The competition among these various interests followed a certain pattern, what we might call the "Middle Eastern Question"—"when some great struggle is underway in Europe, the adversaries, whenever capable of doing so, will seek whatever strategic advantage that can be gained through alliance with a Middle Eastern power, or intervention in a Middle Eastern dispute."[71] (This formulation can now be expanded to include extra-European great powers such as the United States and China.) While it is comfortable to assume that what occurs in the Middle East is merely a local competition for influence in that region, in fact history shows that it is most likely part of a larger struggle for strategic advantage outside the region.[72]

Rood cited, for instance, the Bourbon-Hapsburg conflict, in which Christian France enlisted the Muslim Turks against the Holy Roman Empire over which house would enjoy supremacy in Europe. For the Ottoman Empire, the alliance with a European power served to strengthen its quest for supremacy in the Balkans and North Africa. French efforts in the Middle East have continued with varying success until our own time. And almost invariably French interests and efforts were connected with struggles elsewhere.

British interests in the Middle East are no less long-standing than those of the French. French interests were those of a Catholic, imperial, and continental power engaged in a struggle for supremacy in Europe. Britain's interests were those of a maritime power whose chief impulse was that of fruitful commerce abroad. But first the Spanish and then the French drive for supremacy in Europe compelled British intervention in the international politics of Europe, in order to maintain British control over the eastern approaches to the British Isles. While it was from the pursuit of commerce that Britain's maritime strategy developed, that strategy also had to consider the safety of the British Isles themselves, as well as the commerce upon which the prosperity of the islanders depended.

Both commerce and the struggle for supremacy on the continent of Europe compelled British intervention in the Mediterranean, for the waters of the Mediterranean wash the western shores of the Middle East. As Britain became a commercial and eventually an imperial power in the Far East, matters in the Middle East became a compelling British concern, something that provoked Napoleon, in his war with Britain, to invade Egypt.

Rood noted that the acquisition of the Suez Canal by British Prime Minister Benjamin Disraeli merely confirmed and extended British policy in the region. The canal lay along the most direct maritime route to India and to Australia and New Zealand; that line was regarded as essential for the defense of India and for ensuring that foodstuffs reached the population of the British Isles. In addition to ongoing Franco-British competition in the Middle East, the imperial Russian advance into Central Asia toward India and against the Turkish Empire gave additional cause for British anxiety. The fate of the declining Ottoman Empire deeply embroiled Britain because the breakup of that empire would open the region to penetration and domination by hostile powers that would then lie astride Britain's imperial lines of communication.

The unification and rise of Germany created yet another challenge to Britain across the globe, including the Middle East. To meet the German naval challenge, Britain converted its capital ships from coal to oil. As a result, the lines of communication from the Persian Gulf to Britain became a strategic concern bearing directly on the ability of the British Home Fleet to defend the British Isles and to control the North Sea. Germany, meanwhile, began to cultivate ties with the Muslims and Arabs to penetrate the Middle East commercially, and to construct strategic railways. Once again a power in Europe, bent on supremacy on that continent, found reason in its commercial and imperial interests to enter the realms of the Middle East. Germany would find there an ally (the Ottoman Empire) that would make the Middle East a strategic theater of war waged by Germany for supremacy in Europe.

The stalemate on the Western front in 1914–1918 led Britain and France to attempt to force the Turkish Straits to help their ally Russia, and perhaps force Germany to expend its strength away from the decisive theater. Britain later encouraged and supported the Arab Revolt against the Ottoman Empire as a means to ensure the safety of the Suez Canal and the defense of the oil fields of the Persian Gulf.

The breakup of the Ottoman Empire brought Britain even more deeply into the strategic architecture of the region, especially that of Mesopotamia, which had always been a troubled place for the great powers to try to control (whether under the Byzantines, the Persians, the Seljuks, the Arabs, the Mongols, or the Ottoman Empire). The British conquests in World War I, as part of the general pacification of the Middle East, led to the founding of modern Iraq. Britain, as a mandatory power, undertook to render Iraq an independent nation, one that was self-governing and equipped to maintain internal stability and defend its frontiers. By April 1928, the British Army had been replaced by Iraqi levies paid for by Britain. Iraq still had its disturbances but these were dealt with routinely. Five Royal Air Force squadrons and some armored cars helped to express Britain's interests in a pacified Iraq.

The British Mandate for Iraq ended with Iraq's entry into the League of Nations in October 1932, but the country remained within the geography of Britain's imperial defense. Iraqi oilfields, pipelines, refineries, and landing fields supporting the air route to India and the Far East rendered Iraq part of that defensive system; and the oversight of the Persian Gulf, whether by Britain or a friendly power, was crucial to the defense of British maritime routes to the Indian Ocean. As an example of the continuity of the Middle Eastern Question for Britain, Rood noted that the British reentered Iraq in the First Gulf War (1990–1991) and the Second Gulf War (2003, with ongoing operations thereafter).[73]

With the defeat of France in June 1940, German policy toward the Middle East was reawakened, for here once again were opportunities for the advancement of German strategic interests. The Germans found the Middle East a lucrative arena in which to engage the forces of those who opposed their renewed drive for continental supremacy. In a directive on the Middle East, Hitler stated: "The Arab Liberation movement is our natural ally against Great Britain in the Middle East. In this connection particular importance must be attached to the rising in Iraq. It is strengthening the anti-British forces in the Middle East beyond the frontier of Iraq, disrupting communications and containing British forces and shipping space at the expense of other theaters."[74]

Rood pointed out that the United States, too, has long been a player in the Middle Eastern Question, although, until recently, primarily for commercial, religious, and humanitarian reasons. American strategic concern for the Mediterranean and the Middle East did not become reflected in policy until well after France and other western European nations had been seized by Germany in 1939–1940, and after full-scale battles were taking place in Egypt and the eastern Mediterranean. The United States supported British efforts to maintain their position in North Africa; but, perhaps more importantly, the United States took responsibility for supplying its new Russian ally through the Persian Corridor, which was the route least susceptible to disruption by the Axis. It was vital for the United States and Great Britain to keep the Soviet Union in the war, in order to tie down major Axis forces away from Western Europe. Once again the Middle East had become an important strategic theater in the battle over the control of Europe.

According to Rood, Tsarist Russia's interests in the Middle East and the Mediterranean emerged during the final stages of the "reassembling of the Russian lands after the Mongol conquest, and the establishment of a state that could protect itself from foreign invasion and extend Russian dominion across Siberia to the Pacific."[75] The main lines of modern Russian foreign policy were laid out by Peter the Great; these included access to the open seas and a policy of expansion toward the Black Sea and eventually into the Mediterranean, with its access to the Red Sea and the Indian Ocean and its exits to the Atlantic through the Strait of Gibraltar.[76]

The principal enemy blocking Russia's drive to the south, historically, was the Ottoman Empire and its West European allies, first Britain, then for a time Germany.

The Soviet Union inherited the main line of traditional Russian strategy toward the region. The Hitler-Stalin Pact of August 1939 and the Soviet-Japanese Pact of March 1941 were part of Soviet strategy to see the West disorganized and defeated, to open the door for Soviet influence and eventually domination of the vast areas of the world controlled by the Western powers. This included the Middle East and the Mediterranean. As the European colonial powers receded from the Middle East after World War II, due in part to the success of Soviet strategy, the United States emerged by default as the principal Western power in the region and as the only power capable of frustrating the realization of Soviet aims. Rood contended that it then became Soviet policy to disconnect the United States from that region, to permit the Soviet Union the freedom to settle matters in the area according to its particular ideological and strategic interests.[77]

The newly established American connection to the Middle East rested on Turkey's membership in NATO; on the American policy of securing the survival of Israel; and on friendly relations with Arab states in the Gulf. The American connection at one time extended from Iran to the Horn of Africa and Ethiopia. The Mediterranean lay on the southern flank of NATO Europe and was essentially an American lake in the early years of the Cold War.

Rood argued that Soviet policy attacked in turn each of these anchors of the American connection to the Middle East. The expanding Soviet naval and air presence in the eastern Mediterranean was intended to deny NATO the option to defend its southern flank. Soviet aid to Egypt and Algeria in 1956 led to French and British disengagement from the region. Algeria, Libya, South Yemen, Iraq, and Syria became Soviet client states, to whom military, economic, and ideological assistance was extended. The Soviets coerced or co-opted Austria, Yugoslavia, and Malta into a strategic axis that extended the Soviet Middle Eastern flank into central Europe (see chapter 5). Ethiopia became a Marxist state. The Soviets lent considerable encouragement to those bent on overthrowing the Shah in Iran and to his replacement by an anti-Western regime.

What a happy set of circumstances for the Soviet Union, Rood observed archly, that Islam's extremists, hostile to the West, should have come to power in Tehran. For the Soviet Union did not have to take any direct action toward Iran, such as a direct military thrust, which might have forced a counterresponse from the United States. The extremists performed the function quite well. The civil war in Lebanon served a similar purpose, where the detonation of a few hundred pounds of high explosives disconnected Lebanon from the West. As with Imperial and Nazi Germany, the Soviets seemed perfectly willing to align themselves not only with the forces of Arab nationalism, but also with more extreme forces. One must face the fact, Rood argued, that Soviet policy aimed to array Islam against the West, just as the Kaiser and Hitler had once done.[78]

Soviet policy was aimed to gain that freedom of action in the region, without unduly alarming the West. When Western influence became absent because Western interests had been dissolved or rendered too dangerous to support, Rood argued, events in the Middle East and North Africa could be permitted to develop in a favorable direction for Moscow, with only a minimum of Soviet exertion.

According to Rood, the success of Soviet strategy in managing the Middle Eastern Question was illustrated by the 1973 Middle East War. The Soviets provided the means for Egypt to win the first battle and ensured that the Egyptians would not lose the war. Moscow threatened military intervention that the United States could not counter because it no longer enjoyed air and maritime supremacy in the eastern Mediterranean. The upshot was that Israel lost the Sinai, civilly of course, through the Camp David "Peace Process."

And what did the Soviets get for their efforts, besides the defeat of Israel, a vital U.S. ally, even if the United States did not recognize the defeat as such?[79] Rood cited the Soviet Consul in Sapporo, Japan, who answered that question in a briefing to his staff in June 1975:

> What I consider the most joyous occasion at this time is the reopening of the Suez Canal for the first time in eight years. What it means is that the great sacrifice made by the Soviet Union from the time it supported Israel's war of independence to the cease fire when it supported Egypt are finally being rewarded with the reopening of the Suez Canal. The long cherished ambitions of advancing southward by the Soviet people is finally materializing after more than fifty years since the founding of the U.S.S.R. What the Soviet Union expects to realize through the use of the Suez Canal is the secure command of the sea in order to carry out its security concept in Europe and Asia. The use of the Suez Canal permits the Baltic Fleet, the Northern Fleet, Mediterranean Expeditionary Fleet and the Black Sea Fleet to link with the Pacific Fleet and the Indian Ocean Expeditionary Fleet in the Indian Ocean.[80]

Rood also pointed to an editorial in the *Beijing Review* (January 19, 1978), which described Soviet strategy as follows: "to lay down a strategic cordon around the continent stretching from the Mediterranean . . . to Vladivostok . . . controlling the major sea routes linking Western Europe and the United States and those linking the two with Africa and Asia."[81] The Middle Eastern Question, in Rood's view, had once again become part of the competition for Eurasian supremacy.

Rood argued that the contentious great power relations over Iraq, culminating in the two Persian Gulf Wars, should likewise be viewed in the context of the Middle Eastern Question. Those contentious relations did not begin with Saddam Hussein's invasion of Kuwait in August 1990. Soviet interests in Iraq were clearly manifest with the withdrawal of Iraq from the Central Treaty Organization (CENTO) in 1959. Turkey and Iraq had formed the Baghdad Pact that was at the heart of CENTO in 1955, with the subsequent adherence of Iran, Pakistan, the United Kingdom, and eventually the United States. The revolution in Iraq in 1958 that overthrew King Faisal and his government, culminating in the execution of the king and his principal ministers, was managed by a military coup d'etat. There followed, in 1964, the creation of Iraq as an Arab Islamic Republic. By 1969, the equipment of Iraqi armed forces reflected Soviet influence in the country. Three-quarters of that equipment was then Soviet-made, whereas before the revolution it had been chiefly British or American.[82]

In the period between the overthrow of the monarchy and the invasion of Kuwait in 1990, Rood noted, the annual gross national product of Iraq increased from about $2 billion to over $35 billion. That growth occurred despite the eight-year war with Iran, which ended in 1988. The industrial development of Iraq was greatly assisted by loans and credits from Eastern Europe and the Soviet Union, amounting to nearly $3 billion with an additional $1.2 billion from Communist China. That total was in addition to the military assistance granted to Iraq from the same sources. In short, Iraq had become a client state of the Soviet Union. And yet the People's Republic of China, supposedly a strategic adversary of the USSR, had delivered 1,500 T-59 and T-69II tanks to Iraq by 1988.[83]

The Iran-Iraq War of 1980–1988 seemed, at the time, to be just one more of the sets of rivalries that have often characterized the Middle East since the dissolution of the Ottoman Empire, rather than a manifestation of the Middle Eastern Question. But for Rood, that war had its curious anomalies, not the least of which was the supply of arms to both sides by the Soviet Union or its client-states and by China. The chief suppliers to Iran were Libya, North Korea, and Vietnam. Since those countries were supplied with either Soviet or Chinese equipment, or both, it is reasonable to assume that military support for Iran was endorsed first by the original donors. And in the course of war, there were 625 Soviet and East European military advisers in Iran. All of this occurred while the Soviet Union, Czechoslovakia, and Romania were the chief suppliers of armor, artillery, aircraft, and air defense weapons to the Iraqis. In the process, both Iraq and Iran came to be equipped with the Soviet SCUD ballistic missile and the capability to manufacture and improve such missiles. In 1989, the year before the Iraqi invasion of Kuwait, there were 16,660 Soviet and East European "economic technicians" (with ten thousand more from Communist China) and 1,350 Soviet and East European "military technicians" in Iraq.

The Iran-Iraq War was obviously a reflection of the conflicting interests of those two countries; but, in Rood's opinion, the war was also in

Moscow's interest. Both countries would have to look to the Soviet Union for support and the Soviets would come out ahead regardless of who was victorious.[84]

In 1990, the Cold War was declared to have come to an end; Iraq invaded Kuwait on August 2, 1990. On August 7, 1990, the United Nations Security Council declared the annexation of Kuwait by Iraq to be null and void; but on August 22, the Soviet foreign minister indicated that his country rejected the use of force beyond enforcement of the embargo against Iraq. Rood cited copious evidence that, despite the fact that the Soviet Union eventually aligned itself with the coalition organized by the United States to expel Iraqi forces from Kuwait, Soviet military advisers continued to work with the Iraqi armed forces. In Moscow's scheme of things, support for Iraqi policy had a higher priority than any amiable gesture toward the United States, even though the Cold War had "ended."

For its part, the United States government believed it had good reason to take action against Iraq. Saddam's seizure of Kuwait in August 1990 was not just an international outrage; it also opened the possibility that Iraq would overrun Saudi Arabia, the Emirates, Qatar, and Bahrain. Still, there were many prominent figures in the West who favored a strategy of containing Iraq and relying on international sanctions and disapproval to negotiate some sort of compromise settlement. After all, the United States had tolerated the overthrow of the Shah's regime in Iran, even though Iran had before then been pro-Western.

In the end, of course, the United States-led coalition resorted to force and won a smashing victory over Iraq. But was the victory quite so smashing? Was it a military victory at all? Rood pointed again to certain anomalies. For instance, the Iraqi government sent 120 of its combat aircraft to Iran, supposedly its mortal enemy, within days of the opening of the coalition air offensive. Additional aircraft were sent around February 6, 1991, just before the ground offensive opened. Other than SCUD missile attacks and defensive air patrols by individual Iraqi aircraft over Iraq, and a small incursion into Saudi Arabia, the Iraqi regime chose not to engage coalition forces. The consequences were that the bulk of the Iraqi Army was conserved. By April, five Republican Guard divisions were being employed to suppress internal resistance to the Iraqi regime. Iraq had not been disarmed. The regime remained in control of the country and used its power to suppress Kurdish and other resistance to the regime.

Kuwait had been liberated, but the U.S. Air Force and the Royal Air Force would have to fly 200,000 air patrols over Iraq to suppress air defenses and enforce the "no-fly zones" between 1991 and 2002. In 2003, the United States and some of its allies from the 1990 coalition felt compelled to finish the job against Saddam, in large part because of concerns over Iraq's arsenal of weapons of mass destruction. (We discuss Rood's views of the Second Gulf War in chapter 7.)

Meanwhile, Rood pointed out, Saudi Arabia, for whose defense the United States organized the coalition, suffered the consequences of Christian forces deployed on its soil. To Muslim extremists, the presence of Infidels with their women, driving trucks, flying aircraft, and serving as soldiers and marines, was an abomination not to be tolerated on the same territory where the most sacred Islamic holy places were located. The Saudi regime, guardian of those holy places, was caught between modernization and orthodoxy, Westernization and tradition. It remains a fragile, reluctant ally.[85] One could therefore conclude, Rood argued, that Russia had objectively gained a net strategic advantage from the Gulf War, furthering its efforts to alienate the West from the Middle East, despite the fact that Iraq had been defeated.

## THE CARIBBEAN-CUBAN SALIENT

Rood observed that any power bent upon the reorganization of Europe or Asia will eventually become involved in the Western Hemisphere as well as in the Middle East. It will do so to strengthen its own resource base, to weaken that of opposing Eurasian powers, and above all to retard the ability of the largest indigenous power in the hemisphere, the United States, to intervene effectively in the trans-Atlantic and trans-Pacific regions.

Historically, there have been two main avenues of approach to and from the heartland of North America. First, the St. Lawrence River–Great Lakes route, with its critical southern branch, the "Great Warpath," the 200-mile-wide corridor of lakes, rivers, and portages running roughly between Montreal and Albany. The defeat of France in the French and Indian War (Seven Years' War) temporarily removed that source of threat to the American colonies. Once the United States became independent, it had to deal with the danger of invasion by British and Indian forces, a threat that was removed by Anglo-American rapprochement in the decades following the Civil War (and the granting of constitutional rights to the Canadian Federation by London). Rood concluded that the breakup of Canada and the independence of French-speaking Quebec, which seemed close to occurring in the late twentieth century, might create a renewed strategic threat if Quebec became sympathetic to or aligned with anti-American forces in Eurasia.[86]

The second avenue of approach to the heartland of North America is the Mississippi River, the approaches to which are covered by the Gulf of Mexico and the Caribbean Basin, what we might call the Caribbean-Cuban Salient because of the particular strategic significance of that island. Long before the American Republic was founded, Cuba compelled the strategic attention of those who would rule in North America. The island is located so as to provide the means for commanding the sea routes via the Florida Straits, the Windward Passage, the Yucatan Channel, and the Old Bahama Channel off the Great Bahama Bank. In 1762, during the French and Indian War, it was the British capture of Havana that, in one blow, crippled Spanish power in the West Indies and cut the communications between Old and New Spain. It was clear to those who initiated the expedition against Cuba, as well as those in command of it, that possession of Havana as a military and naval base granted the strategic freedom of action to operate against French and Spanish possessions in Louisiana and Florida.[87]

In 1812, Thomas Jefferson wrote of the importance to the United States of maintaining "the meridian of the mid-Atlantic" as the "line of demarcation between war and peace, on this side of which no act of hostility should be committed." He observed elsewhere that "Cuba alone seems at present to hold up a speck of war to us. Its possession by Great Britain would indeed be a calamity for the United States."[88]

Furthermore, Rood observed, whenever Cuba has been in the hands of a weak regime or one hostile to the United States, American interests have been threatened. In the 1820s, when Cuba was ruled ineffectually from Madrid, pirates operating from the island's innumerable inlets and bays preyed on American and foreign shipping in the Gulf of Mexico. The U.S. Navy and Marines were deployed to deal with these threats, as well as those in and around Puerto Rico. In the course of the U.S. Civil War, Confederate raiders like CSS *Sumter* and Confederate and foreign blockade runners found Cuban harbors to be sympathetic havens in their efforts to evade the ships of the Union Navy. Havana became a great entrepôt for the accumulation and dispatch of war goods and other supplies for import into the Confederacy.

In 1897, Alfred Thayer Mahan reflected upon the strategic importance of the island. He argued that Cuba, as a military and naval base, would be of incomparable value to any power that would influence affairs in North America.

> Regarded, therefore, as a base of naval operations, as a source of supply to a fleet, Cuba presents a condition wholly unique among islands of the Caribbean . . . such supplies can be conveyed from one point to another, according to the needs of a fleet, by interior lines, not exposed to the risk of maritime capture. The extent of the coastline, the numerous harbors, and the many directions from which approach can be made minimize the danger of total blockade to which all islands are subject."[89]

In January 1917, the German government, in the infamous Zimmerman Telegram, offered Mexico a military alliance and financial support. In the event of war with the United States, Mexico was to recover certain territories that it had lost in the Mexican-American War of 1846–1848 (Texas, Arizona, and New Mexico). Not coincidentally, in February 1917, revolts broke out in Cuba threatening the production of sugar, a commodity upon which both the United States and the Allies were dependent. U.S. Marines had to be dispatched to protect the sugar mills. This fact did not escape the notice of the German government. In August 1917, German agents encouraged new revolts, forcing the Marines back into Cuba. Cuba was a place where the Central Powers hoped to tie down American military forces to prevent their deployment into France, where the decisive battles had to be fought.

The Germans did not neglect the opportunity to exploit the Caribbean-Cuban Salient when it next presented itself, Rood noted. In the dark days after the Japanese struck at Pearl Harbor, between January and August 1942, 263 merchant ships totaling a million and a half tons were sunk by German submarines in the Gulf of Mexico and the Caribbean. In two weeks alone during June 1942, thirteen ships were sunk in the Atlantic approach to the Panama Canal. One half of the ships lost to German submarines during this period were tankers. It was not just the ships that were lost, but also Allied merchant sailors, navy crews, and the precious cargoes, all of which had to be replaced if the Allies were to wage war against the Axis. Every merchant ship lost had to be replaced, taking steel and labor for the construction of other war materials. This took time, the one commodity that could not be replaced. German submarines also laid mines in heavily traveled shipping channels. The mere suspicion that a submarine was present in an area forced delays and the rerouting of merchant ships. The U-boat threat tied up scarce air and naval units that might have been employed elsewhere against the Axis. The Royal Navy had to transfer three of its hard-pressed escort groups to assist in the protection of shipping in U.S. waters.

This enormous loss of material and diversion of resources, away from the theater of operations where the decisive battles for the liberation of Europe would take place, was brought about by a handful of German submarines. These submarines operated from bases thousands of miles away from the action. Admiral Karl Dönitz, writing of what the German submariners called the "Happy Time," summarized the strategic concept of the campaign:

> For the conduct of U-boat warfare this gaining of liberty of action in American waters held yet a further advantage. . . . As the attackers we held the initiative, and by rapid switches of the main weight of our attack from one focal point to another we could confuse and surprise the enemy. The Americans obviously could not provide adequate protection for all focal points at all times, and they would be compelled to follow us from one to the other. In this way it seemed likely that we could compel the enemy to a real dispersal of his defensive forces. [90]

Of course, German submarines during this time were also attacking ships along the Atlantic coast of Florida, off the Carolinas, and among the islands of the British West Indies, as well as in the rest of the Atlantic Ocean. Rood believed, however, that the Gulf-Caribbean-Cuban theater was the most serious of these had the Germans (or Japanese) been able fully to exploit it.

The strategic problem of the Caribbean-Cuban Salient reemerged for the United States in 1959, when the Batista regime gave way to a revolutionary force led by Fidel Castro. Within a short period of time, Soviet and Warsaw Pact arms and advisers were flowing into the island. By the end of the next decade, Rood argued, it was fair to say that the Soviets had established a military and naval presence in this critical location (see chapter 5). Rood again cited the editorial in the *Beijing Review* (January 19, 1978): "For years the Soviet Union has wanted to turn Cuba into its unsinkable aircraft carrier, 90 miles from the United States, and make the island the bridgehead for expansion into the Western Hemisphere."[91]

## "OBJECTIVE CONDITIONS"

To the enduring patterns or "problems" of great power behavior Rood added another dimension—what might be called "objective conditions" or circumstances. For instance, he pointed out, we might observe that certain nations or factions seem to be at odds with each other, even fundamental enemies. We know that they are enemies because they tell us so, and there is often a long history to support that assumption. Yet they may objectively share certain common interests with respect to a third party or to the organization (or reorganization) of the international order itself. As a result, their policies, even if conducted independently, may have the objective effect of working against the interest of the third party, or of the international order itself.

For instance, Rood observed, from the late nineteenth century onward, Russia and Japan were mortal enemies in East Asia over the future disposition of China—yet both shared a common interest in expelling the Western colonial powers from the region. During the Cold War, a Muslim resistance, some of it consisting of extremist elements, fought Soviet forces in Afghanistan. Certain elements of the resistance received support from the United States. But at the same time, both the Soviets and jihadists had a common interest in the expulsion of American power and influence from the Middle East. Objectively speaking, in the early twenty-first century, Rood argued, the extremists and the Russians are both working to further the same outcome.[92]

According to Rood, we should not take the public hostility of two powers or groups as reason to ignore the objective effects of their actions. After all, international politics is a complicated thing. Is the objective effect mere coincidence or is organization and deliberate policy at work? It is axiomatic, for instance, that communism and democracy, and communism and fascism, are ideological enemies. Yet communist Russia and democratic Germany cooperated militarily after World War I, and this cooperation continued into the years of fascist Germany. This arrangement helped Germany to work around the restrictions of the Treaty of Versailles and begin rearmament, while German advisers helped train the Red Army. The mechanization of the Red Army and of the German Army was, in effect, a joint Soviet-German enterprise. Junkers built an aircraft factory at Fili in Russia, to build and test prototypes and train airmen for the new German Air Force.[93]

Rood also noted the lack of response by the Soviet Union to the incorporation of Austria and Czechoslovakia into the German Reich in 1938–1939, and the continuation thereafter of Russian exports of raw materials to Germany in exchange for finished goods. This was not a sentimental connection between friendly powers but a matter of high policy. Both powers had a profound animus toward the Western democratic powers and the post–World War I settlement. Germany aimed at the submission of Western Europe and Great Britain. Soviet political warfare against Britain and France was an indication of Moscow's hostile intentions toward the capitalist democracies. With this in mind, no one should have been surprised by the Nazi-Soviet Pact of August 1939.

The advantages to Hitler of the pact were immediately obvious. It freed him for the moment from the threat of a two-front war and allowed him to isolate Poland (assuming that London and Paris would back down again or at least not take the offensive in the West). But what about the Soviets? The pact was part of their policy to see the West disorganized and defeated. Hitler's aim, after all, was the defeat of France and Great Britain, two imperial powers that governed or kept order in vast areas of the world. If Germany defeated France and England, Soviet interests would be served. Therefore the Soviet Union allied itself temporarily with Germany to defeat the Western Allies (with the added benefit of not actually having to fight the Allies, for the moment). Whether Germany won or lost, however, the Soviet Union would wind up with Eastern Europe. If Germany defeated the West, there would eventually be war with Germany, but against a Third Reich surely weakened by the effort. If Germany lost to the West, it would be divided, exposing Western Europe to increasing Soviet influence. But for the moment, Stalin was content to let the German armed forces pay the full price against the ill-prepared West, while the Soviet Union reaped the benefits from the wreckage.

To be sure, Stalin miscalculated. Germany was able to defeat France and isolate Britain much more quickly and decisively than he expected. He also allowed himself to be surprised by how rapidly and viciously Hitler turned against him. This forced Stalin to seek another temporary alliance of opposites with the United States and Britain. But the objective outcome was still along one of the paths that Stalin's policy had outlined: in the end, Germany lost and the Soviet Union gained Eastern Europe (and China).[94]

Rood's line of analysis might cause us to inquire, for instance, if some sort of active organization and cooperation could possibly be at work, say, between Russia and Muslim extremists, just as it once existed between Hitler and Stalin. As Rood would say, you won't know until you ask the question and see what the evidence produces. Even if one cannot find or confirm evidence of active cooperation between two otherwise hostile regimes or groups, one must take objective conditions fully into account. At the very least, if the strategic vectors of the two otherwise hostile groups coincide, to the detriment of the United States, that fact should be duly noted. It is part of the inherent logic of events.

Rood believed that recognition of the inherent logic of war and strategy, of the deeply ingrained problems of international politics, and of objective conditions permitted the development of intelligent strategic forecasts. "Looking ahead to see what can or may happen is an essential part of the development of policies meant to address those crises in international politics created by nations bent on changing the order of things in the international community," Rood wrote.[95] Churchill's "step by step" anticipation of Nazi Germany's strategy in the 1930s was one of Rood's principal examples. He also stressed that Russian strategic policy in the future is likely to follow a predictable path, whether that policy aims to recover what had been lost through the breakup of the Soviet Union or to take advantage of objective conditions that the supposed "end of the Cold War" had created (see chapters 5 and 7).

Rood noted that intelligent strategic forecasts can emerge from unusual places, including novels (for example, Erskine Childers's *Riddle of the Sands*, published in 1903, whose plot was based on the discovery of German plans to invade England).[96] The iconoclastic geopolitical analyses of Homer Lea, *The Valor of Ignorance* (1909), anticipated a great Japanese-American war in the Pacific, including a surprise Japanese attack and an invasion of the West Coast of the United States. Lea's book included a map of sites predicting where the Japanese would land in the Philippines, which corresponded exactly with Tokyo's campaign in 1941–1942.[97]

Governments and their armed forces have also demonstrated that such far-sightedness is possible if they grasp the essentials of politics and strategy. For instance, Admiral George Dewey, after the defeat of the Spanish fleet in Manila Bay in 1898, warned: "I look forward some 40 or 50 years and foresee a Japanese naval squadron entering this harbor, as I have done, and demanding surrender of Manila and the Philippines with the plan of making those islands part of the great Pacific Japanese Empire of the future."[98]

Within a few days after the Munich agreement in September 1938, the U.S. Army-Navy Joint Board concluded that there would be war in Europe within the year. It therefore directed its Joint Planning Committee to make studies and estimates about the courses of action open to the military and naval forces of the United States, in the event of a violation of the Monroe Doctrine by the Fascist powers and a simultaneous attempt by Japan to extend its influence in the Philippines.[99]

On April 4, 1939, the Joint Planning Committee published its *Exploratory Studies*, which was to be the basis for development of *Joint Army and Navy Basic War Plans: Rainbow 1 through 5*. Rainbow 5 was the general scheme under which the United States would wage war in coalition with Great Britain. In dealing with the problem of Japanese aggression in the Pacific, *Exploratory Studies* concluded, very much as Homer Lea had done almost three decades earlier, that:

> The objective of Japanese aggression against the Philippines and against the United States interest in the Western Pacific in general would be:
>
> a. Possession of the Philippines, economic and political.
> b. Capture of Guam.
> c. Elimination of outside interference to Japanese domination of the Western Pacific and Eastern Asia.
>
> If the U.S. Fleet is not in a position to move to the Philippine area in sufficient time to intervene, the Japanese operations against the Philippines will include:
>
> a. Blockading, destroying, or driving off units of the U.S. Asiatic Fleet, except submarines.
> b. Blockade of Manila Bay.
> c. Landing of expeditionary forces on Luzon.
> d. Capture of Manila Bay.
> e. Establishment of airfields and movement of aircraft by flight from Japanese homeland via Formosa.
> f. Occupation of all the Philippine Islands.
> g. Simultaneously Guam will be captured and defenses established.
>
> Japan will undertake these operations when the international situation favors their success. She will prefer starting them when the U.S. Fleet, or a part of it, is in the Atlantic. In such a case the advantage to Japan of blocking the Panama Canal for an extended period would be at a premium.
>
> If the U.S. Fleet is in the Pacific a probable Japanese measure would be attempts to damage Major Fleet Units without warning, or possibly attempt to block the Fleet in Pearl Harbor. Japan would plan the inauguration of these initial measures without warning, and with as little preliminary indication as possible.[100]

Rood emphasized that *Exploratory Studies* did not intend to predict events in a Pacific War but only to set forth what Japan would have to do in order to attain its objectives. Yet the description of what might be expected in such a war reads almost like an outline history of the period between December 7 and 8, 1941, and the surrender of the Philippines in May 1942. Rood found it notable that such a chain of events could be anticipated, based on a reasonable assessment of Japanese policy and military capabilities, once that assessment was placed in the context of geographical space and the inherent logic of war and strategy.[101]

## NOTES

1. For contrasting perspectives on these topics see, for instance, Frank McDonough, *The Origins of the First and Second World Wars* (Cambridge: Cambridge University Press, 1997); and Graham Allison and Philip Zelikow, *Essence of Decision: Explaining the Cuban Missile Crisis*, 2nd ed. (New York: Longman, 1999).

2. Harold W. Rood, "Commentary on Books and Other Works Useful in the Study of International Relations," *Classics of Strategy and Diplomacy*, Ashbrook Center, accessed November 12, 2012, http://www.classicsofstrategy.com/strategyanddiplomacy/rood.pdf, 1.

3. Harold W. Rood, "Soviet Strategy and the Defense of the West," *Global Affairs* 2 (Summer 1987): 2. Harold W. Rood, *Kingdoms of the Blind: How the Great Democracies Have Resumed the Follies that So Nearly Cost Them Their Life* (Durham: Carolina Academic Press, 1980), 3. Rood also formulated the issue this way: "The clash of interests among nations and the conflicts that may arise from them are characteristic of international politics. 'Interests' seems an innocuous term to be secured by astute diplomacy guided by careful policy, behind which is the implication of the application of force when interests are vital, that is fundamental to the survival of the nation as a going concern." Rood, "Commentary on Books," 8.

4. Harold W. Rood, "Early Warning, Part IV," *Grand Strategy: Countercurrents*, June 15, 1983, 2.

5. Rood, *Kingdoms of the Blind*, 3.

6. Rood discussion with the authors.

7. See Rood, *Kingdoms of the Blind*, 277–78, for examples.

8. Ibid., xiv. Rood and William R. Van Cleave concluded in the 1960s that regional nuclear powers in a proliferated world might well explore the tactical uses of nuclear weapons rather than a so-called minimal deterrent or city-busting strategy. William R. Van Cleave and Harold W. Rood, "Spread of Nuclear Weapons," *Military Review* 46 (December 1966): 5.

9. Rood, "Early Warning, Part IV," 2–3.

10. This quote and the following case study of France are taken from Harold W. Rood, "The Strategy of Freedom," *Grand Strategy: Countercurrents*, July 1, 1981, 15–17.

11. Quoted in ibid., 15–16.

12. Ibid., 15.

13. Rood discussion with the authors.

14. Rood, "Commentary on Books," 1.

15. Harold W. Rood, letter to Christopher Harmon (July 19, 2003), Print.

16. Quoted in Hans J. Morgenthau, *Politics among Nations*, rev. 5th ed. (New York: Knopf, 1978), 120.

17. Nicholas J. Spykman, "Geography and Foreign Policy II," *American Political Science Review* 32, no. 2 (April 1938): 236.

18. Nicholas J. Spykman, "Geography and Foreign Policy I," *American Political Science Review* 32, no. 1 (February 1938): 29.

19. Ibid., 28–31.

20. Rood, "Commentary on Books," 6.

21. Van Cleave and Rood, "Spread of Nuclear Weapons," 3, 10. "As nuclear weapons become accessible to more and more countries, even an anticipated development of nuclear weapons by a rival must brook large in a nation's policy calculations. Especially in those areas where nuclear weapons might significantly alter the military balance, nations are likely to attempt to reduce the lead-time for producing nuclear explosives. They might even go ahead with their production in anticipation that some hostile neighbor is about to go nuclear" (p. 4). India, for instance, faced not only a conventionally superior power in China, who possessed an ally that could open second and third fronts (Pakistan, before its dismemberment) but also one that had recently acquired nuclear weapons. For a discussion of the relationship between civilian nuclear energy programs and potential weapons capability, see William R. Van Cleave and Harold W. Rood, "A Technological Comparison of Two Potential Nuclear Powers: India and Japan," *Asian Survey* 7 (July 1967): 482–89.

22. Van Cleave and Rood, "Spread of Nuclear Weapons," 6–7.

23. Harold W. Rood, "Distant Rampart," U.S. Naval Institute *Proceedings* 93 (March 1967): 32.

24. Rood, *Kingdoms of the Blind*, 127–30.

25. Rood thought it is useful in one's reading about the context of the German Problem to review the accounts of events given in J. A. R. Marriott, *The Evolution of Prussia* (Oxford: The Clarendon Press, 1917) and in *The Cambridge Medieval History*, Vol. V, *The Empire and the Papacy* (London, 1898; 1924). Rood also recommended *The Origins of Modern Germany* by Geoffrey Barraclough. The author, a professor of history at Liverpool and fellow of Cambridge and Oxford, began the book in 1944 while on active service in the Royal Air Force. It reflected fifteen years' study of German history by Barraclough, but it also manifested his nation's real-world experience with the modern German Problem. "In January 1946 when this work was finished," Rood noted, "one could still smell in London the charcoal and ashes along the city's streets and see the bombed-site parking lots where once buildings had stood marking the six years of war whose beginnings had nearly cost the British their kingdom and their freedom. The last of the flying bombs (V-1) and the last of the V-2 rockets of which there had been over 10,000 of the former and 1,400 of the latter had arrived on 29 March 1945, nine months before *The Origins of Modern Germany* was published. Along the road outside Oxford, one could see still the great accumulation of aluminum ingots, derived from crashed aircraft, product of the air war against Britain. The last months of the war had inflicted over 33,000 civilian casualties in Britain while 200 British ships had been sunk by U-Boats in Home waters and on the Western approaches." Rood, "Commentary on Books," 2.

26. The following material on the German Problem through unification in 1870–1871, unless otherwise indicated, is drawn from Rood, "Commentary on Books," 2–6.

27. Quoted in ibid., 3.

28. Quoted in ibid., 4.

29. Rood recommended to his students the six or so volumes of *The Franco-German War 1870–71: The War against the Empire and the War against the Republic* (1874) by the German Imperial Staff. Rood, "Commentary on Books," 4.

30. Quoted in Rood, "Commentary on Books," 5.

31. Quoted in ibid.

32. Rood, "Commentary on Books," 6; Rood discussion with the authors.

33. Rood dealt with the revisionist account of the origins of World War I in Harold W. Rood, "The Naiveté of George Kennan," *Claremont Review of Books* 4, no. 3 (Fall 1985), accessed July 18, 2014, http://claremontinstitute.org/index.php?act=crbArticle&id=1556#.U8beZ7EUp2A. Here Rood reviewed George Kennan's The Fateful Alliance: France, Russia, and the Coming of the First World War (New York: Pantheon Books, 1984). Kennan's book dealt with the negotiations that led to the conclusion of the

alliance between France and Russia and the military convention that was the substance of that alliance. Kennan accepted the standard argument, made most prominently by Sidney Bradshaw Fay's *The Origins of the World War* (1928) during Kennan's tutelage in international affairs. Rood thought that the Fay-Kennan explanation of World War I assumed that the strong-willed men who governed in Russia and France, and who sought the alliance of the two countries, were succeeded by men enraptured by the alliance to the exclusion of other considerations. Rood also thought it assumed that solemn words on paper imprisoned policy beyond the influence of reason or external events. Kennan left little room for the possibility of the clash of wills between great nations, each bent on the fulfillment of aims and ideals held to be as important as survival itself. He had no concept of the imperatives of strategy, the vulnerabilities of nations imposed by geographical circumstances, or even the inherent nature of politics. As far as diplomatic history was concerned, Rood cited for his students several illuminating accounts of the circumstances and consequences of the Franco-Russian Alliance, including William L. Langer's *The Diplomacy of Imperialism* (New York: Knopf, 1935) . If one wishes to understand the alliance as part of the general trend in Russian foreign policy in the nineteenth century, Rood recommended the excellent, restrained account given in Barbara Jelavich's *A Century of Russian Foreign Policy, 1814–1914* (Philadelphia: Lippincott, 1964).

34. The following material on Germany and the World War I period, unless otherwise indicated, is drawn from Rood, "Naiveté of George Kennan."

35. Quoted in ibid. For an understanding of the German Problem, Rood recommended that his students study carefully the documents and argumentation in Fritz Fischer, *Germany's Aims in the First World War*, trans. Hajo Holborn and James Joll (New York: Norton, 1967); Fritz Fischer, *War of Illusions: German Policies from 1911 to 1914*, trans. Marian Jackson and Alan Bullock (New York: Norton, 1975); Fritz Fischer, *From Kaiserreich to the Third Reich: Elements of Continuity in German History, 1871–1945*, trans. Roger Fletcher (Boston: Allen & Unwin, 1986).

36. Quoted in ibid.

37. Quoted in ibid.

38. Rood discussion with the authors.

39. Quoted in Rood, *Kingdoms of the Blind*, 22.

40. Quoted in Rood, "Commentary on Books," 5. Rood thought that one could hardly do better to understand the situation in Europe upon the coming to power of the Nazis in Germany than to read with care *The Survey of International Affairs, 1933* (Royal Institute of International Affairs, 1934). The events described in the *Survey* are those of a prewar world still among the vestiges of problems unsettled from the last Great War. The World Economic Conference and the World Disarmament Conference, Sino-Japanese hostilities, and the United States and the Philippines were topics having to do with stability in the international community. As to the independence of the islands, there was only the faintest concern expressed that such independence might create a vacuum of which some foreign power or other might take advantage. Ibid., 12.

41. Rood, "Early Warning, Part IV," 4–5. As to Soviet-German cooperation in the interwar years, Rood cited J. W. Wheeler-Bennett, *Wooden Titan: Hindenburg in Twenty Years of German History, 1914–1934* (1936) and J. H. Morgan, "The Disarmament of Germany and After," *Quarterly Review*, October 1924, as well as his *Assize of Arms* (1946); the latter work was withheld from publication until after the war, according to Rood, to avoid unwarranted criticism of German rearmament in the interest of peaceful relations. Rood, "Commentary on Books," 11.

42. Rood, "Commentary on Books," 11.

43. Rood discussion with the authors, referring them to Unsigned Memorandum, "Documents on German Foreign Policy, 1918–1945: From the Archives of the German Foreign Ministry," 16 July 1941, The War Years, Series D: 1937–1945, Vol. 13: June 23–December 11, 1941, Document Number 114 (Nuremberg Document 221-L), United States Government Printing Office, United States Department of State, 149–56. Excerpts printed in "German History in Documents and Images," Nazi Germany,

1933–1945, Vol. 7, accessed January 15, 2014, http://germanhistorydocs.ghi-dc.org/
sub_document.cfm?document_id=1549.

44. Ibid.

45. Ibid.

46. Rood discussion with the authors.

47. Van Cleave and Rood, "Spread of Nuclear Weapons," 10.

48. Ibid., 9–10. The immediate problem was dealt with through greater West German involvement in NATO's nuclear planning process and Bonn's accession to the
Nuclear Nonproliferation Treaty. The long-term issue persisted, however. The neu-
tron bomb and INF crises of the late 1970s and 1980s turned on whether and how the
United States could reassure the West Germans (in particular) that the U.S. nuclear
deterrent would not be decoupled from Western Europe because of the growing Soviet theater and strategic nuclear threat. For a time it appeared that the West German
electorate might decide to seek security by abandoning the alliance altogether and by
reaching some sort of accommodation with the Soviet Union, which would overturn
the European balance of power altogether—yet another dimension of the persistent
German Problem. Rood discussion with the authors.

49. Rood discussion with the authors.

50. According to Rood, Bienstock's *The Struggle for the Pacific* was based largely on
research done in Prague at the Oriental Institute, at the Russian Archives of the Ministry of Foreign Affairs and its Library, and in the British Statistical Office. The bibliog-
raphy of the book contains French, American, German, British, and especially Russian
sources. Rood cited an important work from Japanese sources, that of Shinsaku Hirata,
*How We Will Make War* (Tokyo, 1933). Rood also noted that Bienstock's theme is one
that twenty-seven years before had been put forth, within the context of that time, by a
Frenchman, René Pinon, in *Revue des Deux Mondes*, February 15, 1904; it was published
just days before the outbreak of the Russo-Japanese War and called "La Lutte pour le
Pacifique " (The Struggle for the Pacific). Rood, "Commentary on Books," 8.

51. Ibid., 8; Rood, *Kingdoms of the Blind*, 13.

52. The following account of Japanese strategy, and quotes from contemporary
sources, unless otherwise noted, is taken from Rood, "Commentary on Books," 9–11,
15–16. Rood noted that the story of the Japan Problem as it impacted China could be
followed further in D. H. Cole, *Imperial Military Geography: General Characteristics of the
Empire in Relation to Defense*, 9th ed. (London: S. Praed, 1937), which was published
from his post in Peshawar on the Northwest Frontier of India.

53. Rood noted that the American communist, an ex-Croatian, Steve Nelson, remi-
nisced about the old days of his party work, during which time he delivered cash to
the Chinese Communist Party as a courier for the COMINTERN. Steve Nelson,
*American Radical* (Pittsburgh: University of Pittsburgh Press, 1981). The Philippine
Communist Party was founded in 1930. Eugene Dennis, of the U.S. Communist Party,
was the COMINTERN representative in the Philippines in 1931. For the COMIN-
TERN's organization and operations, Rood recommended the *Survey of International
Affairs, 1928* (London, 1929), and other years of the *Survey*. Rood, "Commentary on
Books," 16.

54. Harold W. Rood, "China's Strategy: Past, Present and Future" (unpublished
manuscript, 2011), Print, 46–49.

55. Harold W. Rood, "Southeast Asia" (unpublished manuscript), Print, 30–31.

56. Ibid., 34.

57. Rood discussion with the authors. Rood's assessment from the mid-1960s concerning Japan's long-range interest in acquiring nuclear weapons indicated his belief
that the "Japanese Problem" within the Problems of Asia had not necessarily been
resolved forever; or, differently put, that Japan might come to play a major strategic
role in resisting Chinese efforts to establish control over mainland Asia and the Western Pacific. Rood preferred a strengthened U.S. alliance structure with Japan, rather
than an independent Japanese nuclear capability. Should Japan ever acquire nuclear
weapons, however, Rood observed, it would gain greater independence from all the

great powers, including the United States, and would become a more attractive ally for those powers in East Asia that felt threatened by China. (At the time, Rood listed these powers as the Philippines, Indonesia, Australia, India, and perhaps even the then-Soviet Union.) "These diplomatic possibilities open the door for increasing Japanese relations with Communist China under circumstances where Japan can derive the maximum benefits without becoming a Chinese satellite. As Japan becomes a more attractive ally because of increased military capability, so might other nations now dependent completely on the United States for their security find it possible to exercise some choice among alternatives in foreign policy." Van Cleave and Rood, "Spread of Nuclear Weapons," 7–8.

58. The following material on China, Taiwan, and Hong Kong is taken from Rood, "China's Strategy: Past, Present, and Future," 5–7, 10–18.

59. Ibid., 16–17.

60. Ibid., 21.

61. The following information on China and Korea, unless otherwise noted, is taken from ibid., 22–28.

62. Rood speculated that North Korea has been for China a "strategic actor"—an "outlaw state" whose outrageous policies, while serving Chinese interests, permit China plausible deniability for North Korean actions at home and abroad. This includes Pyongyang's exports of ballistic missile and nuclear technologies, which the West considers to be so destabilizing. Rood noted that in 1971, North Korea introduced into Mexico Mexican students recruited at the University of Moscow and trained in East Germany and outside Pyongyang. Rood asked: what possible independent interest did North Korea have in Mexico? In October 1983, North Korean special forces attempted to assassinate the President of South Korea, who was visiting Rangoon, Burma. The explosion killed twenty-one South Korean officials, including the Foreign Minister. Although this terrorist attack is easily explained in terms of the North-South conflict, Rood noted that this attack preceded the coming into power of a regime in Rangoon submissive to Chinese policy. Ibid., 27, 34.

63. Rood, "Commentary on Books," 6.

64. The following discussion of China and Vietnam is taken from Rood, "China's Strategy: Past, Present, and Future," 28–34.

65. Rood noted that Ho Chi Minh, resident of France from 1918 to 1941, was a founding member of the French Communist Party; often visited Moscow, where he studied for a year (1923–1924), where his companions included those who would rise to leadership in the Chinese Communist Party; served as the Soviet COMINTERN's ambassador-at-large in Southeast Asia; and played an important role in the founding of the Malayan Communist Party (1928–1930), when it was an offshoot of the Chinese Communist Party. Ibid., 31–32.

66. Rood concluded that Vietnam, which had a more respectable international image than the "rogue state" of North Korea, also served as a "strategic actor" for China (and the Soviet Union/Russia). In the 1980s, for instance, Vietnam provided arms and training to the Marxist insurgents in El Salvador through Cuba. Ibid., 33.

67. Rood's analysis of Burma and China is taken from ibid., 35–49. These human and physical factors include topography, in which north and south movement is easy along the major rivers while east-west travel is difficult, due to the intervening mountain ranges. Among other things, this has made it difficult for the principal minority groups (32 percent of the total population) to assimilate with the Burmese. The border regions are typically distant from where the Burmese majority dwell, and are peopled chiefly with ethnic groups who are at odds with their Burmese masters and hence susceptible to outside influence. Ibid., 36.

68. Beyond that, Rood noted, was the fact that the United States waged major ground, naval, and air campaigns in the Atlantic, Mediterranean, North Africa, Italy, and Western Europe, as well as in the South and Central Pacific, and also provided major support to the Soviet Union; yet it still had sufficient resources to wage a campaign from India into western China. That is, a great industrial nation, free of a

direct threat to its national territory, was able to take part in operations in China, six thousand miles from the Pacific Coast of North America. For Rood, this suggested that the Chinese (or the Russian-Chinese alliance) would take measures in the future to see that the United States would not enjoy such luxury in the future. See the section on the Caribbean-Cuban Salient, below. Rood, "China's Strategy: Past, Present, and Future," 44.

69. Harold W. Rood, "China's Strategical Geography and Its Consequences," in Vol. 1 of *China and International Security: History, Strategy, and 21st Century Policy*, ed. Donovan C. Chau and Thomas M. Kane (Santa Barbara, CA: Praeger, 2014), 15.

70. The following section on the Middle Eastern Question, unless otherwise noted, is drawn from Harold W. Rood, "The Eastern Question: 'Peace in Our Times'" (unpublished manuscript, 1989), Print. See also Harold W. Rood "The 'Eastern Question' and Beyond," *Global Affairs* 3 (Spring 1988): 196–203. Rood typically referred to the strategic situation of the Middle East, broadly defined, as the "Eastern Question." To avoid confusion with the classic "Eastern Question," which referred to the future of the Ottoman lands in Europe (see J. A. R. Marriott's treatment), we have settled here on the term "Middle Eastern Question."

71. Rood, "The Eastern Question: 'Peace in Our Times,'" 13.

72. Harold W. Rood, "The War for Iraq," Claremont Institute, April 2003, http://www.claremont.org/publications/pubid.285/pub_detail.asp.

73. Rood, "Commentary on Books," 9–10.

74. Quoted in Harold W. Rood, "AVOT—Harold W. Rood on the War in Iraq," Claremont Institute, October 2007, http://www.claremont.org/projects/pageid.2501/default.asp. In 1941, a nationalist government in Iraq repudiated the Anglo-Iraqi Treaty of 1930 and demanded that the British abandon their military bases and leave the country.

75. Rood, "The Eastern Question: 'Peace in Our Times,'" 31, quoting Jelavich, *A Century of Russian Foreign Policy*, 4.

76. Rood, "The Eastern Question: 'Peace in Our Times,'" 32. For this analysis Rood drew from Robert J. Kerner, *The Urge to the Sea: The Course of Russian History* (Berkeley: University of California Press, 1942), 32. Rood recommended Kerner's book to his students as a classic study of geography and politics.

77. The following account of Soviet strategy in the Middle East, unless otherwise noted, is taken from Rood, "The Eastern Question: 'Peace in Our Times,'" 36–63.

78. For instance, according to Rood, the Soviet Union demonstrated its sympathy for Iran in the *Satanic Verses* affair. Ibid., 57.

79. The official American interpretation of the outcome of the war was that it was necessary for the war to end in something of a stalemate in order for future diplomatic progress to take place. Arab honor had been satisfied by early victories in the war. Had Israel been permitted to destroy the Egyptian Third Army by a counterattack across the Suez Canal, the Soviets might have been compelled to make good on their threat to intervene. In any case, according to the standard analysis, if the Israelis had succeeded, the subsequent improvement in U.S.–Egyptian relations and the prospects for a stable Middle Eastern balance of power would have been destroyed. Rood, in contrast (without agreeing), argued that the United States has always treated its interest in the security of Israel as a matter of sentiment, not of strategy. In other words, Israel was not worth fighting for, as Washington demonstrated with its acceptance of the 1973 Arab oil embargo. The survival of Israel was thus seen as being dependent on a general Middle Eastern peace settlement, which leaves the burden of making peace on Israel rather than on its Arab enemies, and their great power patrons. Ibid., 45–46.

80. Quoted in ibid., 54.

81. Quoted in ibid.

82. The following section on the Iraq War and the Soviet Union/Russia, unless otherwise indicated, is drawn from Rood, "The War for Iraq."

83. For details on this relationship and its strategic implications, Rood called attention to Christopher C. Harmon, "Soviets Double-Deal Iran and Iraq" (Claremont, CA: Public Research, Syndicated, 1981).

84. Rood also detailed another set of anomalies relating to the coming to power, at roughly the same time, of Saddam Hussein, the Ayatollah Khomeini, and Nur Mohammed Taraki in Afghanistan. He concluded: "Should one dismiss as a random coincidence the outbreak of the Iraq-Iran War within eight months of the beginning of Soviet military operations into Afghanistan, if eight years later, the Iraq-Iran War ended with a cease-fire within two months after the Soviet Union began withdrawal of its combat forces from Afghanistan? Long-standing Soviet/Russian interests had dictated the invasion of Afghanistan and after eight years, the withdrawal of Soviet forces, leaving Afghanistan devastated in city and countryside, and the Afghanis in a state of internal war that continues to this day [2003]." Rood, "The War for Iraq."

85. Rood made this point in Rood, "The War for Iraq." Rood, as noted in chapter 7, favored military action in Iraq in 2003, as well as the continued deployment of U.S. troops in that country afterward. One might argue that a permanent U.S. garrison in Iraq would generate the same sort of religious and cultural hostility as it did in Saudi Arabia (or at least that such hostility would be played upon for political purposes). The authors suspect that Rood would have argued that these sensitivities would not have been as great in Iraq as in Saudi Arabia.

86. Rood discussion with the authors.

87. The following material on the historical importance of Cuba for the security of North America through World War II, unless otherwise indicated, is taken from Rood, *Kingdoms of the Blind*, 105–8, 130–33.

88. Quoted in ibid., 106.

89. Quoted in ibid., 108.

90. Quoted in ibid., 131.

91. Harold W. Rood, "Grenada: The Strategic Dimension," *Claremont Review of Books* 2, no. 4 (Winter 1983), accessed July 18, 2014, http://claremontinstitute.org/index.php?act=crbArticle&id=1452#.U8bdQLEUp2A. For more detail on Soviet strategy in Cuba, see chapter 5.

92. Rood discussion with the authors.

93. This discussion of the Soviet-German relationship is taken from Rood, "Commentary on Books," 18.

94. Rood, "The Eastern Question: 'Peace in Our Times,'" 36. On this general topic Rood recommended to his students Ernst Topitsche, *Stalin's War: A Radical New Theory on the Origins of the Second World War*, trans. A. Taylor and B. E. Taylor (New York: St. Martin's, 1987).

95. Rood, "Commentary on Books," 8.

96. Rood, "Naiveté of George Kennan."

97. According to Rood, Lea, who studied law at Stanford University, earned the intense criticism of the President of the University, David Starr Jordan, who was a world-renowned pacifist and enthusiast for treaties of arbitration as the means to avoid war between nations. Though physically handicapped, Lea fought in the resistance against the Manchu Empress and became a military aide to Sun Yat Sen. Both fled to Japan to avoid capture by the Empress's forces. While in Japan, Lea discovered that it was Japanese policy to keep China weak, backward, and disunited in order to dismember and conquer her when the time came to solve the problem of China. Lea's concern, most strongly expressed, was that the United States was not ready for war with Japan. On page 175 of *The Valor of Ignorance*, there is a map of the island of Luzon marking the sites for Japanese landings when Japan came to seize the Philippines: Lingayen Gulf and Lamon Bay, the one in Northern Luzon and the other in South Luzon, east of Manila. This turned out to be exactly on the mark in 1941. Rood thought it noteworthy that the 1909 edition of the book had been reportedly checked out of the New York Public Library only three times between 1909 and 1941. Rood, "Commentary on Books," 7, 27.

98. Quoted in Rood, *Kingdoms of the Blind*, 12.

99. Information on U.S. prewar planning is taken from Harold W. Rood, "Early Warning, Part II," *Grand Strategy: Countercurrents*, February 1, 1983, 5–7. The Army-Navy Joint Board comprised, among others, the Chief of Staff of the Army, the Chief of Naval Operations, the Assistant Chief of Staff of the Army for Operations, the Assistant Chief of Naval Operations, the Director of the Army's War Plans Division, and the Director of the War Plans Division of the Office of Naval Operations.

100. Quoted in ibid., 6.

101. By contrast, Rood cited a professor of International Relations at Columbia University who looked ahead in the Far East in the coming months to "an equilibrium on which peace can be based. . . . The Far East seems to be nearer a regime of lasting peace than it was a year ago or five years ago." See Nathaniel Peffer, "Omens in the Far East," *Foreign Affairs* 20 (October 1941): 49–60. Rood, "Commentary on Books," 20.

# THREE

## The Nature of Strategy

### *You Run the Show or the Show Runs You*

*Some of the more difficult issues surrounding war and peace revolve around the problems of the appropriate balance of military power, the use of surprise and the failure to perceive threats, and the approach to deterrence, especially in an age of nuclear weapons. Professor Rood examined these questions in the context of principles of strategy that he gleaned from the practical observation of how states behave. Rood did not believe that these principles were fundamentally altered by modern technology, nuclear weapons, or the advent of cyberspace.*

*There is a large and varied literature on these topics and Rood's approach to them was unconventional, to say the least. Above all, he emphasized the possibility—and desirability—of controlling events by making continuous and maximum use of the strategic point of view, something many scholars regard either as undesirable (and even dangerous) or just not possible, while some have agreed with Rood in the main.[1]*

*Rood 's contribution in this area remains valuable precisely because it is not grounded in the specific technologies or strategies of one era or another, but relies on principles of strategy that have been in operation since before Thucydides. Rood's dictum that in international affairs either "you run the show or the show runs you" is obviously not perfectly achievable as an end-state, but is a forceful reminder that states need to attend to strategy, lest they be driven to war by those more strategic-minded states seeking to overturn the existing international order. Democracies in particular, Rood taught, need to acknowledge this dictum lest they be threatened by states hostile to their political system.*

For Rood, the beginning of strategic wisdom is the appreciation of the enduring factors of international politics described in the previous chapter. These factors include the constant competition of the great powers to organize the international system to their advantage, and the high probability that some great power, sooner or later, will resort to war—at a minimum, the threat of war—to that end. Other great powers, sooner or later, will resist that attempt. The deeply rooted patterns of international politics, and the great powers' preparations for war, provide important clues as to who is trying to do what to whom and thus who will likely be one's adversaries and allies.

In this world of great power competition, "you run the show or the show runs you," as Rood often remarked. Running the show is what strategy is all about. This chapter describes briefly some of Rood's key teachings about strategy:

- the basic objective of strategy, that of achieving a preponderance of force;
- the means by which a preponderance of force may be achieved, through prewar preparations or through the initial phases of war;
- the complementarity (or unity) of diplomacy and military power;
- the value and limitation of strategic surprise as a component of strategy;
- the importance of deception and disinformation;
- the means to manipulate enemies; and
- the conditions for the successful deterrence of war.

According to Rood, the ultimate goal in strategy is to confront an enemy with such a preponderance of forces, and such superiority of strategic position from which to deploy those forces, that the enemy, however much he may resist, can only conform to one's will. (Strategic positions are those that when held in strength by one side deny to the other the freedom of action to use its forces effectively to prevent defeat.) This situation, if realized, would represent complete strategic freedom—the material capability and geographic position to deny a potential enemy any reasonable hope of success in battle. If the enemy insists on fighting in spite of reason, he will be defeated.[2]

> In war, the purpose of grand strategy is so to deploy one's own forces as to deprive the enemy of his freedom to act effectively to carry out his policies: to gain the objectives of the war. To do so one must destroy the enemy's armed forces or their will to resist. The armed forces may be destroyed by forcing them to fight under circumstances of one's own choosing where one enjoys superiority in forces and superiority in strategic position.[3]

Of course, the ultimate objective in strategy—complete freedom of action—is seldom if ever realized. One is always operating somewhat at the margins. The objective conditions of international politics are dynamic. The enemy will actively try to overcome or at least limit that strategic freedom, and seek a degree of freedom of his own. Third parties have their interests and capabilities. There are inherent limits imposed by geography and technology. The resort to war, even under highly favorable conditions, is fraught with uncertainties. Still, according to Rood, strategic preponderance, as much as can be reasonably obtained, is the goal by which national and military policy should be measured.

Rood liked to quote Sun Tzu—"attack by stratagems . . . supreme excellence [in war] consists in breaking the enemy's resistance without fighting."[4] Again, this is an ideal objective. Rood believed that actual fighting—destroying the enemy's armed forces—was typically necessary to drive the point home to the enemy that he had lost, if push came to shove.

If a nation bent on establishing a new order is serious in its purpose, it will certainly attempt to create those strategic conditions that will facilitate its success. That is, it will prepare for war. But the same should hold true, Rood argued, even for a status quo power. He quoted Queen Victoria: "One great lesson is again taught us, but it is never followed: NEVER let the Army and Navy DOWN so low as to be obligated to go to great expense in a hurry. . . . If we are to maintain our position as a first rate Power—and of that no one can doubt—we must with our Indian Empire and large colonies, be prepared for attacks and wars somewhere or other CONTINUALLY. And the true economy will be to be always ready."[5]

Rood thought that preparations for war were perhaps the most important human activity for his students to consider and understand. These preparations reveal most clearly the means and ends of the conflicting powers. Rood cited Thomas Hobbes:

> For as the nature of foul weather lieth not in a shower of rain but in an inclination thereto of many days together; so the nature of war consisteth not in actual fighting but in the known disposition thereto during all the time there is no assurance to the contrary.[6]

And William James:

> It may even reasonably be said that the intensely sharp competitive preparation for war by the nation is the real war, permanent, increasing; and that battles are only a sort of public verification of mastery gained during the "peace" intervals.[7]

Rood argued that the outcome of war—not only who wins and who loses, but the relative costs that the winner and loser must pay—is generally determined by how well one has prepared for war in "peacetime." Preparations for war will include not only accumulating the material means with which to wage war, but also securing access to those localities from where military power may be most effectively employed to overcome resistance and to gain the decision that will accomplish the purposes of policy. Preparations for war will therefore include measures that are material, strategic, economic, moral, psychological, and political in character.[8]

The accumulation of strategic advantages on one side and of disadvantages on the other will help define who can win and who will most likely lose a war. These advantages also establish the cost for avoiding defeat or securing a victory. The particular value of one small advantage over another similar advantage may not be clear, when taken in isolation. But the accumulated effect of many such small advantages, some unnoticed or too easily discounted, rather than a single dramatic event, is typically the way in which one side or the other achieves the capability to wage war successfully. This involves not merely positional or technical improvements but advantages brought about by weakening the will of the adversary, confusing him as to one's objectives, and the like.[9]

The strategic object in "peacetime," then, is to preserve and enhance one's strategic freedom of action. This is easy to say but difficult to do, especially for a status quo power, unless that power constantly keeps in mind the possibility of war. For instance, between 1918 and 1939, France's strategic freedom of action, which was well-nigh complete at the end of World War I, was lost gradually, but no step in the process seemed to portend the magnitude of the final disaster. It always seemed much easier to do nothing, to wait for the next opportunity. But the right opportunity never seemed to present itself and France's strategic freedom gradually evaporated.[10]

To avoid frittering away strategic freedom of action, one must have an understanding of the proper relationship between foreign policy (diplomacy) and military strategy. Rood thought it folly to suppose that the imperatives of strategy do not apply during times of peace. "It certainly is not difficult for the ordinary mind to grasp the difference between being droned at by gentlemen in business or formal attire and being stormed at by shot and shell," Rood wrote. "But to suppose that one process can 'triumph' over the other is to conceive them both in a manner that, while picturesque, is hardly descriptive of how things are in the world, for diplomacy is conducted to attain the goals of policy, and war is conducted for the same reason. The two together complement each other within the realm of international political relations."[11] Diplomacy, properly conceived, improves the state's ability to wage war—and hence, if possible, its ability to deter war. War, when necessary, and when properly conceived and successfully executed, enhances a state's ability, including through diplomatic means, to organize its environment so as to secure peace, justice, and defense.

Above all, diplomacy cannot substitute for military power or make up for its deficiencies. Rood cited Sir Edward Grey in 1912, on the occasion of an attempt to achieve a naval agreement with Imperial Germany: "In the first place you must not rely upon your foreign policy to protect the United Kingdom. That is to say, if you let your margin of naval strength fall below that which may be brought to bear against you rapidly, you are setting foreign policy a task which you ought not to set it. The risk of an attack on the United Kingdom stronger in force than we could meet with the ships we keep in Home waters is not one to be settled by diplomacy." [12]

Clausewitz famously wrote that war is a continuation of politics (policy) by other means. Rood concluded that totalitarian states, following Lenin, reverse the order. Politics is a continuation of war by other means. Rood believed that this formulation is a more accurate understanding of how the world actually works, than is the common presumption of a sharp delineation between two distinct states of human activity (peace/politics on the one hand, war/violence on the other). If politics and war are in their nature inseparable, then strategy—the preservation or accumulation of military advantage, aimed at preponderance and strategic freedom—is at the heart of every important political and therefore every diplomatic exercise. [13]

Rood often cited the negotiations to "end the war in Vietnam" as a classic example of the relationship between diplomacy and military power. The United States thought it could seek a *political* solution in Vietnam as though it were an alternative to a *military* resolution of the war. The North Vietnamese and their allies pursued a straightforward military victory, at the conference table as well as on the battlefield. When American military power and tactical competence altered the conditions of war so as to favor the United States, the North Vietnamese came to the conference table to prevent military defeat. The United States negotiated to reach a settlement, the North Vietnamese to preserve their armed forces and to retain strategic positions in South Vietnam. Thus Hanoi set the stage for its eventual victory in the war, as American patience with the war waned.

The United States used the bombing of North Vietnam to get the North Vietnamese to negotiate a political settlement of the war. The price the North Vietnamese demanded for beginning negotiations was a halt to the bombing of the North. In exchange for a lessening of the Allied military effort against North Vietnam, Hanoi would agree to a political settlement, which to the North Vietnamese meant the establishment of those conditions that would guarantee military victory—including the withdrawal of U.S. military forces from Vietnam. For the North Vietnamese, the conference table was an extension of the battlefield, one more arena for protracted warfare. For Americans, the conference table was an alternative to the battlefield, a place for negotiations—politics, not war. The United States negotiated to achieve an accommodation that would stop the violence. The North Vietnamese negotiated to gain a strategic advantage on the battlefield—to win the war. That was perfectly consistent with the notion that "politics creates favorable conditions for military strategy." Politics had cleared the way for strategy to bring about military victory.[14]

The North Vietnamese case study showed what diplomacy, aimed at securing victory, could accomplish in wartime. For Rood, the classic case of achieving strategic advantages in peacetime, to overturn the international order through incremental changes of circumstances, was that of Germany between 1919 and 1939. The manner in which Germany overcame its unfavorable military circumstances in the twenty years after Versailles illustrates how policy can be made to serve strategy, and how strategy can operate toward winning a war before fighting has broken out.[15] These steps may be accomplished without alarming those who are to be the victims, by moving incrementally while preparing to seize by force the remainder of the prize. Hitler put it this way: "The wise victor will, if possible, always impose his claim on the defeated people stage by stage, dealing with the people that has grown defeated, and this is every people which has voluntarily submitted to force. He may then rely on the fact that not one of these further acts of oppression will seem sufficient reason to take up arms again."[16]

The first incremental step was to rebuild Germany's military capabilities by evasion of the Treaty of Versailles. The foundations of that rearmament were set in place before the Nazis ever came to power. This was accompanied by diplomatic measures that restored Germany to the good graces of the international community, and that made complaints about clandestine rearmament—signs of which could hardly be missed—seem small minded. Even before German forces were systematically expanded, the threat of their use facilitated favorable changes in the strategic environment, without which a successful war against France would have been nearly impossible. This seminal event was the remilitarization of the Rhineland in 1936. The Rhineland, in German hands, protected the industry upon which rearmament greatly depended. Its possession also gave Hitler a certain freedom of action to pursue an eastern policy that would bring disaster to France.[17]

Hitler's support of Mussolini's policy in Africa then won Italy's acceptance of the annexation of Austria. German forces now outflanked the Czech fortified line. That development, coupled with British and French appeasement policies, undermined Czechoslovakia's resolve to resist Germany. The loss of Czech fortifications as a result of the Munich agreement in September 1938, and the occupation of the entire country in March 1939, meant that Poland was now untenable, especially once the Nazi-Soviet Pact was signed. Germany had put itself in a position where it could fight a quick war in the East. In a secret address to leading members of the German press on November 10, 1938, Hitler said:

> It is a fabulous success so great that our present-day world is hardly able to assess it. I myself became most aware of the grandeur of this

success for the first time when I stood in the middle of the Czech fortified line. Then and there I realized what it is to take possession of fortifications representing a front almost 2,000 kilometers long without firing one single shot of live ammunition.[18]

Hitler was understandably jubilant. By threatening war, he had gained moral ascendancy over Great Britain and France, discredited an alliance intended to contain Germany and defend France, and won a strategic victory of enormous consequences at no cost whatever to Germany.[19]

Meanwhile, in May 1938, Germany began construction of a line of fortifications, apparently in great haste, from Kleve on the Dutch border in the north to the Swiss border by Basel in the south. The double belt of fortifications covered a zone from two to twenty kilometers deep along the Belgian frontier with Germany, from north of Aschen to the Schnee-Eifel, with the belt extending along the frontier with Luxembourg. Yet Belgium, Holland, and Luxembourg were three countries that were declared neutral powers and that lacked any capability to invade Germany. Germany had apparently embarked on policies that might lead France and Britain to consider war against Germany under circumstances so compelling that they might contemplate the violation of the territory of the neutral states. It was surely not a coincidence that the Führer Conference from which the directive was issued to begin the Westwall, on May 28, 1938, was the same one from which the directive to prepare for war against Czechoslovakia came. France was thereby confronted with the prospect of a serious war, should France attempt to support its eastern allies by invading Germany from the west. When France's turn came, neither Poland nor Czechoslovakia (nor Russia) would threaten Germany from the east. The march to Paris would be easier for Germany than it had been in 1870 and 1914 (when the Germans never actually reached Paris). Indeed, Rood encouraged his students to realize that this war aim was not something that sprang out of the conflict in 1914, but that it had been central to the strategic objectives of the *Kaiserreich* since the defeat of France in 1870–1871.[20]

Here then was a deliberate and coherent strategy, carried out over a score of years. Yet until the attack on Poland, the strategy was carried out in peacetime. Nations bent on reordering their world will follow such strategic policies, short of war, that enable them to gain success when war comes. The beauty of operating a strategy in peacetime, Rood contended, is that its ultimate victims must either conform to each step in the strategy or go to war. Against the inconvenience and exertion and even horror of war, accommodation, compromise, and appeasement seem reasonable, virtuous, and humanitarian.[21]

The first act of the strategic drama, occupying the Rhineland, posed the greatest risk for Germany and would have been the cheapest for the allies to cancel. Once Germany took the risk and won the strategic advantage, each succeeding action was less risky for Germany because as each new occasion presented itself, effective Allied response became *more* costly. If the allies would not act when the cost of preventing a German success was slight, why would they act when the cost became ever higher? So the Germans reasoned. [22]

## ACHIEVING STRATEGIC SUPERIORITY THROUGH WAR

Rood noted that nations cannot always achieve strategic superiority, and the corresponding military freedom of action, during the run-up to war. Nations seriously preparing for war thus may seek to devise means to remedy material deficiencies during the initial phases of a campaign. Those means include seizing the strategic initiative, particularly through the use of surprise at the beginning of war, and by the employment of novel means of warfare. Deception and disinformation play a major role in each of these elements, as they did during the diplomatic phase. Rood argued, however, that such a strategy worked only for powers that were actually running the show by preparing seriously for war: "Strategic inferiority is the handmaiden of defeat. . . . To wait until war has come before gaining strategic superiority is to entertain the false hope that the enemy will go easy until we get ready; or that they will follow only those courses of action that play to our strengths." [23] The tendency for the inferior, unprepared power is "to rethink the enemy's strategy until one comes up with one that is not threatening." [24]

In August 1914, Germany sought to overcome its great strategic predicament, that of encirclement, by seizing the strategic initiative through the superiority of its initial onslaught in the West. Germany's central object was to weaken France to the point where her revival as a great power was impossible. There was more room for error in the East. Although Germany failed to accomplish this objective immediately, it ensured that from 1914 until 1918 the decisive theater of the war—where war would be won or lost—lay in Belgium and northern France, not in Germany. The Allies lacked the military forces to overcome the Germans in France and Belgium, or to deploy sufficient forces elsewhere to make Germany conform to Allied strategy. Allied forces were insufficient to breach German forces covering the Baltic, to penetrate the Balkans, or to prevent the defeat of the Russian Army. The strategic initiative was not wrested from the Germans until 1918, when American forces began to arrive in great numbers. [25]

Weimar and Nazi Germany, as we have seen, accomplished the remarkable feat of recovering Germany's position after the defeat of 1918. But even Hitler, as effective as his campaign of coercive diplomacy had been in avoiding a two-front war against the great powers, still had not created a situation of strategic superiority on the Western Front. As Rood calculated things, the decisive battle that shattered the French Army and forced the British to withdraw from the continent was fought with super-iority in tanks and in divisions of nearly two-to-one *in favor of the Allies.* [26]

The *Wehrmacht's* success, despite its numerical inferiority, was achieved by the particular combination of forces employed by the German Army, by the manner in which armored and motorized formations were employed, and by the role allocated to the German Air Force in direct support of German troops on the ground. It was not the numbers that were decisive, but the manner in which the aircraft were employed in cooperation with mobile units on the ground. The Germans spread panic among the civilian population by bombing ahead of the panzer troops, but they also attacked military targets as well with the intention of disrupting preparations for defense. German fighters attacked Allied aircraft that otherwise would have been employed against the leading columns of invaders. German dive bombers, on call by the German panz-er and motorized troops, acted as mobile artillery wherever there was a prospect that Allied forces on the ground might delay the German ad-vance. The French Air Force was decimated in the first days of the inva-sion. The Royal Air Force Air Component of the British Expeditionary Force in France and the Advanced Air Striking Force lost 934 aircraft in France; that was half of the entire first-line air strength of the Royal Air Force. [27]

The Allied preponderance of power could not be brought to bear be-cause the Allies were divided and unprepared for coalition warfare. Ger-man diplomacy and deception helped create those divisions. But it took war to bring about strategic superiority in the West. What almost irre-trievably tipped the scales against the Allies was their lack of military preparation, coupled with the strength of German determination. If op-posing military capabilities are anywhere near to being equal, an indeci-sive and uncoordinated defense is no match for a determined and compe-tent attack. [28]

## SURPRISE AND THE FAILURE OF EARLY WARNING

Rood devoted a great deal of attention to the use of surprise as a means by which nations might gain tactical, operational, and even strategic superiority, particularly at the outset of a war. He also studied the oppo-site side of the equation—how nations might recognize and respond to early warning indicators to avoid being surprised. Rood cited Clause-witz, that "war is never an isolated act . . . war never breaks out quite suddenly, and its spreading is not the work of a moment. Each of the two opponents can thus to a great extent form an opinion of the other from what he actually is and does, not from what, theoretically, he should be and should do." [29] As a consequence, there will always be political as well as strategic warnings of the coming of war. The substance of these warnings are indications of the purpose of the attacker and the dimension and the manner in which the war will be conducted. These indications appear well beforehand whether or not they are observed and understood by those who are to be the objects of the war. But the indications are cumulative over a period of time, so that each must be assessed in context with the others. [30]

According to Rood, the purpose of surprise in war is to achieve a material and psychological advantage, one that leaves an adversary unable to respond effectively to the surprise itself and helpless to master the events that the surprise was intended to set in motion. Surprise is used to conserve forces that would otherwise have to be expended to achieve an objective when an enemy is forewarned and prepared. The forces conserved through a successful surprise are available for employment elsewhere. Thus, surprise may accomplish what any battle or campaign is intended to accomplish, but more cheaply. It can reduce an adversary's will and capability to fight a battle or to wage a war effectively; for once an adversary is robbed of his strategic or tactical initiative, he must thereafter conform to his enemy's design, until he can collect sufficient forces to attempt to regain the initiative from his enemy. Forewarning by itself is not sufficient to avoid the consequences of surprise, unless it leads to the adoption of timely measures that frustrate the purpose of the surprise. [31]

The only thing that is worse than being taken entirely by surprise, Rood judged, is to be taken by surprise after repeated warnings that one is going to be taken by surprise. The former is shocking; the latter is devastating and demoralizing. After a successful surprise attack by an enemy whose intentions have for long been transparent, the victims inevitably conclude that there must have been treachery in high places. Yet it is always easier after an event than before to recognize the signs that might have given warning. Before the event, the evidence is subject to doubt, and the precautions against surprise attack are so warlike in themselves that democratic nations are especially reluctant to put them in hand. Even if it is generally understood that war is to be the probable outcome, measures to prepare for that eventuality are almost always bound to be inadequate. Such measures, by their nature, conflict with the ordinary programs of peacetime, upset the lives of people who have grown accustomed to peaceful pursuits, and portray the government as warlike rather than peace-loving, as it is supposed to be. In these circumstances it is the prospect of war that is the threat that is most abhorred, and not the prospect of surprise attack by an enemy. [32]

It might seem impossible to achieve surprise in modern war. This is due to the complicated matters that must be undertaken in order to wage war successfully and the sophisticated technical means to collect technical intelligence possessed by the great powers (and even lesser powers). In addition, the enemy can simply read the newspapers and monitor the modern social media. The indicators of the preparations for war are invariably present, as are the conditions of hostility that lie at the root of such preparations. Strategic surprise is possible only if the victims are willing, to some extent, to acquiesce in the delusion. Either they have to be unwilling to see the preparations for war as what they are, or be unable, in the general noise intended to camouflage the indicators, to discern what is afoot.

Tactical surprise, too, ought not to be a problem at all once it is understood that hostilities can start at any time. But in order to avoid being surprised tactically, it is evidently insufficient merely to discern the indicators of a coming offensive. The preparations for that offensive must be disrupted or rendered inadequate. This seems to imply that those on the defensive must possess enough strategic and tactical competence to either (a) set a trap that the enemy cannot avoid and that will destroy his offensive capacity, or (b) launch a preemptive offensive that will disrupt the preparations of the attacker to such an extent that surprise cannot be achieved, or effective operations undertaken. Neither of these courses is very attractive to a status quo nation in peacetime. "It is very difficult for a nation whose policy is to avoid war to prevent being taken by surprise, without itself putting in hand those measures that may well lead to war," Rood wrote. "The nation on the defensive can hardly expect to avoid being surprised if its opponent is bent on war while it is not." [33]

Take the case of Pearl Harbor, the very exemplar of tactical surprise. It was the result of careful planning; the anticipation of obstacles and difficulties, with measures taken to overcome them; tactical organization appropriate to the action to be taken; the painstaking training of those who carried out the operation; and the rehearsal of the forces that would be employed in the attack. Beyond that, there was the courage and audacity of those upon whom the success of the operation depended. But there can be no tactical surprise if the forces to be surprised know what is coming and are prepared to handle it.

Rood stressed that the Japanese attack on American forces in the Pacific in December 1941, which included the strike on Pearl Harbor, was not a true *strategic* surprise to the United States. Speaking with the Japanese Ambassador to the United States on October 8, 1940, Secretary of State Hull observed that it was clear now that those dominating the external policy of Japan were, "as we here have believed for some years, bent on the conquest by force of all worthwhile territory in the Pacific Ocean area without limit as to extent in the south and in southern continental areas of that part of the world." [34] Here was a clear appreciation that Japan was determined upon war and that its objectives were not limited to the mere adjustment of international boundaries to favor Japan. Japan's intent was rather to overthrow the existing order and to impose a new order in Asia. That meant, inter alia, war with the United States.

This strategic appreciation was coupled with political and operational intelligence gained by breaking certain Japanese codes. The highest civilian and military officials in the Roosevelt administration were well aware by late November 1941 that Japan was about to embark on a major military offensive in the Pacific, one that would involve, in all likelihood, American territory. War warnings were issued to senior military commanders throughout the Pacific theater, including those at Pearl Harbor. And yet, still psychologically in a peacetime mindset, those commanders found it difficult, if not impossible, to translate that appreciation in such a way as to avoid tactical surprise.[35]

The American contribution to the effectiveness of the Japanese attack on the Pacific Fleet at Pearl Harbor was thus many sided. There was a neglect of political, strategic, and tactical intelligence; an underestimation of the enemy; and the simple failure to take those precautions that, however troublesome and expensive, would become second nature in war.[36] To these things were added the advantages that the Japanese enjoyed from the outset. They knew long before the attack on Hawaii that they were going to have to go to war in the Far East if Japan were to carry out its policies. The men who flew against the U.S. Fleet at Oahu knew from the moment they took off from the carriers that they were at war with the United States. The Americans who were on duty that day at Pearl Harbor, in contrast, did not know in their bones that they were about to be at war with Japan, whatever their leaders in Washington might have concluded.

One of Rood's favorite case studies of successful tactical and strategic surprise was that achieved by a coalition of Arab powers over Israel in the October 1973 Middle East War. Israel and its great power patron, the United States, did not suspect that war was in the offing. They neither anticipated the Arab plan of attack nor appreciated the newly acquired means that made the attack possible. The root cause of that strategic surprise, Rood argued, lay in Israel's previous short and decisive defeat of the Arab armies and air forces. This helped create a state of mind in Israel and elsewhere about Israel's military competence, and about Arab inability to wage war successfully. The 1956 war had demonstrated Israel's military superiority. The 1967 war simply confirmed it. It was easy to assume that the Arabs would not dare to expose themselves to another defeat on the battlefield when harassment and diplomacy seemed to promise more fruitful consequences for the Arab powers. The Arabs, particularly the Egyptians, and their Soviet patrons, understood and played upon this perception.[37]

In Rood's analysis, one of the most important contributing causes that led to the surprise was the nature of Israel's relationship with the United States. Although the United States remained concerned about the defense of Israel, its view was that the security of Israel depended on peace in the Middle East. U.S. influence could be exercised over Israel to that end by controlling the delivery of arms to the country. The United States could not, however, influence the Arabs in the same fashion since the hard-line Arab states could depend on the Soviet Union for the arms necessary to wage war against Israel. Therefore, Israel found its freedom of action to be limited by its ties to the United States; Egypt, Syria, and Iraq found their freedom of action against Israel enhanced by their ties to the Warsaw Pact.

There were a number of circumstances that had changed in the Middle East and North Africa following the June War of 1967. These changes should have provided long-range warning that the favorable strategic conditions for Israel (and the United States) no longer existed and that resort to war had become a feasible option for the Arabs. Not the least of these was the overthrow of Libyan King Idris and the replacement of his government by a military junta led by Muammar al-Gaddafi, in September 1969. The almost immediate result of that was the withdrawal of the United States and Britain from the bases that they had been free to use: Wheelus Air Base, Tobruk, and Al Adem. The loss of Wheelus Air Base meant that the United States could not influence Egyptian policy toward Israel by deploying forces into Libya. Libyan airfields could not be used for refueling transport aircraft flying material to Israel in an emergency, and the U.S. Sixth Fleet could no longer enjoy the support of land-based aircraft in the waters off Libya and Egypt.

Beyond that, Libya became a Soviet client-state, receiving great quantities of Soviet arms. As a client of the Soviet Union, Libya was unlikely to support the policies of the Western powers; as an Arab state it was likely to be hostile to Israel; and, as a state well armed by the Soviet Union, it was beyond the reach of influence of any of the Western powers. Thus Libya joined the ranks of those hard-line Arab states hostile to Israel. Egypt's freedom of action to wage war against Israel was enhanced by the removal of British and American bases from Egypt's western flank.

Generally unremarked upon during this shift in the regional strategic balance, according to Rood, was the role played by Yugoslavia. While the ordinary interpretation of relationships in the Middle East and southeastern Europe held that Yugoslavia was nonaligned—committed neither to East nor West—"nonaligned" in the case of Yugoslavia meant political support for Soviet and Egyptian policies in the Middle East. Fighters from the Soviet Union used the airfield at Kragujeva in Yugoslavia to refuel on their way to the Middle East. Despite the "nonalignment" of his country, in Rood's opinion, President Tito of Yugoslavia had become a spokesman for both Soviet and Egyptian policy in respect to Israel.

Not the least significant change in circumstances was the activity of the Soviet Navy in the Middle East and elsewhere. Before the June 1967 War, the Soviet fleet had established bases on the Red Sea coast and at

Berbera, in Somalia, soon after the British Labour government had written off the splendid base at Aden. Within a month of the Egyptian defeat in the Sinai, a dozen Soviet warships steamed into Alexandria and Port Said. From that time onward, it seemed that the Soviet Navy was ubiquitous in the eastern Mediterranean and the Red Sea. This posed a direct challenge to what had been Western naval supremacy in those seas.

All of these items, if viewed as a whole, should have constituted a strategic warning that the Soviet Union was preparing for war in the Middle East, according to Rood. A warning should also have been conveyed by the fact that early in 1970, the Soviet Union began an extensive improvement of Egyptian air defenses, including surface-to-air missile (SAM-3) installations and interceptor aircraft. By April 1970, it had become clear that not only was Soviet materiel being given to the Egyptians, but that Soviet personnel were actually manning the new air defense installations along the Suez Canal and flying interceptor missions over Egypt. These installations provided air-defense coverage right across the canal into Israeli-held territory from north of Al Qantara south to Suez. The presence of Soviet missiles and aircraft across the canal deterred the Israeli air force from undertaking any offensive strikes into Egypt beyond what was termed the "Suez Canal battle zone." Western media at the time reported that the Soviets had taken over three Egyptian military airfields, increased the number of Soviet ground troops and airmen to 15,000, and built 450 concrete shelters for Egyptian and Soviet aircraft.

It was not remarkable that the Soviet Union should improve Egyptian air defenses because the key to Israeli victory in the 1967 war had been the quick establishment of Israeli air superiority over the battlefield. The new air defenses and the training of the Egyptian Army and Air Force were perfectly consistent with the Soviet commitment to help Egypt defend itself. Yet it was not Soviet policy merely to maintain the status quo but to see Israel expelled from the Sinai. The Soviet-installed air defense system was so placed that it could cover not only the Egyptian side of the Suez Canal, but also a wide strip right across the canal on the Israeli side. While no one outside Egypt and the Soviet Union seemed to believe the Egyptian Army capable of getting across the canal, if it were to do so it would enjoy the cover of a first-rate Soviet air defense system. It may not have been evident at the time, but what the Soviet Union had accomplished for its ally was to cover with its own forces the installation of the Egyptian air defense, while deterring Israeli interference with that process.[38]

That was not the conclusion drawn by the Israelis or their Western patrons, Rood observed. Both London and Washington had concluded in 1970 that "the Russians now seem to want neither true peace nor war in the Mideast, but an indefinite continuation of controlled tension."[39] Any evidence that seemed to confirm this relatively comfortable view of the situation tended to be accepted by Israel and the West. This was certainly easier to believe than the apparent alternative interpretation of events, that the Soviet Union would wish to expose its Arab allies to another defeat like that suffered in 1967.

To this point, Rood's analysis largely tracks with the common postwar assessment of events as to why Israel and the United States were surprised in October 1973. But here Rood added one major additional bit of strategic deception. The apparent breakdown of Soviet-Egyptian relations before the Arab attacks, in Rood's judgment, was orchestrated to mislead the West as to the peaceful intentions of the Soviet Union and the improbability of war.

In July 1972, President Sadat of Egypt announced that he had ordered all Russian military advisers and experts out of Egypt. The Middle East News Agency reported that the Egyptian President had rejected "the placement of any conditions on the use of weapons" and "vowed that Egyptian political decisions would be made 'without any permission from any side, whichever it is.'"[40] It was reported that Sadat had told a secret session of the Egyptian parliament that all Russian naval units, except two under repair, had been withdrawn from Egyptian ports. The editor of the Cairo newspaper *Al Ahram* indicated that this was because the Soviet Union and the United States had agreed, in their recent summit conference in Moscow, to isolate the Middle East conflict to avoid a superpower confrontation. The Soviet news agency TASS reported from Moscow, meanwhile, that "Russian military personnel would be withdrawn from Egypt because they had finished teaching the Egyptians how to master Soviet military equipment."[41]

It is easy to see how such a statement could be interpreted as face-saving on the part of the Soviet Union, which, it appeared, had suffered a real political defeat at the hands of Egypt. But Rood found it curious that on July 19, the same day that the Russian advisers were "expelled," Russian members of the Egyptian-Soviet Friendship Society arrived in Cairo from Moscow to celebrate Egyptian-Soviet Friendship Week. But then it was also made clear at that time that, although some Soviet advisers might be leaving, their numbers did not include those Soviet instructors working in Egypt under contract.

The belief that the Soviet Union and Egypt were seriously at odds seemed based chiefly on reports originating from either Cairo or Moscow, Rood noted. But Czechoslovakia, a country whose policies were unlikely to diverge from those of the Soviet Union, continued to enjoy warm relations with Egypt even after the Egyptian "ouster" of Soviet personnel. Czech relations with Cairo had been close from 1955, when Czech arms were first shipped to Egypt. In January 1973, the Czech foreign minister visited Cairo at Sadat's invitation. "Identity of views" were expressed that condemned "the expansionist policy of Israel supported by American arms" and acknowledging "the vital importance to both countries of the friendly assistance of the U.S.S.R. in every sphere." [42] Not only were Czech-Egyptian relations warm—Czechoslovakia was the third largest trading partner of Egypt—but those relations extended into trade union activities, journalism, and a number of other endeavors.

As if to confirm the depth of Soviet-Egyptian differences, Rood noted multiple reports originating in Cairo that suggested that the Soviets were attempting to undermine Sadat. They also emphasized how the Russian withdrawal had weakened Egyptian military capability. It was reported further that the Russians had withdrawn their SAM-4s and SAM-6s "which would have been especially useful to the Egyptians in extending air cover into the Israeli-held Sinai if the Egyptians crossed the Suez Canal." [43] As "one well-informed European diplomat" said, "It is almost certain that the Russians are making the point to the Egyptians that since they have been asked to pull out, they are going to pull everything out, no matter how that affects Egypt's defenses." [44]

An obvious conclusion to draw was that Egypt was now less capable of waging war than it had been before the Soviets had been asked to withdraw their advisers from the country. The possibility that the Egyptians themselves might be able to run a sophisticated air defense system was treated as a remote one; it was one of those false and dangerous articles of faith that the Arabs in general, and the Egyptians in particular, found such things beyond their capability, Rood observed. Defense sources in London, for example, expressed doubt about the effectiveness of Egyptian air defenses now that the Soviets were gone. The fact that Moscow had begun airlifts of personnel and arms to Syria did not at the time seem significant, because the whole thing simply confirmed what everyone knew: Moscow had been forced to change its emphasis in the Middle East because of "the expulsion" of Soviet advisers from Egypt. On August 11, 1972, Israeli Defense Minister Moshe Dayan said that the "expulsion of Soviet military forces and advisers from Egypt would enable Israeli armed forces to redeploy along the Suez Canal truce line and reduce call-ups of reservists for active duty." Dayan added: "The Russians' departure . . . leaves Egypt in no doubt that any area of Egypt would be subject to instant Israeli retaliatory strikes and, thus, constitutes an important deterrent to military adventures initiated by Egypt . . . in the event of renewed fighting we would have had to expect to encounter the Russians in battle whereas now the situation has changed." [45]

From Rood's perspective, the fact of the matter was that, once the Egyptian air defense system was installed, the Soviet forces were free to leave if that suited Soviet policy. Since the myth persisted that the Arabs could not be expected to operate sophisticated military equipment without Soviet help, the Soviet withdrawal simply reinforced the psychological conditions that set the stage for a surprise attack. Before "leaving," the Soviets had also supplied the Egyptian Army with the equipment to carry out bridging operations for the crossing of the Canal, and had trained Egyptian soldiers in how to conduct such a crossing. The strong air defense not only inhibited preemption by the Israelis; it also provided the essential cover against attacks by Israeli tactical air, if Egypt set out to cross the Canal.

By the end of 1972, then, Rood observed, the psychological conditions had been set for acceptance of the notion that war in the Middle East was unlikely; that the Soviet Union was certainly not in a position to encourage the Arabs to attack Israel; and that if the Arabs went ahead anyway, the outcome would be the same as it had been in past wars with Israel. If war came at all, it would be because of some provocation growing out of general regional tensions—but certainly not out of any Arab intention to go to war.[46]

Despite warlike preparations on the part of the Arabs, despite the indicators of war so easily seen, and despite the formidable weapons supplied by the Soviet Union, nothing would shake the notions of Arab incompetence and Israeli military superiority. Worst of all, in Rood's view, U.S. and Israeli intelligence at the highest level made the cardinal mistake of judging the Middle East situation in the light of their political preferences rather than indisputable fact. The strategic facts demonstrated warlike preparations on an elaborate scale. The wishful preferences excluded the possibility of war.[47]

We might ask of Rood: Was the apparent breach between Moscow and Cairo in 1972–1973 really a carefully orchestrated strategic deception? Or, as common wisdom would have it, did the Egyptians truly resent the Soviets' patronizing attitude and efforts to restrain them? If the latter case was true, then subsequent Soviet support for the Arab war effort, including the USSR's threat to intervene if the Israeli counteroffensive went too far, merely represented a belated effort by Moscow to avoid losing all influence in the Middle East. According to this line of analysis, the Kremlin was actually playing catch-up, not running the show, and playing a losing hand at that.

The postwar move by Egypt to improve relations with the West and even with Israel seems to favor the common analytical wisdom. But the objective fact, Rood would counter, was that the appearance of Egyptian and Soviet animosity in the run-up to the war served to promote surprise, whether that was the intention or not. As a result of war and diplomacy, Israel lost the Sinai and along with it the physical and moral sense of security that it had obtained with the 1967 war. The common wisdom has it that this loss of territory was, and still remains, a necessary precondition for peace in the Middle East. And of course, no one doubts Israel's conventional military superiority today. To this, Rood would point out that no one doubted Israel's superiority in 1973, either. Egypt's alignment can change with an assassin's bullet or a violent street demonstration, perhaps orchestrated or at least exploited by some interested outside power.

To be sure, Rood did not believe that surprise everywhere and always establishes the conditions for military victory. First, one side might possess certain geostrategic advantages that will, time and circumstances permitting, offset the tactical and operational benefits of surprise. The attack on Pearl Harbor, for example, did not lead to the strategic defeat of the United States, however devastating the attack seemed at the time. While the strikes against Pearl Harbor facilitated the Japanese campaign in the Malay Archipelago, it did not do more than delay the American riposte in the Pacific. The Japanese were not able to exploit the American defeat at Pearl Harbor (and in the Philippines) to cripple American military power elsewhere. Above all, the continental United States remained beyond the strategic reach of Japanese forces. That meant that Japan could not interfere effectively with American preparations to wage war in the Western Pacific. Therefore Japan rather quickly lost the strategic initiative to the United States despite the fact that the United States placed the highest strategic priority on the war against Germany. The limits of military surprise in this case, according to Rood, were a function of the geographic location of the United States in relation to Japan and of the overwhelming comparative industrial and military potential of America. When such conditions were more evenly balanced, however, Rood thought that surprise indeed might spell the difference. [48]

Second, the ultimate strategic objectives of the two parties should be taken into account when judging the value of surprise, according to Rood. When Argentina landed its forces in the Falkland Islands in 1982, the British government was clearly taken by surprise. Yet nowhere was it supposed that the objectives of Argentine policy were anything but the acquisition of a portion of British-held territory, to which Argentina had for some time laid claim. Argentina did not contemplate the overthrow of the British constitution or the submission to Argentine sovereignty of the British people. When Britain responded by forcibly reoccupying the Islands, there was no evident policy or effort on the part of the British government to conquer the Argentine. That is, the war was not intended by either side to encompass the destruction of the other, the overthrow of the regime in power, or the occupation of the homeland of either adversary. The surprise inflicted on Britain in the Falklands may have been embarrassing, but it was hardly devastating and did little to affect the outcome of the war, Rood argued. The policies of both Argentina and Britain were evident to each other before and during the war and those policies clearly defined the war as limited in both objective and means. [49]

On the other hand, Rood pointed out, if one belligerent clearly aims to overthrow its adversary's government and to occupy its territory, while the adversary fights for limited objectives (and believes the other side is doing so also), then the conditions for decisive strategic and tactical surprise are well in place. This behooves the aggressor to deceive its adversary about the extent of its ambitions, as Nazi Germany did in the 1930s.

## DECEPTION, DISINFORMATION, AND SUBVERSIVE INFLUENCE

In order to study nations' preparations for war and to comprehend their search for strategic advantage, Rood argued, one must appreciate the fact that one or both sides will attempt to deceive the other. If, as Churchill said, truth in war is so precious that it must be protected by a bodyguard of lies, then the same holds in "peacetime." "Behind propaganda and disinformation," Rood commented, "is high state policy."[50] As we have seen, Rood believed that, although the surprise achieved by the Arabs in the 1973 Middle East War resulted from Israeli and American self-deception, that state of mind had been encouraged and reinforced by an active campaign of deception on the part of Moscow and Cairo.

During the 1930s, both Nazi Germany and the Soviet Union employed propaganda against the United States to support isolation and neutrality as American policies. Great powers, especially dictatorships, will use witting or unwitting agents of influence as conduits for disinformation. Rood noted the bestselling book by Joseph E. Davis, *Mission to Moscow* (1941). Reflecting on his time as U.S. Ambassador to the Soviet Union, Davis expressed his conviction about the sincerity and friendliness of the Soviet Union and the Russian people toward the United States. Davis paid a special tribute to American journalists, including Walter Duranty, who had been the *New York Times'* correspondent in Moscow from 1920 to 1935. Duranty's reporting from the Soviet Union earned him a Pulitzer Prize in 1932. It would later be discovered that Duranty had been a useful tool for the Soviet government while working for the *New York Times*. Among other things, Duranty covered up the great famine in the Ukraine and other parts of the Soviet Union, which resulted from Stalin's attack against the "kulaks."[51]

The Germans worked through agents such as academics inclined to their cause, recently arrived German-Americans, isolationists, and Roosevelt haters, Rood observed.[52] German propaganda toward Great Britain was no less ambitious. For instance, Dr. Ernst Woerman, Minister Plenipotentiary and Counselor of the German Embassy in London, lectured the Members of the Royal United Services Institute in December 1937 on "Germany of Today," which was published in the *Journal of the Royal United Services Institute* (August 1938). It was a reassuring lecture that cast a favorable light on developments in Germany and their implication for peace in Europe. He especially noted how British public opinion had eased the crisis over the reoccupation of the Rhineland. Rood cited the remarks of Helmuth Brückner, the Nazi governor of Lower Silesia, delivered through Otto Tolischus to the *New York Times* from Breslau:

"France has nothing to fear from us. We do not want any land in the West. Our problem and the problem of Europe and the world is in the East. We do not want war, we want disarmament." The problems were caused by someone else: "We are perfectly familiar with the plans of Poland and her friends. Poland is a great admirer of preventive war."[53]

Rood documented many such public avenues of Nazi deception and disinformation. By 1938, for example, there were sixty German newspaper correspondents in Britain engaged in propaganda and espionage. German propaganda, carried out by agents of influence, appealed to the Cliveden set, to the fox hunters and their class; while Soviet propaganda and espionage were aimed at using the universities, where cells were recruited and influence exercised through the Bloomsbury group.

Public deception by the Germans continued even during the war. As Hitler explained in a high-level conference shortly after the invasion of the Soviet Union (referenced in chapter 2), Germany would hold to the same propaganda line in the East that it promoted after its occupation of Norway, Denmark, the Netherlands, and Belgium.

> In these cases too we said nothing about our aims, and if we were clever we would continue in the same way. We shall then emphasize again that we were forced to occupy, administer and secure a certain area; it was in the interest of the inhabitants that we should provide order, food, traffic, etc., hence our measures. It should not be recognizable that thereby a final settlement is being initiated! We can nevertheless take all necessary measures—shooting, resettling, etc.—and we shall take them. But we do not want to make any people into enemies prematurely and unnecessarily. Therefore we shall act as though we wanted to exercise a mandate only.
>
> It was essential that we should not proclaim our aims before the whole world; also, this was not necessary, but the chief thing was that we ourselves should know what we wanted. In no case should our own way be made more difficult by superfluous declarations. Such declarations were superfluous because we could do everything wherever we had the power, and what was beyond our power we would not be able to do anyway. What we told the world about the motives for our measures ought to be conditioned, therefore, by tactical reasons.[54]

From the 1950s through the 1980s, various groups in the West protested against American policy overseas in Vietnam, Nicaragua, El Salvador, Cuba, and other situations where U.S. interests were being contested. "Hands off (fill in the blank)" was the typical rallying cry. Rood had no doubt that many sincere and loyal Americans were merely exercising their constitutional rights to free speech (rights he strongly supported and defended). Rood's analysis revealed, however, that certain of these organizations served as front groups and cut-out organizations that were intended to obscure Moscow's influence over activities that supported Soviet foreign policy. They hid behind a façade that appealed for

solidarity against war and injustice and for human rights, noninterven-
tion, and other "legitimate" causes. Rood observed that within days of
the Iraqi attack on Kuwait, in 1990, many of these same organizations
began organizing demonstrations, marches, and protests against any
U.S.-led intervention. The same pattern held true in the run-up to Operation Iraqi Freedom in 2003.[55]

How can statesmen and scholars recognize the bodyguard of lies that
permeate international politics and conceal preparations for war? Rood's
method of strategic analysis relied heavily on stripping away strategic
deception, and self-deception, to reach a considered judgment about the
true objectives of the great powers. He used the long-term problems of
international politics as a template to predict the general behavior of
particular states. He sought to identify objective conditions—such as the
long-term commonality of interest between the Soviet and Chinese communists—to "connect the dots" and to determine whether such objective
conditions were a matter of high policy rather than coincidence. One
useful starting point for Rood was to challenge constantly the conventional wisdom, especially when the conventional wisdom conveniently
suggested that all was well in the world, that war was distant or impossible.

Rood believed that the serious strategic analyst can most readily cut
through the deception and the platitudes of the common wisdom by
"following the money," to use the famous expression from the Watergate
era. A nation's purpose can be determined and understood less by what
its leaders say and more by how its national power is developed and
employed. Statements about policy made by national leaders have little
meaning unless actions and the notable expenditure of resources lends
them substance. No action that costs money, requires the investment of
resources, and is troublesome to undertake lacks purpose or reason behind it, according to Rood. When money is spent, or when troops, ships,
and aircraft are accumulated and deployed, or when diplomacy and
propaganda are exercised, we should expect that policy is at work.[56]

Rood stressed that the expenditure of resources, the accumulation and
deployment of military hardware, and the exercise of diplomacy and
propaganda, are all matters of public record and thus discernible from
so-called open sources. Hitler may have preached peace in one place and
threatened war in another; but what told the tale was the extent and
nature of the buildup of Germany's military power and the practical
effects of its diplomacy. Rood insisted that there is little about the world
that any citizen of the United States cannot know if he or she merely
follows the story in Western newspapers and other commonly read peri-
odicals (a task made much easier, at least in terms of access to sources, in
the age of the Internet). Details may be hidden and particulars may remain secret, but the pattern will become clear if one is prepared to do
one's homework and to apply common sense. One must constantly ask of

seemingly random events, cui bono—who benefits? The answer to the question, cui bono, will point at least to whose strategy is at work, and for what purpose.[57]

Rood was keen to discern anomalies from the "noise" of international relations—to take a page out of Sherlock Holmes, the curious incidents of dogs that do nothing in the night, when they ought to be barking. As an example, Rood pointed to an anomaly reported in the pages of the Nazi Party newspaper, *Völkischer Beobachter* (October 14, 1933), concerning the trial of those accused of burning the Reichstag. Hitler had blamed the communists for the fire and used it as a pretext to "suspend" the democratic Weimar Constitution. Van der Lubbe, a Dutchman, was arrested for the act. Four of the other men allegedly involved in the fire were Bulgarian and German communists. Yet in the Reichstag trial, according to the Nazi newspaper, the one German and three Bulgarian communists were found innocent of any charges and were ultimately released from jail and put on a plane to Moscow. Perhaps this was German justice on display, to see that innocent men were set free—or perhaps something else was at work.[58]

In more recent times, Rood pointed out, it might have struck one as odd that, as of the early 1980s, the island of Cuba had 197 airfields, with thirty-three having runways in excess of 2,400 meters, while Norway, with a coastline as long as that of Cuba but an area three times as large, had ninety-three fewer runways and five fewer runways in excess of 2,400 meters. This, despite the fact that Cuba, unlike Norway, has no general aviation, as all Cuban aircraft are owned and operated by the government. What made the Cubans so aviation minded, one might ask. One might also ask why Guinea-Bissau, with a per capita GNP of $141 per year, with a land area of 36,260 kilometers and a population of 827,000, then enjoyed the services of fifty-three airfields, eight of which had runways up to 2,400 meters, while Belgium, with a land area only slightly smaller, ten times the population, and a per capita GNP ninety times that of Guinea-Bissau, had seven fewer airfields. Yet Guinea-Bissau had only two transport aircraft while Belgium had fifty major transport aircraft in its commercial airlines. Belgium had general aviation as well. Perhaps a clue, Rood speculated, lay in the fact that the army of Guinea-Bissau was equipped with Soviet tanks, armored personnel carriers, and artillery. Its navy was equipped with Soviet naval craft and the air force with Soviet-made transports and helicopters. But perhaps more important, Cuban military personnel were stationed in the country, and Cuba and Guinea-Bissau had more than a speaking relation with one another.[59]

It was no anomaly that nonaligned Yugoslavia would be heavily armed, in order to deal with a threat to its independence from the Soviet Union. But if that were the case, Rood observed, it was surely strange that Yugoslavia was well armed with Soviet and Eastern bloc weapons. It was also strange that nonaligned Yugoslavia permitted the Soviets to use its military facilities as a way station to supply Egypt and Syria during the 1973 Middle East War.[60]

Rood's favorite example of the silent dog in the night involved the Soviet attempt to deploy nuclear-capable ballistic missiles and medium-range bombers in Cuba in 1962. The anomaly was not the fact that the Soviets would attempt to do so but rather the manner in which the deployment was discovered.

> What should have struck every intelligence analyst in Allied services as a gross anomaly demanding explanation was that missiles and bombers were brought into Cuba and erected without any effort at camouflage or secrecy. . . . The aerial photographs released to the public in the United States could hardly have been more revealing. . . . The photographs . . . show Soviet military vehicles lined up as though for Saturday inspection and personnel tents dressed in orderly ranks. Control cables can be seen stretched between the emplacements. There were even indications of where the nuclear warheads for the missiles might be stored. The rockets, their prime movers and erectors are easily identified as the same type that had been photographed in the military parades as early as 1959 and 1960. There could hardly have been any mistake about what the Soviets were doing in Cuba.
>
> Either the Soviet rocket crews who emplaced the missiles, their commanders and the Soviet High Command knew nothing of camouflage and cared nothing for secrecy or, the lack of camouflage was as deliberate as was the placing of the rockets in the first place.[61]

To decipher the anomaly, Rood took a critical look at the outcome of the crisis. The conventional wisdom focused on the success of finely tuned American crisis management skills, which avoided war and led to the Soviets' agreement not to deploy "offensive" weapons in Cuba. This was generally taken to be a "political" victory for the United States because the Soviets had apparently backed down and also because the two sides, having stared into abyss of nuclear Armageddon, had new incentives to explore opportunities for peace. The Soviets had blundered, as the conventional wisdom would have it, because the nuclear weapons, even had they been successfully deployed, would not have had any "military" significance.

Rood challenged the conventional, "political" interpretation of the crisis, which he felt the Soviets played upon to their advantage.

> The missiles and bombers were intended to accomplish some objective of Soviet grand strategy. The manner of installation and eventual removal of the Soviet rockets and bombers were as much a part of the Soviet gambit as was the installation in the first place. . . . What the Soviet Union created with its rockets and medium bombers in Cuba was to create an incident that was certain to draw world attention to the island and equally certain to place the United States in a position where some response had to be made.[62]

Lost in the American self-congratulations was the fact that the Soviet Union had been offered a quid pro quo by the Kennedy administration to settle the crisis. The United States would provide assurances that it would not invade Cuba as long as the Soviets did not deploy "offensive" (read: nuclear) weapons on the island.[63] The Soviets, however, had already provided Fidel Castro with military equipment and personnel, long before President Kennedy's attention had been called to the deployment of rockets and medium bombers. The United States did not deem this equipment to be "offensive," and therefore worthy of a crisis with the Soviet Union.

Nor over the subsequent years after the missile crisis did the United States object to the fact that Soviet Tu-95 bombers were flying regular reconnaissance runs between Murmansk and airfields in Cuba. Soviet naval units, including attack submarines, regularly deployed in Cuban ports, so regularly that it might be said that the Soviets had "bases" in Cuba. Soviet fighters and ground-attack aircraft were also present. In 1979, the Carter administration discovered the existence of a Soviet combat brigade in Cuba that, upon closer examination, had been there all along. As a consequence, Rood, writing in 1981, concluded:

> The Soviets' risky venture ended by being hardly risky at all; what they gained from it was the acceptance by the United States of a Soviet military, naval, and air presence in the Western Hemisphere. Cuba had become and remains a defended base for Soviet and Cuban military and political operations in support of Soviet strategy.[64]

A skeptic of Rood's arguments might argue that, if the Soviets' strategic objective was to secure Cuba for military purposes, it would have been a better strategy to conceal the missiles until a propitious moment and then announce their existence to the world. Why should the Soviets deliberately show their cards prematurely by allowing the United States to "discover" the missiles? Perhaps high policy was not at work here; perhaps the Soviets were simply careless or unlucky and made the best deal they could under the circumstances.

To this, Rood would respond that the Soviets were not prepared to fight a war in 1962, a war that they knew they would lose. To secure Cuba as a future operating base, the Soviets had to raise the stakes for the United States by ostentatiously installing the missiles, while providing room for a diplomatic "solution" before the nuclear warheads arrived. If things went too far too soon, the American government (under pressure from "hawks," as the Soviets believed) might be provoked not only into military action against Cuba, but against the USSR itself.[65]

We should note that after the dissolution of the Soviet Union, American and Soviet participants from the 1962 crisis met to document their impression of events. Soviet archives were opened for a time, at least on a limited basis. To our knowledge, no evidence has emerged that would support Rood's interpretation of the anomaly of the nonconceal-ment of the Soviet missiles — that it was done deliberately to provoke a crisis, rather than an accident that inadvertently precipitated a crisis. To which Rood would respond: nothing emerged from such exchanges that disproved his argument, either. If there is greater continuity of policy between the Soviet Union and the Russian Federation than most are pre-pared to admit, why should Soviet/Russian leaders, past or present, ac-knowledge the success of a stratagem that served them so well? As to the archives, Rood would ask: who controlled them at the time and who controlled them when they were "open" to researchers? The KGB? Its successor, the FSB? Surely, those agencies have never been known to destroy or doctor documents.

But let us assume, Rood might say, that the Soviets did not cook up the 1962 crisis from beginning to end. The Kremlin's actions from 1960 onward certainly showed that Soviet leaders put an extremely high value on their relationship with Cuba. The objective outcome of the missile crisis was that the problem of the Caribbean-Cuban Salient was once again fully in play for the United States. By the mid-1970s, to make mat-ters worse, sixty thousand Soviet-equipped Cuban forces, transported by Soviet aircraft, were fighting wars in Africa. Cuba had also become a point of supply for Marxist forces throughout Central and South Ameri-ca. Yet the United States, despite occasional periods of anxiety, effectively continued to recognize Cuba as being within the Soviet sphere of influ-ence, against which it could not take military action without "violating" the 1962 understanding. And as of this writing, Cuba remains commu-nist, with strong ties to Russia.

Whatever one believes about the possibility that deception was at work during the Cuban missile crisis, the general lesson that Rood was trying to impart was the need to avoid accepting the common wisdom, especially when that wisdom is comforting. He would have his students challenge such comfortable assumptions by uncovering anomalies in international politics and attempting to explain them.

## MANIPULATING ENEMIES

Guided by the strategic dictum, "you run the show or the show runs you," Rood perceived a particular pattern of deception and control at work in communist and other dictatorships. If there is opposition to the regime, it is sensible to help organize and direct it, in order that it may not get out of hand and may be neutralized or exploited and destroyed. For instance, Rood pointed out that the KGB penetrated and ran major "anti-Soviet" opposition groups in Poland and the Ukraine in the years after World War II. When the Bulgarian government in the 1970s at-tempted to overcome the resistance of ethnic Turks to assimilation, it assigned an officer of state security to join an underground Turkish liberation group; he eventually became its leader until the movement was smashed.[66]

With this principle in mind, Rood found the 1989 "incident" in Tiananmen Square to be worthy of further inquiry. The period of student unrest began in April with the death of Hu Yaobang, former Party General Secretary, who had been forced to resign for "bourgeois liberalism." Education in China is a national enterprise aimed at strengthening the nation while equipping it with citizens able to render China a modern industrial, commercial, and military power. Higher education is a privilege extended to students who are qualified and prepared, particularly the sons and daughters of the elite: party and government officials, directors and managers of industrial and commercial enterprises, the leadership of the People's Liberation Army, and other such worthies. Given the importance of higher education, Rood argued, party political cadres and members of the state security apparatus are surely present among the faculties, student bodies, and student associations, as guardians of orthodoxy and loyalty to China and the ruling regime. Rood found it difficult to imagine that the organization of demonstrations in Tiananmen Square, which took place over a period of eleven months or more, escaped the notice of those "minders" assigned to monitor that which transpires in the universities. Rood argued that it could not be ruled out that those "minders," under the directions of the State and Party, provoked and helped organize the demonstrations.[67]

What purpose could these demonstrations, if provoked and then put down brutally by the Chinese regime, possibly serve? The repression taught important lessons to the workers and farmers that make up the bulk of China's population: that is, the government will not tolerate nonsense from university students (among whom include the future leaders of the country). Their good discipline is essential to the future of the country, to its unity and defense. The internal management of the huge Chinese population is as important as the management of the country's border regions, and the government and party demonstrated the ability and willingness to preserve good order. Rood thought that Tiananmen Square, albeit on a smaller scale, could be understood as falling into a continuum of Chinese communist policy that included the pursuit of the "Gang of Four" and the Cultural Revolution, which likewise served the purpose of rooting out dissidents and the disloyal.

The climax of events at Tiananmen Square, Rood noted, occurred during Soviet General Secretary Gorbachev's visit to the People's Republic of China, a major diplomatic occasion that mandated significant coverage by the foreign media. Why would the Chinese leadership allow things to play out as they did (assuming that it was in control) in the full glare of international public attention, risking widespread global criticism and a chilling of relations with other major powers, such as the United States?

But in the long term—and the Chinese always think in the long term—exactly what price did the Chinese actually pay in wealth, power, and security, those things that really mattered to them? The objective fact is that the PRC is now booming economically and steadily building up its military capability, with the Tiananmen sanctions ineffective or long forgotten. In Rood's view, the Chinese demonstrated to the outside world, with the foreign media allowed to report events, the regime's ruthlessness and determination to keep China unified and in good order, so that it might continue to progress as a major power in the world. And so it has.[68]

## DETERRENCE, RIGHTLY UNDERSTOOD

The doctrine of deterrence is not a creature of the nuclear age. Rood noted that deterrence relies, after all, on a judgment of human nature and rationality. Thus the Roman dictum, that to prepare for war is the best means to assure peace. But deterrence has different connotations to different leaders at different times.[69]

Rood believed that it is possible to deter a hostile power from going to war to achieve its objectives. It is possible, but not certain, even in the best of circumstances. Deterrence is a laudable goal but, like peace, it can never be achieved directly. A policy based on the deterrence of war is highly likely to fail if it becomes a substitute for rigorous high-level strategic thinking, appropriate military policy, and the means to execute that strategy and policy in wartime. The mere existence of nuclear weapons, "threats that leave something to chance," "sufficiency," and the like are merely variations on the comforting assumption that there will be no war.[70]

For instance, when the United States enjoyed a nuclear monopoly, and later nuclear superiority over the Soviet Union, its military objective, in the event of war, was to be able to defeat the USSR, limit damage to the United States, and achieve its political objectives (put more directly, to win the war). This goal was not out of line with American military capabilities. As a result, the *political* objectives of American policy (most importantly, to deter a Soviet invasion of Western Europe) were achieved. We cannot know if the Soviets were in fact deterred, Rood wrote, only that they did not attack. Had they attacked, the United States and the West would have stood a good chance of militarily preventing Soviet victory.[71]

By contrast, the belief that *minimum* deterrence will halt the advance of those powers determined to alter the status quo had achieved the status of a hallowed tradition in the West, even before the nuclear age. On November 7, 1938, after the Sudeten crisis had apparently been resolved in favor of peace, the British cabinet met to discuss the service estimates. The air staff had long requested parity with the German *Luft-waffe*, by which it meant "a force of equal striking weight" with that of Germany. For the British cabinet, however, parity in the air was equated with "effective deterrent strength." British air power would be *sufficient* if it protected the country and acted as a *deterrent*, "so that whatever the strength of the German air force, Germany itself would risk destruction if they [sic] attacked us."[72]

Needless to say, the Cabinet's position—to maintain "effective deterrent strength"—became the operating assumption that drove British strategic policy. Prime Minister Neville Chamberlain hesitated to authorize an increase in the British bomber force, because it would require "more borrowing of money," and because it would appear rather difficult (in Chamberlain's opinion, at least) to represent the acquisition of heavy bombers by the RAF as "in any way defensive." For the British to concentrate on producing Manchester and Halifax bombers would only invite Germany to build a super bomber. Further, a bomber force was not cost effective: one heavy bomber would cost as much as four fighters. Thus, the heavy bomber program of the Royal Air Force, which would have provided the means to threaten Germany, was postponed. The definition of "effective deterrent strength" did not raise, in German eyes, the risk of Germany's destruction if Germany attacked Britain, for Germany's leaders knew that Britain did not have the material capability to destroy Germany. To them, this was the salient fact.

Britain was not the only nation to have fallen prey to such wishful thinking. In January 1932, President Herbert Hoover ordered the Pacific Fleet to remain in Hawaiian waters after its winter concentration. Units of the Imperial Japanese armed forces had just attacked the city of Shanghai, and Hoover hoped that the presence of the U.S. Fleet in the Pacific would deter further Japanese moves against China. It did not. In any case, there were no fuel oil reserves in the Philippines, should the Fleet require them. In fact, there was barely enough tanker capacity to support Fleet operations in the Pacific for more than thirty days. But President Hoover had already made it clear that he would not fight for Asia.

A similar situation occurred in October 1940, when the American government debated the disposition of the U.S. Pacific Fleet: should it remain in Hawaiian waters or, with the exception of the Hawaiian detachment, should it be stationed on the West Coast? President Franklin D. Roosevelt directed that the fleet be retained in Hawaii in order to exercise a "restraining influence on Japan." The commander in chief of the U.S. Fleet argued that the presence of the fleet in Hawaii might influence a civilian political government, but Japan had a military government that knew that the fleet was undermanned, was unprepared for war, and had no train of auxiliary ships (without which it could not undertake active operations). Therefore the presence of the fleet in Hawaii could not exercise a restraining influence on Japanese actions.

The Japanese, in fact, were not deterred from initiating hostilities against British, Dutch, and American territories in the Far East the following year. Japan did not act upon the *political* signal of basing the U.S. Pacific Fleet in Hawaii, which President Roosevelt had intended as a sign of America's determination. The Japanese government instead evaluated the *military* value of the Pacific Fleet. That value did not rest in its location at Pearl Harbor, Rood concluded, but rather on the fleet's ability to advance across the Pacific, where it might interfere with Japan's strategic operations.

This did not mean that Japan ignored the Pacific Fleet. On the contrary, Rood noted, the Japanese gave the military potential of American forces full credit. Those forces that might have deterred (i.e., prevented) the Japanese from achieving their strategic objectives became prime targets upon the initiation of hostilities. The main Battle Force of the U.S. Pacific Fleet was surprised at Pearl Harbor. American B-17 bombers based in the Philippines came under attack. The Royal Air Force in Malaya was all but destroyed. Having eliminated those military assets, Japan was then temporarily free to seek to create its Far Eastern Empire without significant opposition.

Prior to World War II, the American and British goal of deterrence rested on an attempt to influence the *political* decision of their opponents to go to war. In other words, Rood pointed out, deterrence meant the ability to register one's displeasure toward an adversary, in the belief that that would be sufficient to determine his actions. But Germany's or Japan's decision to go to war was based on assumptions that the Allied powers could not comprehend. It did not matter to the Allies that they lacked the ability to prevent, physically and undeniably, their enemies from carrying out a particular course of action. But to their enemies, without that there would be no deterrence.

Many individuals in the democracies pointed to the obvious economic and strategic weaknesses of both Germany and Japan as another reason that these nations would not go to war and thus why a serious rearmament was unnecessary. But the German government believed that this was the precise reason that it must go to war. On November 17, 1937, Hitler explained the situation to his top military and civilian officials:

> Case 1. Period 1943-45. After this we can only expect a change for the worse. The re-arming of the Army, the Navy and the Air Force, as well as the formation of the Officers' Corps, are practically concluded. Our material equipment armaments are modern, with further delay the danger of their becoming out-of-date will increase. In particular the secrecy of "special weapons" cannot always be safeguarded. Enlistment of reserves would be limited to the current recruiting age groups and an addition from older untrained groups would be no longer available.

In comparison with the re-armament, which will have been carried
out at the time by the other nations, we shall decrease in relative power. Should we not act until 1943/45, then, dependent on the absence of
reserves, any year could bring about the food crises, for the countering
of which we do not possess the necessary foreign currency. This must
be considered as a point of weakness in the regime.

Over and above that, the world will anticipate our action and will
increase counter-measures yearly. Whilst other nations isolate themselves we should be forced on the offensive.

What the actual position would be in the years 1943-1945 no one
knows today. It is certain, however, that we can wait no longer.

On the one side the large armed forces, with the necessity for securing their upkeep, the aging of the Nazi movement and of its leaders,
and on the other side the prospect of a lowering of the standard of
living and a drop in the birth rate, leaves us no other choice than to act.
If the Führer is still living, then it will be his irrevocable decision to
solve the German space problem no later than 1943-45.[73]

Deterrence, Hitler understood, works both ways. In 1936, Rood noted,
he was not deterred from occupying the Rhineland, despite the overwhelming superiority of the British, the French, and others. German military leaders were frightened by this enormous gamble and strongly opposed it. Hitler gave strict orders to the small German occupying force: it
must withdraw at the least sign of opposition. But free Europe, tired and
fearful from the last war, stayed its hand, because it could not bear to
contemplate the renewal of the struggle and the consequences that might
befall it as a result. Hitler, himself a product of the Great War, drew
somewhat different conclusions about the nature of deterrence.

Rood offered additional reflections on the nature of deterrence in the
context of the so-called INF (Intermediate-Range Nuclear Force) crisis in
Europe in the early 1980s. Against considerable public opposition in
Western Europe and the United States, NATO had agreed to deploy U.S.
Pershing II missiles and Ground Launched Cruise Missiles (GLCMs) in
response to the buildup of Soviet theater nuclear forces, particularly the
SS-20 missile. Rood, of course, strongly supported measures that re-
dressed the military balance in Europe, which he believed had come to
favor the Soviets. He was concerned, however, that NATO's rationale
reflected the tendency in the West to rely on political rather than military
deterrence. This rationale was based on the enormous destructive power
of nuclear weapons. In other words, the United States and NATO had
come to believe that the very existence of nuclear weapons would, if they
were properly located, make certain courses of action impossible for the
Soviets, just as the existence of the Pacific Fleet and its location in Hawaii
was believed to inhibit the Japanese. Rood concluded, however, that the
Soviets, although respecting the destructiveness of nuclear arms, treated

them just as any other weapon, to be used when appropriate, and not otherwise.

Given Soviet objectives and their views on nuclear war, prudent Western statesmen rightly viewed with concern the deployment of SS-20 and other nuclear-capable systems. These Soviet deployments did have obvious political objectives: to intimidate European governments, to weaken the NATO alliance, and to serve as instruments in future arms negotiations. But they also had a definite military purpose. In the event of war, these Soviet nuclear weapons would be used to achieve specific strategic and tactical goals that could otherwise not be achieved, or that would not be achieved so readily.

Because of the West's preoccupation with political deterrence, Rood contended that the debate over theater nuclear modernization in Europe had virtually no connection with reality. One side of the Western INF debate argued that the deployment of GLCMs and Pershing IIs did not increase the security of the West because nuclear war was impossible (and therefore any new weapons were superfluous), or because the weapons made nuclear war more likely. The other side contended that the new deployment was needed to signal NATO's continued resolve to resist the USSR. But neither position fully considered what *military* application these new NATO weapons might have. If they could, in combination with other Western forces and arms, defeat the Soviet Union in war, then they might have some deterrent value. If they rendered the possibility of Soviet victory significantly less likely than otherwise, then too they might have some deterrent value. But if they were intended as a political signal to the Soviet Union, then they were probably useless.

Rood did not mean to say that the Soviet Union did not take into account the presence of nuclear weapons in the U.S. and NATO arsenals, even if the West was uncertain as to their military application. Just as Japan sought to eliminate those forces that could threaten its objectives, so the Soviet Union would have acted, had war occurred in Europe. Soviet Frontal Aviation had as one of its principal missions the destruction of the enemy's nuclear capability. One of the tasks that Soviet tactical writings assigned to reinforced tank battalions, following a breakthrough operation, was the destruction of the enemy's means of delivering nuclear weapons. If the Soviets achieved strategic surprise in launching an invasion, it was widely assumed that they would have a "grace period" before nuclear weapons were used against them, because twenty-four to forty-eight hours were required to obtain political authorization to release and use NATO's nuclear weapons.

In this context, Rood commented on the ongoing controversy over whether NATO should detonate a nuclear device over the Baltic as a warning in the event of a Soviet attack. This explosion would presumably have reminded the Soviets of the existence of NATO's nuclear force, perhaps deterring a further Soviet advance before full-scale theater or strategic nuclear war began. This option might have relieved some pressure on certain Western European leaders, but Rood believed that, again, it had no connection with reality. The Soviets were well aware of the existence of the West's nuclear weapons. If NATO wished to deter the Soviets at such a point, and if it believed that the Alliance's resolve must be shown, then it should target the leading elements of the Soviet invasion force, or some other militarily important assets.

Some Western leaders argued that deterrence of the Soviets was feasible because, unlike Hitler and the Japanese leaders, the men in the Kremlin were political optimists and therefore less prone to take risks, since they believed history was on their side. Rood countered that if the Soviet leadership still believed in the inevitability of the triumph of socialism, then it need not fear changes in technology, such as the development of nuclear weapons, which could not deflect the tide of history as socialism understood it. Others in the West argued that the Soviet leadership was actually steeped in realism, not political ideology, and was moved instead by fear that its empire would be broken up. In either case, Rood said, it remained a fact that the Soviet Union had prepared to fight with nuclear weapons. It made no difference whether those preparations were made out of desperation or ambition; the mere possession of nuclear weapons by the West itself did not constitute an effective deterrent.[74]

## NOTES

1. Sir Lawrence Freedman's important new book, *Strategy: A History* (New York: Oxford University Press, 2013), is highly skeptical of the efficacy of strategy as traditionally understood. Paul Kennedy, *The Rise and Fall of the Great Powers: Economic Change and Military Conflict from 1500 to 2000* (New York: Random House, 1987), sees the great powers as being inexorably drawn into imperial overstretch over time. Joseph S. Nye, *Soft Power: The Means to Success in World Politics* (New York: Public Affairs, 2004) introduces a different view of strategy. Colin S. Gray, *Modern Strategy* (New York: Oxford University Press, 1999) reflects on the enduring characteristics of geopolitics and strategy and considers why strategy is difficult, yet necessary.

2. Harold W. Rood, "Soviet Strategy and the Defense of the West," *Global Affairs* 2 (Summer 1987): 3; Harold W. Rood, "The Strategy of Freedom," *Grand Strategy: Countercurrents*, July 1, 1981, 17.

3. Harold W. Rood, *Kingdoms of the Blind: How the Great Democracies Have Resumed the Follies that So Nearly Cost Them Their Life* (Durham: Carolina Academic Press, 1980), 133.

4. Quoted in ibid., 83.

5. Quoted in ibid., 76.

6. Quoted in Harold W. Rood, "Early Warning, Part IV," *Grand Strategy: Countercurrents*, June 15, 1983, 7.

7. Quoted in ibid.

8. Rood, "Soviet Strategy and the Defense of the West," 3. Here, Rood specifically cited "measures that are both material and strategic." The authors have included the additional factors, which are consistent with Rood's general argument.

9. Rood, *Kingdoms of the Blind*, 268.

10. Rood, "The Strategy of Freedom," 16.

11. Rood, "Early Warning, Part IV," 2.

12. Quoted in Rood, *Kingdoms of the Blind*, 22.

13. Ibid., 95; Harold W. Rood, "Early Warning, Part I," *Grand Strategy: Countercurrents*, December 1, 1982, 7.

14. Rood, *Kingdoms of the Blind*, 241–43.

15. A critic of Rood's position could point out that although the Germans successfully invaded and occupied Norway, the Low Countries, and France in 1940, they still lost the war. Rood would counter that Germany's ultimate defeat was due in large part, if not completely, to a series of strategic errors later in the war; and that France and the others suffered terribly and unnecessarily from their strategic folly in the interwar years.

16. Quoted in ibid., 191.

17. Rood considered the case of German strategy in the interwar years in "Soviet Strategy and the Defense of the West," 6–9.

18. Quoted in Harold W. Rood, "Early Warning, Part II," *Grand Strategy: Countercurrents*, February 1, 1983, 2.

19. Ibid.

20. Rood, "Early Warning, Part IV," 8; Rood discussion with the authors.

21. Rood, "Soviet Strategy and the Defense of the West," 9.

22. Rood, *Kingdoms of the Blind*, 269–70.

23. Quoted in ibid., 80.

24. Quoted in ibid., 66n.

25. Rood, "Soviet Strategy and the Defense of the West," 3–4.

26. Rood, "Early Warning, Part I," 6.

27. Ibid., 6–7.

28. Rood, *Kingdoms of the Blind*, 270.

29. Quoted in Rood, "Early Warning, Part IV," 3.

30. Ibid., 3–4. On the matter of strategic warning, Rood recommended Roberta Wohlstetter, *Pearl Harbor: Warning and Decision* (Stanford, CA: Stanford University Press, 1962).

31. Harold W. Rood, "Early Warning, Part III," *Grand Strategy: Countercurrents*, March 15, 1983, 2.

32. The following section on tactical and strategic surprise and Pearl Harbor, unless otherwise indicated, is taken from Rood, "Early Warning, Part I," 2–5.

33. Rood, "Early Warning, Part I," 8; Rood, "Early Warning, Part III," 2.

34. Quoted in Rood, "Early Warning, Part II," 6.

35. Rood, "Early Warning, Part IV," 3.

36. Rood noted that in November 1940, the Fleet Air Arm of the Royal Navy attacked the Italian fleet at anchor in Taranto with torpedo bombers, inflicting considerable damage to the Italian ships. The possibilities of carrier air strikes on Hawaii were demonstrated by a carrier of the U.S. Pacific Fleet in 1938. Fleet Problem XIX in March of that year included carrier air operations by the air group from USS *Saratoga*. In order to evade defending air patrols from Oahu, *Saratoga* approached Pearl Harbor from the northwest behind a weather front, launched aircraft, which evaded detection, and carried out a mock raid on the naval base. A continuation of the fleet exercise included a sneak attack on Mare Island Navy Yard off San Francisco Bay, where defending forces were once again caught unaware. Rood, "Early Warning, Part I," 3.

37. The following case study of surprise and the 1973 Arab-Israeli War, including quotations from contemporary press sources, unless otherwise indicated, is taken from Rood, "Early Warning, Part III," 2–10.

38. Rood commented in 1983 that "a no less sobering consideration is the density and location of the Warsaw Pact air defense system that stretches from Finland south to the Austrian border with Czechoslovakia and extends from the very eastern border of West Germany back into Warsaw Pact country. Will it be a surprise one day to discover that all of those thousands of anti-aircraft missiles and guns are no more

defensive in character than the ones the Soviet Union installed for the Egyptians along the Suez Canal?" Rood, "Early Warning, Part III," 10.

39. Quoted in ibid., 5.

40. Quoted in ibid., 5–6.

41. Quoted in ibid., 6.

42. Quoted in ibid., 8.

43. Quoted in ibid., 6

44. Quoted in ibid.

45. Quoted in ibid., 7.

46. Ibid., 8.

47. Ibid., 10.

48. Rood, "Early Warning, Part I," 8.

49. Rood, "Early Warning, Part IV," 2–3. As it turned out, of course, the military government in Argentina fell because of its defeat in the Falklands War (or, as it would have it, the Malvinas War).

50. Jeffrey Hanson, "A Collection of Prof. Harold W. Rood's Quotations," in *Memories of Professor Bill Rood, Scholar and Gentleman, from his Students, Colleagues, and Friends*, ed. Patrick J. Garrity, Christopher Harmon, and Colleen Sheehan (unpublished manuscript, January 2012), Print, 34.

51. Ibid.

52. Harold W. Rood, "Commentary on Books and Other Works Useful in the Study of International Relations," *Classics of Strategy and Diplomacy*, Ashbrook Center, accessed November 12, 2012, http://www.classicsofstrategy.com/strategyanddiplomacy/rood.pdf, 2. For greater detail on this point, Rood recommended Selig Adler, *The Isolationist Impulse* (New York: Collier, 1961) and Z. A. B. Zeman, *Nazi Propaganda* (Oxford: Oxford University Press, 1973). The Soviet Union worked through its agents in the Communist International to organize peace demonstrations on college campuses and through labor unions and church groups. At the same time, the Pacific Coast Manager of Intourist, the Soviet travel agency in the United States, was conducting espionage through an agent in U.S. Naval Intelligence, collecting information concerning the Japanese. Here Rood referenced "Russian Spies Sentenced," *New York Times*, March 21, 1939, 10.

53. Quoted in Rood, "Commentary on Books," 19.

54. Unsigned Memorandum, "Documents on German Foreign Policy, 1918–1945: From the Archives of the German Foreign Ministry," 16 July 1941, The War Years, Series D: 1937–1945, Vol. 13: June 23—December 11, 1941, Document Number 114 (Nuremberg Document 221-L), United States Government Printing Office, United States Department of State, 149–56. Excerpts printed in "German History in Documents and Images," Nazi Germany, 1933–1945, Volume 7, accessed January 15, 2014, http://germanhistorydocs.ghi-dc.org/sub_document.cfm?document_id=1549.

55. This brief study of organizations consistently opposed to American foreign policy is taken from Harold W. Rood, "The War for Iraq," Claremont Institute, April 2003, http://www.claremont.org/publications/pubid.285/pub_detail.asp.

56. Rood, "Early Warning, Part IV," 8.

57. A substantial number of Rood's students at Claremont also studied political philosophy and saw certain affinities in the respective methodologies. "We studied political philosophy with Harry Jaffa, who studied with Leo Strauss. Strauss's famous maxim for reading great books was that, 'The problem inherent in the surface of things, and only in the surface of things, is the heart of things.' [Rood's] approach to reading the book of the world was strikingly similar. He uncovered the heart of things, above all the strategic designs of America's adversaries, almost entirely from open sources." Marlo Lewis, in Garrity et al., *Memories of Professor Bill Rood*, 51. "While Harry Jaffa taught us how to divine the theoretical depths of classic philosophical texts and recognize their esoteric elements, Professor Rood taught us a similar technique: how to think counter-intuitively about historical and current events, which is also an esoteric skill." Steve Hayward, in ibid., 40.

58. Rood, "Commentary on Books," 18.

59. Harold W. Rood, "Grenada: The Strategic Dimension," *Claremont Review of Books* 2, no. 4 (Winter 1983), accessed July 18, 2014, http://claremontinstitute.org/index.php?act=crbArticle&id=1452#.U8bdQLEUp2A.

60. Rood, *Kingdoms of the Blind*, 159.

61. Harold W. Rood, "Cuba: Payment Deferred," *National Review*, November 27, 1981, 1402.

62. Ibid., 1404.

63. Subsequent scholarship has also revealed what was widely suspected at the time: that the United States also agreed that it would withdraw its nuclear-armed Jupiter missiles from Turkey.

64. Rood, "Cuba: Payment Deferred," 1404. At the time, Paul Nitze and Charles Burton Marshall had also remarked upon the strategic advantages that the Soviet Union had gained as a result of the Cuban missile crisis (although Rood's interpretation of Soviet strategy was unique, to the authors' knowledge). Rood discussion with the authors.

65. Rood discussion with the authors.

66. Rood discussion with the authors; Harold W. Rood, "China's Strategy: Past, Present, and Future" (unpublished manuscript, 2011), Print, 11.

67. The Tiananmen case study is taken from ibid., 7–12.

68. It might be objected that student demonstrations and the rebellion of youth are a fact of life in modern regimes of all types—witness the widespread unrest on American campuses in the 1960s, which led in some cases to government counteractions (e.g., at the extreme, the unauthorized National Guard shootings at Kent State University). Yet presumably those demonstrations were not controlled by the FBI in order to eliminate dissidents. To which Rood would reply: there is an obvious difference between democratic and totalitarian regimes and the way in which political opposition is treated. More to the point, he would say, the leaders of China surely would not have missed the point that student demonstrations in the West, however well meaning, had led to a change in American policy toward the Vietnam War, a change that objectively favored the foreign enemies of the United States. Rood believed that Chinese leaders must have been bemused that such a thing could ever be allowed to happen—and that they would be determined it not happen in China. Rood discussion with the authors.

69. Harold W. Rood, "Political, Not Military: The Flaws of Western Deterrence," *Grand Strategy: Countercurrents*, December 1, 1981, 13.

70. The following analysis of deterrence, including the discussion of Japan and Germany in the 1930s and the Intermediate Nuclear Force (INF) case study from the early 1980s, unless otherwise noted, is taken from ibid., 12–19.

71. As to the robustness of deterrence in 1982, after the Soviets (in Rood's opinion) had overturned the military balance in Europe, Rood wrote: "Today, we cannot know if the U.S.S.R. will ever feel compelled to invade Western Europe. One can only judge that the Soviets have not been deterred from systematically developing the means to do so. The West has, over the same period, gradually neglected many of those political and military steps that might cause the Kremlin to pause, or that might offer a reasonable chance of success if the Soviet Union forces the issue." Ibid., 19.

72. Quoted in ibid., 13. Emphasis added by Rood.

73. Quoted in ibid., 15–16.

74. Rood was well aware that U.S. and NATO nuclear targeting plans, and those for U.S. strategic nuclear forces, were not based on "city busting" operations; they included strikes against Soviet and Warsaw Pact military and military-related targets. Even so, he was concerned that the logic of "political" deterrence had so permeated high-level military as well as civilian officials that Allied nuclear operations would have no strategic coherence. He judged that the Soviets knew this and would act accordingly. Rood discussion with the authors.

# FOUR

# The Democratic Strategy Deficit

## *Political, Not Military*

*Professor Rood postulated that democracies are deficient in attending to strategic matters. This is not unique to Rood's teaching. But his examination of this issue—always in the context of looking at real-world examples and problems—suggests many of the inherent weaknesses democracies share as they attempt to manage their affairs within the international system. Those weaknesses, he argued, are largely political and not military in nature. While there is no question in Rood's writing and teaching that he has chosen the side of the democracies in their conflicts with authoritarian governments, he is not sentimental in his treatment of either the democracies or the conflict. Democracies will prevail if they retain and act from a strategic point of view; otherwise they are at grave risk.*

*Many others have argued that the position of the democratic world, and the United States specifically, is not as precarious as Rood's analysis often suggested. Indeed, some have written that, since the end of the Cold War, the game is up for the authoritarians and history itself has ended, although they speak these days in somewhat more muted tones. Others see things perhaps as darkly as Rood but point to other more systemic problems as the roots of conflict. Their work is worth examining as an often stark but worthwhile contrast to Rood's.[1]*

*But the essence of Rood's analysis begins with the argument that, because war can be the result of the pursuit of strategy, and because strategy is a constant pursuit in international politics, some sort of war is likely coming; that states not wedded to the Western canon are preparing for it; and that the great democracies must maintain the ability to wage and win it, hopefully at acceptable costs. The solution is a government, and indeed a citizenry, more attentive to the problems of strategy. The student of international politics would do well to ponder whether such a thesis can be responsibly set aside and what might take its place.*

For Rood, the Cuban missile crisis and the INF debate, discussed in chapter 3, typified the false distinction between "political" and "military" objectives that has typically haunted the strategies of the Western democracies. The root of the problem, Rood argued, is the dangerous inclination by democratic peoples to discount the likelihood of war. "The belief in the impossibility of war, coupled with the failure to contemplate the consequences of defeat, explain the weakness that democracies display in providing for their own defense," Rood concluded. "Military policy must fit the requirements for successful strategy and successful strategy does not derive from the notion that war is impossible."[2]

As we will consider in this chapter, Rood sought to understand what we might call the democratic strategic deficit, especially by contrasting the liberal democratic and totalitarian views on the nature of politics and war. Rood concluded that democracies were particularly susceptible to strategic and tactical surprise, as they were predisposed to avoid war and to assume that other types of regimes shared that assumption. Rood thought that democracies might overcome this deficit through strong and responsible executive leadership, and through a military establishment that took seriously its responsibility to be prepared for war, in the first place, and, if necessary, to win it.

Although he emphasized the harder edges of political life that stemmed from the inherent nature of man, Rood did not consider himself to be a relativist or amoral realist. As a political scientist, he believed that he could dispassionately evaluate the strengths and weaknesses of democratic regimes in the realm of strategy. But as a citizen and civilized man, he passionately believed in the intrinsic worth of liberal democracy and its moral superiority to the lawless totalitarian regimes that had grown up during his lifetime. He thought that by diagnosing the problem of the democratic strategy deficit, he might warn his fellow citizens of the perils they faced and suggest ways to overcome their habitual strategic blindness. "The survival of democratic regimes does not lie alone in the elegance of their principles but in their capacity to apply power to those who would destroy them," he wrote in *Kingdoms of the Blind*.[3]

One might object here that the Age of Totalitarianism—of Nazi Germany and the Soviet Union—is now safely behind us. There are no Hitlers and Stalins these days, only authoritarians and klepto-crats who may kick over a table here and there, but who have neither the desire nor the ability to rule the world. The stakes are much less high and international politics and war correspondingly less important. To which Rood would reply, tyrants may become more subtle without becoming more just. That aside, regimes not based on the rule of law—label them whatever you will (dictatorships, autocracies, theocracies)—inevitably will have a different view of politics and war than those based upon the rule of law (which, in our time, are predominately democratic). Drawing that contrast as clearly as possible, Rood believed, would illuminate the strategic challenges that democracies face at any point of history.

Regimes that are constitutional and democratic, according to Rood, are dedicated to the protection of the weak and the helpless from the unwarranted exercise of power by the state or from elements outside the apparatus of the state who would molest or exploit them. Such precepts of constitutional government and democracy do not ordinarily operate within the international community. Totalitarian regimes, convinced of the ubiquity of politics and the irrefutable nature of the truths they purvey, see no reason to exercise restraint in compelling the powerless to conform to those truths. Those who have the power to threaten the existence of the totalitarian regime must be rendered powerless, co-opted, or destroyed. Any who express doubts about the totalitarian regime's monopoly of truth threaten the regime's existence.[4] Totalitarian regimes distinguish between those who will perpetuate the regime and those who will not; they distinguish between friends and foes, without ambivalence or ambiguity. They make no distinction between foreign and domestic enemies.[5]

Totalitarian regimes, in short, are constantly at war with their own citizens and with free peoples outside of their borders. This struggle may not manifest itself immediately as a shooting war. But the totalitarian thinks of "politics" and "diplomacy" as a means to prepare for a shooting war. War and the preparations for war will be totalitarian; that is, unlimited in their means as well as their end. "Dictatorial regimes often use international discourse as the arena for gaining strategic advantage in relationships that are seen to be fundamentally competitive, where winning will bolster the regime and where losing will threaten the regime."[6] Rood quoted political scientist Edward Mead Earle (1939):

> It is a statement of fact in the light of which otherwise confusing phenomena become quite intelligible. For example, economic policies which, judged by the accepted criteria of economics, border on the insane become altogether rational if considered as quasi-military measures. Governmental controls of the press, the radio, the church, the school likewise are explicable by reference to the obvious fact that under modern conditions nearly all phases of life must be subordinated to the exigencies of war. . . . In Germany, Japan and Italy, the concept of the totalitarian state and the concept of the totalitarian war are inextricably connected.[7]

By contrast, Rood observed, it is *not* a commonly held view in democratic societies that war and politics are the same thing. Such a view of war is incompatible with the notion that politics comprises discourse, argument, negotiation, compromise, and accommodation.[8] Optimism about the future of the human condition is the strength and beauty of the democratic regime, but its principal weakness is in the realm of defense and the conduct of war. It is in the nature of politics and of the human condition that justice, peace, and defense of the community require, from time to time, the application of force. Remembrance of that fact of life is difficult for free men and women, accustomed to peaceful pursuits. As a result, the citizens of free societies are not universally expert in those things necessary to defend a free society, nor should they necessarily be.[9]

Because the exercise of power and the application of force have been diffused and confined by constitutional restraints and the rule of law inside the democratic regime, it is the dominant assumption among democrats that similar restraints will always be exercised within the international community. Because war is coercion and violence, it is seen by democratic regimes to be inimical to democracy (and may even be considered unnatural). Rood observed that a strong sense of guilt manifests itself within the democratic regimes when force has to be applied in the interest of preserving the regime and protecting its citizenry.

> It is difficult to accept that the United States, by its very existence and condition, is an offense in the eyes of some peoples abroad. Making nice to such peoples doesn't change their view but only reinforces their hostile inclinations. Making nice is seen not as strength but as weakness to be exploited. It is in the realm of statesmanship that the choice must be made when to exercise civility and extend help and when to impose will.
>
> It is an unavoidable reality that, while there are in the world entities that wish no harm to others, there are those, as well, who are not merely careless of harming others but find fulfillment in it. That is, there are friends and there are enemies.[10]

In the attack on the United States on September 11, 2001, Rood commented, the instant reaction was of shock and anger at such a manifestation of deadly purpose against the United States. But a secondary response, after the smoke had settled, was to question why we had evoked such hatred. What had the United States done wrong to provoke holy war on its own territory?[11]

One could see the same manifestation in the aftermath of the war with Japan, Rood noted, when it was safe to speculate on such things. What on earth did American political leaders do over the years that would lead Japan to attack the United States in December 1941? The fact that the Japanese government might have long-range and global strategic objectives, the accomplishment of which would require war against the United States (and others) at the appropriate time, was an intolerable truth, for if a democratic nation must always be on guard against attacks and the loss of strategic independence, and must from time to time go to war to secure itself, the world is not the comfortable place that democratic peoples like to think it is.[12]

Rood pointed out that democracies are typically commercial regimes. To a greater or lesser degree, they believe that trade is not a zero-sum game. War, by contrast, is seen as inherently destructive, in which even the so-called winners typically emerge with less than that with which they began. Rood characterized the logic of American economic liberalism: "There's nothing to be gained from foreign relations; so long as trade goes on in the world, what other foreign relations should there be? We should be enemies with no one, friends with all, and carry on commercial relationships because those are the relationships that add to everyone's prosperity."[13] While Rood agreed with this as an ideal, he would have pointed out that in order to sustain a world in which we are free to carry on commercial relations, it will still be necessary to pay attention to strategy.

Rood often cited the British "ten year rule," implemented during the 1920s, as the classic example of how the assumptions of permanent peace and the primacy of economic matters can insidiously deform democratic government policy. In preparing their annual estimates, the British armed services were instructed by the cabinet to proceed on the assumption that "no great war is to be anticipated for ten years." The rule was not intended to be an iron-clad principle against which all defense expenditures were to be judged. It was supposed to be an assumption reexamined annually in the light of the world situation. In fact, however, the rule became for British military and strategic policy what appeasement was for British foreign policy: the means to avoid disruption of "business as usual." The consequences were the deterioration of Britain's strategic position abroad and of the armed services and their supporting industries. Government decisions that should have, in all prudence, been based on strategic imperatives and military realities were based instead on financial arguments of only transient merit. Ironically, the ten-year rule was formally dropped in 1929, and Britain indeed found herself in a great war exactly a decade later. But the spirit of the rule continued into the 1930s, with all the deleterious effects that history records.[14]

The loss of Singapore in 1942 was one of those effects, caused by an early disbelief (shared by Churchill) in the possibility of war with Japan. During the 1920s, Britain realized the economic savings that could be achieved by employing aircraft for policing the empire in the place of masses of infantry. Singapore's fate was sealed by the infelicitous conclusion that airplanes and landing fields were cheaper to erect than fortifications, and less costly to maintain than ground forces. This fit well into an imperial strategy designed to deal with internal unrest and the problems of local border control, such as that in Iraq or Waziristan.[15]

But against a serious, great-power strategic threat such as that posed by Japan, Singapore could not be held because Malaya could not be defended. Malaya could not be defended, in part because it had been cheaper to build the landing fields close to the coast rather than inland, where they could not be protected from amphibious attack. And no one, save perhaps the Japanese, would, until very late, suppose that Japan might have access to airfields in southern Indochina—or that British aircraft would be needed elsewhere, to defend Britain herself from invasion. Who in 1924 could imagine a France so helpless after a German attack that she could not deny the Japanese the use of an airfield at Saigon, which was within easy bombing range of the air bases in Malaya and Singapore? If one could not credit the revival of German military power and the German preparation for war, then surely one could not imagine a defeated France.[16]

British leaders, for reasons of false economy and strategic optimism, preferred to focus on the (cheap) defense of the empire rather than on dealing seriously with the German military threat in Europe. That threat, it was assumed, could be defused through appeasement, or at least deflected to the east, against the Soviet Union. Rood cited Wing Commander J. C. Slessor, Royal Air Force, India, who wrote in the August 1937 issue of the *Royal United Services Institute Journal* (awarded a Gold Medal by the Institution): "The British people will never again agree to provide infantry by the millions," as they did in the Great War. Wing Commander Slessor's essay reflected his concern for the defense of India and the internal security of that country, which dictated the limits on the numbers of the British Field Force to be sent to France and Belgium in the event of war in Western Europe. The wing commander asserted that for a war in Europe, Britain could only afford to send to the Continent one light division (mechanized) and three armored divisions, to be followed by, *after* six months of war, enough forces to bring the strength up to two light and six armored divisions, and four support divisions.[17]

Wing Commander Slessor's view of how Britain should assist France under attack by Germany coincided with the policy laid down by the British government, Rood noted. The Royal Navy would impose a blockade on Germany, while securing the maritime approaches to the British Isles and defending the maritime lines of communication between Britain and its Empire. The Royal Air Force would provide for the air defense of Great Britain and British bases in the overseas Empire, while providing an air striking force for attacks against the Continental enemy. The British Army should therefore provide only a small field force to assist France, while conserving the principal strength for imperial defense.

A Colonel Beardon, CBE, replied in the *Journal* (February 1938) to the Wing Commander's prize essay in an article, "Defense and Defeat." Beardon argued that a British policy of "limited liability" in respect to the defense of France would lead to disaster. If Britain were not to suffer the worst consequences, it would have to exert all of its power if France was to be defended and Germany defeated. He urged: "Let us therefore face facts and eschew ostrich-like postures which can but . . . confuse our own people, dismay our allies, and incur the laughter and contempt of our possible enemies." Within a month of publication of Colonel Beardon's article, Germany had seized Austria, in violation of the Treaty of Versailles, the Covenant of the League of Nations, and the Austro-German Pact of June 11, 1936.[18]

Yet Britain's thralldom to the easy path would remain in effect for some months, Rood observed, following the assumption that war would not come, and if it did come, it would be fought on terms favorable to the British. This conclusion was reached despite the experience of 1914–1918, when the fullest exertions of Britain and France had barely sufficed to attain a stalemate on the Western Front (one that was broken only by the intercession of an American Expeditionary Force of almost two million men). Germany, by contrast, assumed that war would come in a manner for which its democratic adversaries were not prepared. The Germans planned to fight the war in order to ensure that the stalemate on the Western Front would not be repeated.[19]

## DEMOCRATIC "REALISM": FACING THE MUSIC

Rood thought that the democratic strategy deficit was not only the product of misguided thinking about international relations, but also the view of those often characterized as "realists," such as the American diplomat and author, George F. Kennan. Dean Acheson was said to have remarked of Kennan that he has "never grasped the realities of power relationships, but takes a rather mystical attitude toward them."[20] Rood whole-heartedly agreed with this characterization.

Rood frequently cited a quote attributed to Kennan: "A war regarded as inevitable or even probable, and therefore much to be prepared for, has a very good chance of being fought."[21] Rood concluded that if a nation followed Kennan's logic, its military strategy would be designed to support diplomacy that aimed merely at avoiding war, rather than preparing for it. War, not totalitarianism, was the enemy to be resisted. Kennan's formulation of the American doctrine of containment in his famous "X" article embodied for Rood this fallacy by postulating the need to devise "political" means to deal with a "political" threat.[22] According to Rood, Kennan did not believe that the true threat was that Eastern totalitarianism might overcome, subdue, and ultimately extinguish the Western democracies. The peril was war itself. Implicitly, the peril did not come from the new barbarism, but from the possibility that someone might struggle against it. Rood thought that such a strategy would bring on war more surely, and make it more costly to wage, if it did not lead to outright defeat.

Rood thought that Kennan's views on the matter were fully evident in his dispatches and private reflections in the run-up to World War II. In October 1938, shortly after France and England awarded Germany the Sudetenland in order to avoid war, Kennan, stationed in Prague, had reflected: "[T]here can never be any solution of the ills of the day which will satisfy Jack and Tom alike. It is comforting to reflect that if no good wind can fail to blow ill, no ill wind can fail to blow good. Change will always involve suffering, but one can at least hope that such changes as occur will lead in the direction of greater economic security and greater racial tolerance for people sadly in need of both." Kennan then went on to say:

> The adjustment [to the new era in Central Europe]—and this is the main thing—has now come. It has come in a painful and deplorable form. But it has relieved the Czechoslovak state of liabilities as well as assets. It has left the heart of the country physically intact. Finally, and perhaps most important of all, it has preserved for the exacting tasks of the future a magnificent younger generation—disciplined, industrious, and physically fit—which would undoubtedly have been sacrificed if the solution had been the romantic one of hopeless resistance rather than the humiliating but truly heroic one of realism.

On December 8, 1938, Kennan wrote: "I have seen no indications of any desire on the part of Hitler to make Germans out of the Czechs. Their role is that of a vassal—and the vassal's role has always been easier to execute than that of the independent younger brother."[23]

Rood thought that a true realist would see things rather differently from Kennan. When the Germans demanded and received the Sudetenland from the hands of England and France, the Czechs lost those splendid fortifications behind which the excellent Czech Army could conserve its strength to defend its homeland. The loss of the fortifications, the demoralization induced by the Western sell-out of Czechoslovakia, and the discrediting of the Czech government, which had been forced to accede to the terms of the Munich agreement, left Czechoslovakia exposed to the pleasures of German foreign policy. On March 15, 1939, the German Army occupied what had been left of Czechoslovakia after the Munich Agreement.

Kennan's impressions of those events were written in "Personal Notes, dated March 21, 1939, on the March Crisis and the final Occupation of Prague by the Germans." Therein is included the following: "A Jewish acquaintance came. We told him that he was welcome to stay around there until he could calm his nerves. He paced wretchedly up and down in the anteroom, through the long morning hours. In the afternoon, he decided *to face the music* and went home."[24]

The music that the Jewish acquaintance would ultimately face was probably extermination, Rood commented grimly. Although the full horrors of the Holocaust were perhaps then unimaginable, Rood found it difficult to understand how George Kennan, serving in Europe at a time of virulent official anti-Semitism and violence in Nazi Germany, could have written so coolly about that man's fate. But for a "realist" of Kennan's stripe, the fate of the Jews, like that of the Czechs, was of secondary importance to the peaceful "adjustment" of relations in Central Europe.

Rood noted that Kennan, in writing about his early days in the U.S. diplomatic mission to the Soviet Union, had recorded how the Soviet foreign minister Maxim Litvinov really wanted to be a librarian. Kennan had observed: "[F]rom this human confession I begin to realize what I am never to be allowed to forget: that these Soviet Communists with whom we will now have to deal are flesh-and-blood people, like us—misguided, if you will, but no more guilty than are we of the circumstances into which we all were born—and that they, like us, are simply trying to make the best of it."[25]

While urging moderation in dealings with the Soviets, Kennan would later describe Leonid I. Brezhnev as "a moderate, in fact a conservative man who, whatever other failings of outlook he may have, is a man of the middle, a skilled balancer among political forces, a man confidently regarded by all who know him as a man of peace."[26] To Kennan, the Soviet Union was not a totalitarian regime, but merely an authoritarian one, much like prerevolutionary Czarist Russia.

In Kennan's world, according to Rood, there was no tension created by the fundamental conflict between totalitarianism and democracy. Russian totalitarianism and Western democracy were incidental to any relationship between the West and the empire of the Soviet Union. Matters needed but follow the course of moderation dictated by the moderateness of Soviet leadership. All of the issues of human freedom that underlie Western institutions were but an aside to the important thing: the avoidance of conflict.

Rood asked his students to think of the Czech Jew going out "to face the music," of Comrade Litvinov forced by the circumstances of his birth to be foreign minister of the Soviet Union instead of a librarian, and then judge whether Professor Kennan, and "realists" like him, were suitable guides to the cataclysmic struggle that was then in progress around the world.

## DEMOCRATIC IDEALISM: THE LESSONS OF HISTORY

The so-called democratic realists like Kennan wanted to deal with the totalitarian threat by focusing on the avoidance of war; which meant, in Rood's opinion, abandoning politics and resigning themselves with equanimity to the will of the stronger. The opposite extreme—democratic idealism—proposed to eliminate the strategy deficit and prevent war by

transforming totalitarians, and everyone else for that matter, into democrats. For those holding this perspective, democratic regimes are viewed
as better members of the community of nations than are non-democratic
regimes, and less likely to implement long-term policies threatening to
other countries. Disputes among democracies, even if they are at times
rancorous, seem easier to settle by softer means than going to war.[27]

Democratic idealists argue that authoritarian regimes or dictatorships
are more difficult to reason with because their frames of reference are at
odds with those of democratic regimes. Dictators often use international
discourse as the arena for gaining strategic advantage in relationships
that are seen to be fundamentally competitive, where winning will bolster the regime and where losing will threaten the regime. In an ideal
world, where every nation that mattered was a democracy, disputes between nations would be subject to compromise and accommodation in
the same way that they were resolved between contending parties in
domestic politics. Democratic idealists have a variety of suggestions as to
how to bring about democratization of the world, or at least about how to
democratize the most threatening regimes.

Rood would agree with the democratic idealists when it came to their
analysis about the differences between regime types, but he approached
the solution differently, from the perspective of history. He stressed how
difficult it is for a nation and its peoples to become democratic; how the
circumstances need to be just right for this to occur; and how long the
process takes. He cited the slow process by which the United Kingdom
and the United States became modern liberal democracies, despite the
most favorable of conditions.

For instance, Rood noted, the constitutional evolution of the United
Kingdom took over seven hundred years. The quarrels between King
John and his barons, neither of which were democratic, forced the king to
issue the Great Charter of Liberties known as the Magna Carta in 1215.
This was no more than the careful spelling out of the king's customary
obligations to his subjects as they were understood to have been "since
time immemorial." The principle, both implicit and explicit in the charter,
was that the king must respect the rights of his subjects and that, if he did
not, he could be compelled to do so by law. The king swore that no
freeman could be arrested, imprisoned, outlawed, exiled, or otherwise
destroyed, save by the lawful judgment of his peers and by the law of the
land. No payment to the king, save those already customary, could be
compelled unless by common counsel of the kingdom. That would become, by the end of the thirteenth century, the principle that matters of
national importance, like taxation, could only be decided by common
consent of the realm.

The emergence of parliament as the agency for expressing the common consent of the realm took another four hundred years. Over the
following two centuries, the elected House of Commons became the body

upon which national government would be based. A democratically elected House of Commons only evolved beginning with the Reform Act of 1832, and through subsequent acts extending the franchise until 1918, when women over age thirty were granted the vote. The long evolution of the United Kingdom into a parliamentary democracy took place amid wars, internal uprisings, conflicting partisan interests, and all the diverse machinations and frictions that a community generates in the name of politics and government.

The Americans who dwelt in the British North American colonies were more fortunate than their British cousins. They came to rule themselves out of necessity when the English were distracted from that task by civil war at home and threats to the kingdom and empire from abroad. The defeat of France and its expulsion from North America in 1763 after the close of the French and Indian War—the Seven Years' War in Europe—found the colonies so attached to self-rule that they resisted the reassertion of English authority. English efforts to restore imperial control over the colonies became intolerable, and within a little more than a decade the colonies asserted their independence and fought a war to secure it. Yet it was another twelve years after the Declaration of Independence before the colonies, now states, had a constitution for their federation. Seventy years later, the Constitution was challenged by the Southern states in a great and bloody civil war.

If that war settled, at last, the terrible issue of slavery, it would be another century before Americans, descendants of those slaves, would have their rights as citizens finally embedded in law in the Civil Rights Act of 1964 and the Voting Rights Act of 1965. Even in a nation founded on the principle of democratic representation, the progress toward democracy was hardly instantaneous, or without pain and conflict.

What about the prospects for democracy in a nation that had been liberated from tyranny, whether that tyranny was homegrown or imposed from outside? France, for instance, had returned to the rule of its own people between the liberation of Paris and the final clearing of the last German forces from France in May 1945. While Allied and Free French forces struggled to clean France of Germans and to advance into Germany, however, Rood pointed out, France did not immediately settle into good order. The black market, organized crime, political retribution for the defeat of 1940, and collaboration with the Nazis set the atmosphere for reestablishment of civil government in France. Not the least of the difficulties was the struggle with the communists who had helped the Germans to defeat France in 1940. All of that took place amid the necessity to restore public services and civil government, deal with the consequences of Nazi looting of the country's resources, and repair the damage left by Allied bombing and the battles for the liberation of France. It was fourteen years after the liberation of Paris before the French people could settle on a Constitution that seemed like it might endure. But at least the French people dealt with such matters themselves.

Nazi Germany was a different problem altogether, Rood pointed out. The Allied invasion of northwest Europe at Normandy, and later in southern France, aimed at the destruction of the German armed forces, the conquest of Germany, and the overthrow of the Nazi regime. German forces continued resistance until the eve of the surrender of Germany, May 8, 1945. Although German citizens flew white flags of surrender in their towns and villages, Germany, unlike France, was not a welcoming country. If there was defeat and surrender on the one hand, there was defiance on the other. Civil-affairs teams followed the Allied armies to secure control of local governments, while counterintelligence corps units rounded up those on the Allied wanted lists. Allied soldiers in occupation carried arms at all times. The black market raged, stoked by thievery from army supply depots by some displaced persons and Allied deserters, while ordinary public services were slowly restored at the local level.

Rood noted one example—the city of Saarbrücken, on the border with France, which saw the ending of hostilities in late March 1945. There followed the Allied roundup of SS special units in the Saar region and the removal of principal Nazis from the administration. Inhabitants were issued Military Government of Germany registration cards, to be carried at all times. The inhabitants were forbidden to leave the localities where they were registered; they were warned to turn in all firearms, explosives, and edged weapons, with heavy penalties for those who were found with such things in their possession. The restoration of Saarbrücken as a functioning city with minimal public services like transportation, water, and electricity took until 1950. Reconstruction would take another decade or more.

Allied occupation policy aimed at de-Nazification, demilitarization, decentralization of government, and democratization. This was in the Western Occupation Zones; the Soviet Zone followed the edicts of Stalin and suffered the imposition of a communist regime. The important difference between the liberation of France and the occupation of Germany was that Germans were to be treated as defeated enemies. As the 21st Army Group put it, defining military government in Germany:

> In the liberated friendly territories . . . we are dealing with our allies . . . we therefore respect their sovereignty and their institutions. . . . [I]n Germany . . . it is the duty of commanders to impose the will of the Supreme Commander upon the German people. Germany . . . must now do as ordered. Military government is the instrument by which these orders will be conveyed and enforced.[28]

German defiance and hostility toward the Western powers was moderated by the Red Army's presence in the Eastern Zone, Rood remarked. That encouraged the Germans in the Western Occupation Zones to cooperate in the restoration of order and the reconstruction of local government and of the public services—all accomplished less by military force than by the threat of the Russian bayonets across the zonal border in the East. Soviet policies in Berlin, East Germany, and throughout Eastern Europe did nothing to dissuade the West Germans from doing otherwise. It was all helped forward by a certain respect for authority on the part of Germans, Rood believed, and their inclination to work hard at the physical tasks of reconstruction and the political tasks of reconstitution.

Rood pointed out that the re-democratization of France and the democratization of Germany were not central objects of American strategy during World War II. Nevertheless, having achieved what was the central strategic objective—that of defeating and disarming Germany, thus dealing at least provisionally with the German Problem—the United States had a certain freedom of action (but not a responsibility) to promote or rebuild democracy, because highly favorable circumstances allowed it.

In the case of modern Iraq, as we will see in chapter 7, Rood argued that, as noble as it was to remove an evil tyrant and to help a tyrannized people achieve a liberty they have never known, this was not why the United States went to war. It went to war because, in his opinion, strategy demanded it. Two circumstances should have cautioned the occupying powers from expecting Iraq to evolve quickly into a stable democracy. First, Rood contended, Iraq had never before been a place where political freedom has flourished. Political turbulence was the principal tradition that Iraqis had to look back upon since the country's independence from four centuries of rule by the Ottoman Empire, which had suppressed turbulence by force. The more recent dictatorship used terror and force as the basis of civil government. Second, the American-led coalition predictably faced hostility and resistance to what many Iraqis saw as a foreign, infidel occupying force. They could hardly appreciate that the war fought within their land was a discriminating one, aimed not at the destruction of their country but only at the Iraqi regime's ability to resist its overthrow.

Rood did find hope for a decent outcome, defined as an Iraq that was a stable and comfortable place for ordinary citizens to live and prosper. He believed that Iraq had the wealth in its people and resources to become a prosperous state. The restoration of order in Iraq, sufficient for this process to begin, required resolution, determination, patience, and the deliberate and discriminating application of force where necessary. As was the case in Germany in 1945 (Rood thought that Italy might actually be a better example), whatever resentments the peoples of Iraq might harbor against their liberators would be set against concern for the safety of person, family, and community, and the promise of prosperity. But he acknowledged that such an expectation, with its hope and promise, was subject to political passions, deeply rooted animosities, and resistance to foreign intervention.

Miracles, Rood wrote, could not be expected. Therefore strategy must remain the lodestar for democratic peoples, not the desire to create a democratic world. Whether such a world would actually be as peaceful as the democratic idealists believe can be consigned to the realm of theoretical speculation, because it is certainly not on the horizon. Nations that threaten our security will always be with us, and it is the object of strategy—and statesmanship—to deal with them.

## THE CONSTITUTIONAL OBLIGATION OF DEFENSE: THE ROLE OF THE EXECUTIVE

History has demonstrated, Rood acknowledged, that democratic societies are capable of providing for the provision of their defense, as well as for the execution of justice and the preservation of peace, despite the challenges they face due to the democratic strategy deficit. These successes could be credited ultimately to the courage, strength, and common sense of the people, animated to defend their liberties and constitutional order. As we recall from chapter 1, Rood insisted that the obligations to defend the realm did not cease when free societies came to believe that the just powers of government derived from the consent of the governed. Of course, there is no way that free men who govern themselves can be held accountable, as were kings and their councilors, for failure to carry out the obligations to preserve the community. If free men will not see to their obligations, there are none who can do it for them.

In Rood's view, this does not excuse the competent authorities from meeting their responsibilities, however. Citizens have a right to expect that government will take whatever steps the law allows to forestall attacks on the country, and to keep the country in a condition where it is capable of waging war successfully, if necessary. In the American democratic system, Rood concluded, this role seems to have fallen most notably on the executive, the functional equivalent of the king and his councilors. Rood cited the oath of office of the president: "I do solemnly swear (or affirm) that I will faithfully execute the office of President of the United States, and will to the best of my ability, preserve, protect and defend the Constitution of the United States." The Constitution, in this case, did not mean just the formal document describing the structure and nature of government, but also a more general meaning to include that, which in a kingdom, would be called the community of the realm.[29]

While Congress has the power to raise armed forces for the defense of the country and to find the money that will pay for it, it is the president who, although a civilian, enjoys the special position of commander in chief of the armed forces of the United States. Congress has the sole authority to declare war, but nations beyond the reach of Congress may not wait upon such niceties and may wage war against the United States without permission, as it were. In either case, only the president can lead in war and by implication, in the preparations for war. Presidents who have taken their constitutional obligation most seriously have demonstrated how forceful defensive action is possible even in a democracy.

Abraham Lincoln's actions during the Civil War were offered by Rood as a case study in responsible executive leadership in defending the realm (civil wars inherently involve questions of domestic peace and justice as well). In his first inaugural address, Lincoln explained his position on secession and the sanctity of the Union:

> The Chief Magistrate derives all his authority from the people, and they have conferred none upon him to fix terms for the separation of the States. The people themselves can do this also if they choose; but the executive, as such, has nothing to do with it. His duty is to administer the present government, as it came to his hands, and to transmit it, unimpaired by him, to his successor. . . .
>
> In your hands, my dissatisfied fellow countrymen, and not in mine, is the momentous issue of civil war. The government will not assail you. You can have no conflict, without being yourselves the aggressors. You have no oath registered in Heaven to destroy the government, while I shall have the most solemn one to "preserve, protect and defend" it.[30]

When it was rumored that the Maryland legislature might be assembling to vote on secession from the Union, the president instructed General Winfield Scott: "if it shall be to arm the people against the United States, he is to adopt the most prompt, and efficient means to counteract, even, if necessary, to the bombardment of their cities — and in the extremest necessity the suspension of the writ of habeas corpus."[31]

When a group of citizens appealed to Lincoln to go gently in administering military measures in Louisiana so as not to harm the interests of those who truly favored the Union but who felt helpless to act, the President responded:

> What would you do in my position? Would you drop the war where it is? Or would you prosecute it in the future with elder stalk squirts, charged with rose water? Would you deal lighter blows rather than heavier ones? Would you give up the contest, leaving any available means unapplied? I shall not do more than I can, and I shall do all I can to save the government, which is my sworn duty, as well as my personal inclination.[32]

It had not escaped the attention of Lincoln, Rood observed, that failing to preserve the Union would not only lead to division between North and South. Under the terms of the Southern Confederacy, there was nothing to prevent that entity from itself splitting into lesser units even as the confederate states split from the Union. All those things for which the Union had been formed in order to avoid would come to pass, along with a renewed opportunity for foreign meddling in the two or more nations' domestic politics. In Rood's view, Lincoln properly exercised executive authority, taking necessary measures of the "extremest necessity," as FDR did in the run-up to World War II, and as presidents such as Truman and George W. Bush (in the days after September 11) did in later years.[33]

## MILITARY POLICY, DOCTRINE, AND PLANNING IN A DEMOCRACY

In addition to strong executive authority, Rood concluded that the armed forces of a democratic nation had a vital role to play in the defense of the realm—not merely the obvious one of fighting well when called upon to do so, but also in making those prewar preparations that would render their combat service strategically effective and in the national interest.

At first glance it might seem that, in a democracy, the armed forces can do no more in peacetime than follow the strategic assumptions of their civilian masters. If those assumptions prove to be wrong, the armed forces will be ill-configured for any war that follows. This is a variation of the problem of the democratic strategy deficit, because only too often political officials operate on the assumption that there is not going to be a war, or if there is one, that the enemy will obligingly fight it in the most convenient way possible.

Rood's analysis of the run-up to World War II by the British and French seemed to confirm this conclusion. "An oft-spoken criticism of the British Army, after Dunkirk and Narvik, was that it had prepared for the last war: not the one they were called on to fight in 1939. That was sheer hyperbole," Rood wrote. "Within the successive constraints of the British Treasury, constraints laid down by successive British Governments, the Army in France in 1940 actually did far more than could reasonably have been expected. The problem was that the Army could hardly apply the lessons of the Great War without the British Government's having done so *first*." In 1919, Rood noted, the War Cabinet decided that "no expeditionary force [on the European continent] will be required." The organization, equipment, and training for any European war were simply ruled out. Duff Cooper, financial secretary to the War Office in 1933, said: "The British Army are not designed for Continental wars. The purpose of the British Army is to maintain order in the British Empire only." And, later: "The Army is not likely to be used for a big war in Europe for many years to come."[34] The following year, Duff Cooper became secretary of state for war.

Rood believed that there was one revealing, contrary example of over-coming the democratic strategy deficit in this area—the development of military policy by the U.S. armed forces between World Wars I and II. The U.S. Army and Navy (and the Marine Corps) successfully anticipat-ed the nature of the future war despite political guidance that, in retrospect, would have pointed them in exactly the wrong direction.[35]

According to Rood's research, military policy in the interwar years, conceived and formulated by the armed services, linked doctrine and strategy. Policy defined the kind of organization, and the nature of the training and the types of equipment, required to carry out a particular strategy. Policy provided direction to those assessing the requirements for waging war. Once war began, policy was to recede, to be replaced by strategy, so that the national strategy would determine the military re-quirements for victory. Both policy and strategy were to be derived from the same doctrine, although policy, in the case of the interwar period, designated no particular enemy. Policy was designed to provide the basis for American victory in war; strategy was intended to defeat a specific enemy or set of enemies. Military policy became, in effect, the national strategy, once the president and Congress designated the enemy by a declaration of war.

The U.S. armed forces in the interwar years, Rood concluded, had based their military policy on the proposition that war is an instrument of national policy. Derived from that general proposition was the doctrine of the offensive: in general, wars are won by attacking, disorganizing, and destroying the armed forces of the enemy. Military policy, therefore, was designed to provide a military organization capable of carrying war to an enemy, that is, capable of implementing an offensive strategy. An offensive strategy, in turn, required the dispatch of the U.S. Army and Navy overseas, and the acquisition of bases within the theaters of opera-tion from which the offensive could be conducted. These bases would be obtained by agreement or seizure if they were not already under effective American control.

The paradox, Rood noted, was that this military policy based on no-tions of offensive warfare evolved during the time when American politi-cal leaders were denying consistently the existence of any national inter-est outside the Western Hemisphere. Even the brief intervention in Eu-rope from 1917 to 1918 was considered an aberration by the president and Congress. This paradox between American foreign policy and American military policy seems even more pronounced when it is con-sidered that the same men who made foreign policy were constitutionally responsible for the formulation of military policy. Yet it appears that military policy was actually made within the armed forces themselves rather than by Congress and the president, as might have been supposed.

Congress provided what seemed to be a military policy designed to deal with an attack on the continental United States. This appeared to be the only contingency for which Congress was willing to allow and the only contingency that seemed to be possible as an outcome of an isolationist foreign policy. Congress and the president appeared to be providing a military policy to deal solely with the threat of invasion of the United States, and after 1938, the threat of invasion of the Western Hemisphere. President Roosevelt and his congressional allies might have been aware of the military implications of a German defeat of Great Britain, or of a Japanese advance to Australia, but there was no effective political means for bringing such a viewpoint into the open. [36]

Strategically, according to Rood, the United States, following an isolationist national security policy, could have conceived a military policy based on a rigid coastal defense, reinforced by the fleet in home waters. A coastal defense on the scale of the Maginot Line could have been built between 1920 and 1940 to counter any threat of invasion. The fleet, sortieing from continental harbors under the cover of shore-based aircraft, could have dealt with any attack launched from bases in Europe or Asia. The cost in peacetime of such a rigid system would have been large, but certainly nothing like the cost of a major overseas war.

Congress and successive administrations did not choose to insist upon or fund such a military posture, however. The armed forces drew the appropriate conclusions. The army and navy remained unburdened by any illusions about the ideals for which the United States had fought in World War I. Senior officers realized that nations went to war because they had conflicting interests that could often be resolved in no other way. The operative ideal of the armed forces remained the waging of war in the national interest. The military defense of the United States was only one aspect of the national interest, even if it was best served by armed forces capable of winning wars through offensive action.

In this time period, Rood argued, the army and navy were the only agencies in the government prepared to accept war as a legitimate act of policy and not simply as an expedient for the defense of the physical borders of the country. Political expediency before World War II kept the president disassociated from strategic planning in the war and navy departments, except where the planning could be shown to relate directly to the continental United States. It was not until the middle of 1941 that the services received a firm directive from the president concerning the kind of war for which they should plan. By that time, the army and navy had already set the basic strategy for the war based entirely on military imperatives. When war came at the end of 1941, the strategic plans of the services became the national strategy because for twenty years no politician had bothered to explore any realistic alternatives.

Rood recounted the ways in which the doctrine of war that the services had evolved was reflected in their organization and training. The doctrine furnished a strategy for defense of the nation or for the pursuit of national objectives abroad. Nations intent upon attacking the United

States could best be dealt with overseas, thus eliminating the prospect of battles fought on the home soil. In the same way, nations interfering with the pursuit of American aims abroad could be dealt with at a safe distance. And once engaged in war, the armed forces could be confident that they could conduct war with minimum of civilian interference. Since the nation possessed the power to wage war overseas, it was militarily logical to conduct campaigns intended to deprive the enemy of his freedom of action, which meant his freedom to attack the continental United States or to interfere with the national aims abroad.

Rood asserted that it is the nature of military operations that success or failure is signaled, if not ultimately defined, by gaining or losing territory. The closer the territory is to the enemy homeland, the more significant is the effect of a territorial loss on the enemy's ability to act. The Army and Navy applied this general rule to the expected conduct of foreign policy (although foreign policy, except when it was implemented by war, was not their concern). Rood concluded that American foreign policy during the 1920s and 1930s was philosophical, not territorial, and devoted to goals that had the haziest definition: peace, disarmament, world order, sanctity of treaties, and international law. Since the goals of American foreign policy were philosophical rather than territorial, there was no way in which they could be implemented, except by the assurance of other nations that they shared the same goal.

Faced with the active and aggressive foreign policy of Japan, Germany, and Italy, the philosophical goals of American foreign policy were ineffective as a definition of national aims. While Japanese territorial expansion might be deplored as morally defective, the advantages gained by Japan could only be countered by material resistance, that is, the application of force. The Japanese, Germans, and Italians were conducting foreign policy as a "two-person, zero-sum" game. Each advantage they gained was a loss for their opponents. Since they were conducting foreign policy within the definition of Clausewitz, they resorted to war when war furthered their policy. Inevitably, if that pursuit of advantage continued, a time would come when the United States would be faced with a loss that would restrict American freedom of action. This was the threat to which the American Army and Navy responded, and the basis for their preparations for war.

The army and navy had the right answers to the right questions, as Rood saw things. With singular restraint they merely asked for what the country would readily give them in the way of material support, deferring those items that they felt certain to get once war came. They concentrated upon fulfilling the prerequisites for an organization capable of being turned into an offensive military machine. If they could not have sufficient men in peacetime, they could at least provide a reservoir of well-trained officers capable of holding senior command. After the end of World War I, for example, the army chose not to consolidate all of its strength into one or two full-strength divisions. Instead, it chose to retain many skeleton and paper organizations, sacrificing tactical unity for a large command framework to be filled when an emergency occurred. It favored a wide mobilization base over immediate combat readiness. If the services could not have enough of the right kinds of weapons, they could develop necessary prototypes, so when war did come the American Army and Navy would have to fight only the opening engagements with weapons from World War I. One might suppose that control of the purse would shape military policy, but the effect of fiscal economy on the armed forces restricted only the size of their organization, not the doctrine on which they were based.[37]

Military education also played an important role. It was nearly impossible to rise to a senior rank in the army without having passed through the army's educational system, which was the chief means for indoctrination in the principles of offensive warfare. Rood's review of the official and unofficial military literature for the period between 1900 and 1940 revealed the degree to which the doctrine of offensive warfare had been accepted by the army. The army went to special lengths to counteract any experience from World War I that suggested the reliance on static or trench warfare. For instance, an essay by a general staff officer in the *Infantry Journal* (October 1919) argued that the campaign of 1918 had demonstrated again that "war is motion" and that "only the unlimited offensive brings decisive results." A 1939 manual issued by the Command and General Staff School concluded that "the principle that decisive results can seldom be achieved except by an offensive applies to the army of a nation on the defensive as well as to any other. . . . Decisive results can be obtained only by the *offensive*. . . . Even if the attitude of the nation as a whole is defensive, the enemy forces can be defeated and driven from invaded territory only through the attack. It may be advisable to attack first in order to secure initial advantages or to forestall the growing superiority in the hostile forces."[38]

Rood concluded that the navy's conviction about offensive doctrine had been well crystallized even before the First World War. Concepts of offensive naval warfare were taken from Alfred Thayer Mahan, as well as a variety of European authorities, including Julian Corbett. The navy's adherence to a doctrine of offensive warfare was rationalized into a conception of coast defense that left the fleet free to operate against the enemy instead of waiting for the enemy to attack. The "fighting fleet" had no part in the actual defense of the coast. The fleet's function was to operate against the enemy fleet (which required the defense of forward bases and the seizure of bases from the enemy) and thereby to achieve command of the sea. If the fleet operated effectively, the coasts of the nation would never be subjected to attack. (The navy also had a clear enemy against which to plan offensive warfare: Japan.)

The peculiar nature of naval organization lent itself to indoctrination by word of mouth rather than by literary effort. The navy, with its ships in constant operation, could use any occasion when ships were at sea to further tactical indoctrination. The indoctrination that the army had to carry on in its schools was carried on in the navy mainly on the bridges and in the wardrooms of ships of the fleet. The Naval War College fulfilled the role of the preserver of offensive doctrine for the navy.[39]

Rood pointed out that, through a clever rationalization of defense, the armed services were able to preserve the framework of their offensive organizations. The navy argued convincingly that its role as the first line of defense required the fleet be always in a high degree of readiness. Citing the need for economy, the navy was able to convince Congress that the ships of the fleet were a valuable capital investment, best maintained by being in constant operation. The heavy expenditure of a large fleet in both the Atlantic and the Pacific could be avoided by providing ships capable of carrying on extended operations between both oceans. Such operations required the same kind of establishment for the fleet as that required for an overseas war. In this way, the navy appeared to be preparing to fulfill a continental defense mission while remaining capable of projecting the fleet overseas.[40]

The army's offensive mission was more difficult to rationalize, since the army was required at the time to send only enough troops overseas to defend American possessions in the Western Hemisphere. Whereas the navy was fairly explicit in its preparations for offensive war overseas, Rood found that evidence of the army's commitment to the equivalent—a major expeditionary force—was more diffuse. It was, nevertheless, there to some degree. Economy was again used as a convincing argument with which to gain support for the kind of establishment that would cover the contingency of an overseas war. Acting in a defensive role, the army might have been expected to man permanent, coastal fortifications to hold off an enemy while the navy cut the enemy's sea communications. Extensive fortifications along the seacoast and the open borders of the United States would have been extremely costly. The army argued that a system of mobile defense could provide the same level of security. A small, highly mobile army, using the well-developed transportation networks of the United States, could move rapidly to the threatened coast or frontier to repel an invasion. In order to conduct a mobile defense, the army required divisions, corps, and armies, all independent of territorial command. Such a field force was precisely the kind of organization required to mount an overseas expedition.[41]

Rood stressed the point that civilian political officials made no effort to change the leadership of the army and navy into hands that would implement a defensive-only strategy. Presidents did not exploit their authority and the one who was capable of doing so, Franklin Roosevelt, closely shared the views of the army and navy toward international politics (although FDR's strategic views initially envisioned only air and naval support for overseas allies, not a major U.S. expeditionary force). Yet it was not FDR's internationalism that led the armed forces to adopt an offensive strategy. Rood's examination of the internal preparations of the army and navy led him to conclude that the offensive strategy of the United States in both the Pacific and European theaters of war was a simple and logical extension of American military doctrine. The development of a fleet organized around aircraft carriers, battleships, and cruisers, supported by patrol aircraft, fleet oilers, and long-range submarines, was a material expression of the navy's intention to defend the United States by carrying the war to the enemy. The study and development of the techniques of amphibious warfare was an effort to provide for the acquisition of advanced bases so that war could be waged in enemy waters.

The army's effort to organize and equip mobile units that could function in the field, independent of territorial commands within the continental United States, was likewise an indication that the army entertained the prospect of expeditionary forces. Since an initial mobilization of four million men and a full mobilization of twelve million men were anticipated, this could only mean that the army expected to be called upon to operate outside the United States. The significant joint army and navy war plans, starting with Orange and ending with Rainbow 1–5, were an empirical response to the changing capabilities of potential enemies—but also to the unchanging demands of offensive doctrine. They were expressions of the services' intent to mount anything but a static defense of the continental United States.

Orange required the dispatch of expeditionary forces in support of the navy's advance to the Western Pacific. Even Rainbow-1, the least ambitious of the war plans initiated in 1938, provided for strategic dispositions well outside the United States, which would leave the armed forces in a position to operate with an offensive strategy. The plans reflected the service conviction that the most advantageous war for the United States was one fought outside the Western Hemisphere. In choosing to operate from advanced bases, the army and navy assured themselves a degree of freedom to mount offensive strategy once the United States declared war. If the United States was forced onto the defensive, enemy attacks on advanced American bases would divert the enemy's energy from the important target, the continental United States. Successful enemy attacks on the outposts left the army and navy space and time in which to prepare a counteroffensive. On the other hand, battles fought and lost close to the United States gave the enemy decisive advantage by compelling American forces to conform to the enemy's choice of action. A nation forced to fight close to its homeland cannot afford to lose a battle, since its loss may be decisive; whereas, a force fighting at a distance from its homeland may lose a battle without giving decisive advantage to the enemy.[42]

When war planning and foreign policy finally began to parallel one another after the fall of France in June 1940, Rood concluded, it was the result of a change in foreign policy rather than a change in the orientation of the army and navy. It was through such military planning, culminating in Rainbow-5, whereby civilian authorities belatedly concluded that German and Italian hegemony in Europe was a threat to the national interest of the United States. And the philosophy that underlay the strategy of "Germany first, Japan second," derived from offensive doctrine designed to deny the initiative to the enemy. Rainbow-5 followed the implacable logic of military doctrine: the greatest danger to the United States was from the nearest and most powerful enemy. Support of Britain deprived the enemy of a decisive advantage, and provided the United States with an advanced base from which to mount an offensive strategy.[43]

It might seem remarkable that a conservative (in the bureaucratic sense) organization like the armed forces was better able to anticipate the geopolitical situation for the United States in a Pacific or European war than were the elected officials of government. For Rood, this bespoke the firmness with which the services held to their own doctrine. That firmness might be dismissed as the natural working of authoritarian organizations motivated by a single goal: to wage war effectively. In fact, Rood argued, the armed forces were punctilious in their respect for civilian authority, and fully recognized their subordination to the president and Congress. They in no sense plotted war; they simply prepared for the worst. In the event, they were proven correct. The army and navy were doctrinally and organizationally prepared for war in 1941 because they were convinced war would come. Without such a belief in the value of their métier, the services could not have sustained their organizations or campaigned for public support.

In reflecting on Rood's analysis, we might observe that the 1920s and 1930s in the United States were an exceptional time for such effective military planning and innovation to take place. (And even then, the transition from peacetime planning to performance in combat was very uneven, particularly for the U.S. Army.) Civilian authorities may not always be so indulgent. The day-to-day burdens for the contemporary American armed forces—maintaining an overseas presence with ever-more-limited resources—coupled with the need to recover from the fatigue of fighting the wars in Iraq and Afghanistan, do not lend themselves to getting long-term things correct. To which Rood would say, responsible military officials still must prepare for the worst—that war will come, and will not be the comfortable sort that civilians might allow. They must draw the appropriate conclusions about how to fight that war.

## NOTES

1. Francis Fukuyama, *The End of History and the Last Man* (New York: Free Press, 1992); Samuel P. Huntington, *The Clash of Civilizations and the Remaking of World Order* (New York: Simon & Schuster, 1996); Thomas L. Friedman, *The World Is Flat: A Brief History of the Twenty-First Century* (New York: Farrar, Straus and Giroux, 2005); and Robert D. Kaplan, *The Revenge of Geography: What the Map Tells Us about Coming Conflicts and the Battle against Fate* (New York: Random House, 2012), provide a range of views on the future of international politics and the role of ideology and culture as the cause of, or solution to, human conflict.

2. Harold W. Rood, *Kingdoms of the Blind: How the Great Democracies Have Resumed the Follies that So Nearly Cost Them Their Life* (Durham: Carolina Academic Press, 1980), 15–16, xiv.

3. Ibid., 4. At the time Rood wrote *Kingdoms of the Blind* (the late 1970s), democracies were in the distinct minority in the international community, something that compounded their problems.

4. Ibid., 3.

5. "The terror waged against those in Germany who opposed or offended him [Hitler] gave evidence of the nature of the regime and the dimension of the war that was coming," Rood wrote. "How could one expect the Nazis to behave differently to foreigners than they were prepared to behave toward their own people." Ibid., 3–4; Harold W. Rood, "Early Warning, Part IV," *Grand Strategy: Countercurrents*, June 15, 1983, 5.

6. Harold W. Rood, "The Long View: Democracy and Strategy in Iraq," *Claremont Review of Books* 3, no. 4 (Fall 2003), accessed July 18, 2014, http://claremont.org/index.php?act=crbArticle&id=1143#.U8lQ3_ldWSo.

7. Quoted in Harold W. Rood, "Early Warning, Part II," *Grand Strategy: Countercurrents*, February 1, 1983, 4.

8. Rood, *Kingdoms of the Blind*, 238–39.

9. Harold W. Rood, "A Free Society in an Unfree World: Peace, Justice and Defense" (unpublished manuscript), Print, 42–43.

10. Rood, "The Long View: Democracy and Strategy in Iraq."

11. Ibid.

12. Ibid.

13. Harold W. Rood, "Excerpts from answers to audience questions about the fate of Eastern Europe after 1945, Lectures of July 14, 1981 and March 3, 1980," in "Notable Statements by Harold Rood," ed. Christopher Harmon (unpublished manuscript), Print, 3.

14. Rood, *Kingdoms of the Blind*, 40.

15. Ibid., 42–43.

16. Ibid., 41–42.

17. Born in India, Slessor had served in the Royal Flying Corps as pilot officer in Egypt and the Sudan, and then in France for a year during World War I. After the war, he served in the Royal Air Force in India for two years. While writing his prize essay, he was Wing Commander of No. 3 Wing, RAF, in India, providing support of British and Indian troops engaged in suppressing an insurrection in Waziristan. That is, Rood emphasized, Slessor was not an armchair strategist but a long-serving professional writing from experience. Harold W. Rood, "Commentary on Books and Other Works Useful in the Study of International Relations," *Classics of Strategy and Diplomacy*, Ashbrook Center, accessed November 12, 2012, http://www.classicsofstrategy.com/strategyanddiplomacy/rood.pdf, 13.

18. Ibid., 14.

19. In contrast to the democracies, Germany's totalitarian enemy in the East, the Soviet Union, likewise was preparing seriously to wage war. The Red Army and Air Force had engaged the Japanese Empire from August 1938 through August 1939. The Soviet Union's arms production had been prodigious. In 1938, the Red Army had, it

was estimated, twelve thousand armored fighting vehicles and the Red Air Force eight thousand first-line aircraft. This amount was aside from Soviet Forces in the Far East. Ibid., 13–15; Rood, *Kingdoms of the Blind*, 45.

20. Quoted in Harold W. Rood, "The Naiveté of George Kennan," *Claremont Review of Books* 4, no. 3 (Fall 1985), accessed July 18, 2014, http://claremontinstitute.org/index.php?act=crbArticle&id=1556#.U8beZ7EUp2A. Unless otherwise indicated, Rood's assessment of Kennan and his "realism" is taken from ibid.

21. Rood, *Kingdoms of the Blind*, 276, quoting "George Kennan's Message," *Christian Science Monitor*, July 22, 1977, 31.

22. X [George F. Kennan], "The Sources of Soviet Conduct," *Foreign Affairs*, July 1947, 566–82.

23. Rood, "The Naiveté of George Kennan," citing George Kennan, *From Prague After Munich: Diplomatic Papers, 1938–1940* (Princeton: Princeton University Press, 1968), 5–6, 9.

24. Rood, "The Naiveté of George Kennan," citing Kennan, ibid., 86 (emphasis added by Rood).

25. Rood, "The Naiveté of George Kennan," citing George Kennan, "Flashbacks," *The New Yorker*, February 25, 1985, 52–69.

26. Rood, "The Naiveté of George Kennan," citing George Kennan, "The Time Has Come to Exorcise the Ghost of Stalin: Today's Soviet Regime Is Headed by a Moderate, Regarded by All Who Know Him as a Man of Peace," *Los Angeles Times*, December 18, 1977, Part 1-C, 3.

27. The following account of democratic development, unless otherwise indicated, is taken from Rood, "The Long View: Democracy and Strategy in Iraq."

28. Quoted in ibid.

29. Rood, "A Free Society in an Unfree World," 40.

30. Quoted in ibid., 46.

31. Quoted in ibid., 46–47.

32. Quoted in ibid., 47–48.

33. Rood contrasted this with a decline in the sense of executive responsibility for defense in the 1970s. This was exemplified for him by the failed military raid to rescue Americans held hostage by the Iranian revolutionary regime. The raid was a fiasco— of the eight helicopters sent to the first staging area (Desert One), only five arrived in operational condition. After the decision was made to abort the mission, one of the helicopters crashed into an EC-130 aircraft containing extra aviation fuel. The resulting fire destroyed both aircraft and killed eight servicemen. Rood praised the bravery of those who volunteered for the mission, but courage clearly was not enough. Rood cited the observation of former Secretary of Defense James Schlesinger that the raid could be taken as an illustration of the overall state of the defense establishment. "The deficiencies in equipment that caused the failure in Iran have their counterparts throughout the armed services and their presence reflects the state of mind of those who head the defense establishment," Rood wrote. "This weakness is bound to be reflected in the morale and the efficiency of those forces upon which the country must call in time of great emergency." Harold W. Rood, "Courage Alone Is Not Enough Today" (Claremont, CA: Public Research, Syndicated, 1980).

34. Quotations and information in this paragraph taken from Rood, *Kingdoms of the Blind*, 42–43.

35. Unless otherwise indicated, the arguments in this section are drawn from the Introduction (9–23) and the Conclusion (367–73) of Harold W. Rood, "Strategy Out of Silence: American Military Policy and the Preparations for War, 1919–1940" (PhD diss., University of California, 1960).

36. The notion of hemisphere defense, rather than continental defense, which became increasingly prominent in the late 1930s, served as something of a political as well as strategic bridge to large-scale U.S. intervention in Europe. Many leading officials, including President Roosevelt, Secretary of State Hull, and other prominent public figures, expressed fears over Nazi and Japanese activities in South America and

near the Panama Canal. This led to an expanded definition of America's security perimeter and greater demands being placed on the armed services—for example, by legitimating the need for some expeditionary capability. "It helped the Army and Navy to achieve a higher level of preparation than otherwise would have been possible," Rood noted. Ibid., 306–7.

37. Ibid., 264–84.
38. Quotations and text from ibid., 104–15, 132–34.
39. Ibid., 142–60.
40. Ibid., 45.
41. Ibid., 46, 204–7.
42. Ibid., 364–65.
43. Ibid.

# FIVE

# The Russian Problem

## A Study in Grand Strategy

*Professor Rood regarded the Russian Problem as the central strategic challenge facing the West, even after conventional wisdom had declared the end of the Cold War. This was in part because he did not see the Soviet-American conflict — as many scholars did — as largely sui generis, but rather as part of a grander strategic-historical problem that had been working itself out since the consolidation of the Duchy of Muscovy after 1480. In his view, that problem flowed from deep historical, cultural, and geopolitical impulses that transcended epochs and ideologies.*

*For this reason, there is not much in Rood's teaching about "who started the Cold War?" or "whose fault was the Cold War?" — questions that dominated much of the postwar scholarship and sometimes even the political debate on the Russian Problem. For Rood, this would be like asking whose fault is it that water runs downhill. For insight, he often pointed to Russian scholars and statesmen who he believed understood best the problem of Russia. It is useful for students also to look at those who disagreed with his description of Russia's impulses, the magnitude of the problem, and the causes of sustained conflict with the West.*[1]

*Rood explored many specific subproblems of the generic Russian Problem through his provocative analyses of the 1962 Cuban missile crisis and the 1968 "Prague Spring" (among other events), and in his award-winning essay on the significance of the Vietnam War. These were among his best works. Whether one agrees with the general conclusions or the specifics of his analyses, each points to useful ways to think about international problems that students and statesmen can apply to today's strategic challenges.*

In chapter 2, we summarized Rood's analysis of some of the enduring problems and patterns of international politics, such as the German Problem. He paid special attention to what he thought was the most important challenge of his time—the Russian Problem (what became the Soviet Problem and is now again, seemingly, the Russian Problem). We deferred its consideration because Rood thought that Soviet actions could not be understood apart from a full consideration of the nature of strategy in general (chapter 3) and the peculiar difficulties that democracies faced in dealing with aggressive totalitarian regimes (chapter 4). The Soviets, Rood argued, were aggressive, totalitarian, and practitioners of a patient but well-conceived strategy. This strategy, in his mind, pointed to preparations for war.

Rood was criticized at the time by his academic colleagues for exaggerating the Soviet threat ("the Russians are ten feet tall"). After the dissolution of the Soviet Union, the notion that the Kremlin's strategy had been well conceived seemed to be questionable, to say the least. We address these challenges to Rood's thought later in this chapter and in chapter 7. For the moment, we would point to Churchill's judgment that a sensible strategy that fails because of factors that could not be fully anticipated is not rendered any less sensible thereby. Men can only peer so far into the future. Even in apparent failure, a sensible strategy often yields unexpected fruits down the road. It can sometimes be revisited under more favorable conditions. Seen in this light, Soviet strategy can surely be examined with profit. Certainly it was coherent and had its roots deep in history and geography. It may provide a template for the geopolitical challenges we face in the future.

Russia—the Soviet Union for much of the twentieth century—has represented a "problem" for the other great powers since the time of Peter the Great. According to Rood, Russian grand strategy was characterized by the persistent drive to open waters. This meant not only Russian access to, and control over, many of the marginal seas of Eurasia—such as the Barents Sea and the Norwegian Sea, the Baltic, the Mediterranean, the Red Sea, the Persian Gulf, the Sea of Japan, and the Sea of Okhotsk—but also the ability to prevent hostile powers from operating near those seas. If successfully accomplished, this strategy would have left Russia the dominant Eurasian power, given Russia's long-standing ability to control or influence events in Eastern and Central Europe and Central Asia. Russia's geopolitical ambitions were reinforced by the political-religious notion that it was destined to be the "Third Rome." During the nineteenth century, Britain acted on the assumption that Russian expansionism, especially into southwest and south-central Asia, presented a threat to the British Empire.[2]

In the twentieth century, the traditional Russian Problem was compounded by an aggressive ideology that had global, not merely continental, ambitions.[3] The Soviet Problem became one for the United States in the power vacuum after World War II. The nations in Europe and Asia with an interest in preventing the Soviet Union from expanding could no longer do so without strong U.S. support. This meant that Soviet grand strategy now aimed to remove the American strategic presence from Eurasia. Moscow shared its anti-American animus and its basic ideology with China, once the communists took power there with Soviet assistance. The "problems" of Russia and China, according to Rood, had to be viewed as interrelated, even though obvious political and strategic differences emerged between the two communist powers.

Rood dismissed the popular image of bumbling Soviets in ill-fitting suits, addicted to vodka and cushy dachas. To the contrary, Rood argued, the Soviet Union was

> run by a band of professionals whose predecessors have passed on, not only the reins of power, but the knowledge and experience accumulated in years of service to Party and State. There is not a man amongst them who had not served his apprenticeship in the lower ranks of the Party, the bureaucracy, the Secret Police, or the Army. Alongside such men as ran the Soviet Union, the leaders of Nazi Germany were amateurs. Those who led the Communist Party of the Soviet Union, and who operated the Soviet government, were experts in totalitarian politics; those who were not experts did not survive the process of indoctrination to emerge as leaders.[4]

## POLITICAL-STRATEGIC INDICATORS OF WAR

Rood insisted that the nature of the Soviet regime conveyed political indicators of things to come. Those indicators were reinforced by how the Soviets treated those lands and peoples that fell to them under the Hitler-Stalin Pact of August 1939 and that were overrun by the Red Army by the close of World War II in Europe.

> Some territories like eastern Poland, Latvia, Lithuania, and Estonia were simply annexed to the Soviet Union. Upon others were imposed direct Soviet administration, which was succeeded by regimes that mirrored the Soviet. . . . Czechoslovakia attempted to re-create the constitution that had been destroyed by the Nazis in 1939, but its regime was overthrown, to be replaced by one imposed by the Soviet Union, in 1948, three years after the ending of the war. And these regimes were not temporarily imposed to see the countries of Eastern Europe through the difficult period of recovery from the devastation of the war, they were established as permanent features of the political landscape in Eastern Europe. The policies that perpetuate the regimes have transcended changes in the leadership of the Party and State in the Soviet Union. The violent rising of East Germans against the Communist regime in their country was put down by 17 Soviet divisions when the Soviet Union was led by Joseph Stalin [with a collective leadership]; the uprising in Hungary in 1956 was put down by Soviet troops when the Soviet Union was led by Nikita Khrushchev; and it was under

Brezhnev that Czechoslovakia was invaded by 25 Warsaw Pact divisions in 1968. Today [1983] the Soviet Union is led by the man [Yuri Andropov] who ran the Soviet secret police under Brezhnev and who managed the suppression of the Hungarian revolt in 1956 under Khrushchev.[5]

As one of many such examples, Rood quoted from a 1969 article by A. M. Suslov, member of the Soviet Communist Party Politburo, and acknowledged theoretician of Party doctrine. Comrade Suslov described the progress made in "the worldwide revolutionary process of replacement of capitalism by socialism." In 1919, according to Suslov, 16 percent of the world's territory and 7.8 percent of the world's population were subject to "socialist" rule; by 1969, 25.9 percent of the world's territory and 34.4 percent of the world's population were under "socialist" rule. Those figures, Rood noted, were compiled before Libya became an ally of the Soviet Union, before Cuban and Soviet troops secured Ethiopia, before North Vietnam came to rule all of Indochina, and before the Soviets invaded Afghanistan. Suslov concluded: "The ideas of Lenin are conquering the minds and hearts of millions of people. Loyal to Lenin's behests, relying on the ever stronger internationalist unity of the working class, of all the revolutionary, liberation and anti-imperialist forces, the Communists will do their utmost to carry to a victorious end the great struggle."[6]

Rood took seriously the statements of Suslov and other Soviet officials that the end of their policy was to be the establishment of socialism and communism throughout the world. Such things might have been dismissed as the idle dream of party bureaucrats, expressed merely to revive the flagging spirits of jaded party regulars, if not for the fact that the policies described were then in the process of implementation, and that the Soviet Union was acquiring the military capability to support them. Judged by such statements, and by Soviet actions and activities, the conflict between the Soviet Union and the West could not be said to turn on a mere dispute over some border territory, the adjustment of which would restore amicable relations. Cuba, Nicaragua, Africa, and Indochina were not border territories to which the Soviet Union could be said to lay claim. The establishment of "socialist" regimes in those areas, through the active and material support of the Soviet Union and its allies, suggested that arguments such as Suslov's were intended as an explicit statement of Soviet policy.

Based on this evidence, Rood argued that the Soviet Union and the community of powers that it led were embarked on a worldwide struggle against the West over the issue of how the world should be organized. The conflict being waged, therefore, was not like that of the modern German Problem over how Europe and the Middle East should be organized, but over how the *world* should be organized. So long as the nations of the West continued to claim the right to rule themselves under the principles to which they adhered, Rood concluded that there was a high probability of war. He was convinced that war was certain unless the United States and its allies took immediate steps in the 1980s to remedy a situation of nascent Soviet strategic superiority.[7]

Some critics of Rood's position would argue that Soviet aims were in fact much more limited than this. Whatever the high-blown rhetoric of officials such as Suslov, the Soviets were actually trying to address the military vulnerabilities and domestic problems that had always plagued Russia. They merely wanted security and recognition as an equal of the United States. But even if one granted unlimited ambitions to the Kremlin, Rood's critics would say, its leaders were certainly not foolish enough to try to obtain world domination through war. On the one hand, communist doctrine assured them that history alone would bring about the triumph of socialism. On the other hand, the existence of nuclear weapons meant that the resort to war would lead to the destruction of the socialist project.

Rood acknowledged that it was not always easy to distinguish between Soviet dispositions that were merely precautionary and those that added materially to the USSR's military capabilities. For example, the elaborate civil defense program that had been developed in the Soviet Union, along with the formidable force of interceptor aircraft and surface-to-air missiles, could be seen as precautionary measures in an unstable world. Furthermore, as the United States had no such civil defense program, and an air defense system sufficient to control U.S. airspace only in peacetime, and no surface-to-air missiles, it could be assumed that the United States saw no need for such precautions. This might simply have meant that the Soviet Union had a less sanguine view of international politics than did the United States.[8] But there were anomalies in Soviet military dispositions that could not easily be explained in terms of mere sensible precautions taken in a disorderly world, and that instead pointed to serious Soviet preparations for war.

## EARLY WARNING: TRACKING SOVIET ANOMALIES

One such anomaly, according to Rood, was the extraordinary effort expended by the Soviet Union in the area abutting the North Pacific.[9]

In May 1978, the Soviet Union began fortifying the islands lying just north of Hokkaido, the northernmost of the Japanese Home Islands. In the course of the next two years, where formerly there had been nothing but Soviet Border Guards, there was a build-up to over ten thousand troops, the construction or extension of air bases, and the installation of coast artillery and air defenses; so that by 1982, there was a formidable force in place where before there had been none. At the same time, on the

Island of Sakhalin, air bases were going in, or were being expanded where they had already existed. By the end of 1982, the Soviet Union had deployed MiG-21 aircraft into Etorofu, which, along with Shikotan and Kunashiri, had been newly fortified. About 250 miles north of the fortified islands, the Soviet Union installed a submarine base on the island of Simushir.

All these measures, along with the build-up of Soviet naval forces in the Pacific that took place during the same period, might be simply precautionary. But, Rood asked, precautionary against what contingency? The great build-up began after the withdrawal of U.S. forces from South Vietnam and after the general reduction in U.S. naval, ground, and air forces in the region. By 1982, the Soviet Union had deployed, with its Pacific Fleet, eighty attack submarines plus twenty-four nuclear ballistic missile submarines. Meanwhile, the entire U.S. attack submarine force had been reduced to eighty-four, with only thirty-eight of those submarines based in the Pacific. While the number of U.S. carrier air groups had been reduced from sixteen to twelve, half of which were assigned to cover the entire Pacific and Indian Ocean and their approaches, the Soviet Union had not only deployed one or more carriers to the North Pacific, but also deployed Backfire bombers and 110 SS-20 missiles, with 330 nuclear warheads.

Rood noted an article in *Asiaweek* magazine (September 12, 1980), commenting on this build-up of Soviet forces north of Hokkaido: "Their Hokkaido activities are closely tied to securing vital sea routes in the event of an Asia conflict and with the eventual goal of separating Japan from the United States and mainland China."[10] But what, Rood asked, would occasion a conflict in the North Pacific? Soviet merchant ships moved freely in and out of Far Eastern harbors, carrying on trade with the rest of the world, including the Western Hemisphere. Soviet fishing fleets and those of their allies in Europe and Asia fished in the Gulf of Alaska and off both coasts of North and South America, without apparent hindrance (except those imposed by fishery treaties). Did the Kremlin think that the United States was about to contest it for possession of the Kuriles? Did the forty-eight combat aircraft that the United States stationed in Alaska, along with the 8,092 soldiers deployed there, threaten the Soviet naval base at Petropavlovsk?

And why, Rood asked, should the North Korean Army have been increased in size during the same period when U.S. ground and air forces in South Korea were reduced? In 1975, the North Korean Army had 410,000 men with one tank, three motorized and twenty infantry divisions, equipped with 1,130 tanks, and an air force of 216 combat aircraft. In 1982, there were 700,000 men in the army, with an increase to forty divisions, equipped with 2,650 tanks, while the air force had seven hundred combat aircraft. At the same time, the South Korean Army had been reduced by forty thousand troops to 520,000 troops with 860 tanks, and the U.S. ground forces in Korea reduced from thirty thousand to 28,732.

And what was going on in Southeast Asia? During the war in Vietnam, North Vietnam had an army numbering 480,000, of which 220,000 were deployed in South Vietnam, Cambodia, and Laos. But that was when the U.S. and South Vietnamese forces numbered close to 600,000. In the early 1980s, while there were still 200,000 Vietnamese troops in Cambodia, the size of the Vietnamese Army had grown to one million men. Moreover, there were now Soviet naval and air forces deployed in Vietnam, as well.

For Rood, the anomaly here was that the strength of U.S. forces in the Far East had been reduced, while that of its allies had not been increased, and yet the Soviet Union and its allies had substantially strengthened their forces during the same period. Why should the Soviet Union be taking measures to block the approaches to Vladivostok and turn the Sea of Okhotsk into a Russian lake, when it had not seemed necessary to do so in the 1950s and 1960s, when the United States enjoyed strategic nuclear superiority over the Soviet Union and naval and air superiority in the North Pacific? In Rood's view, what the Soviet Union and its allies had apparently done was to prepare for war. Did they do it because they expected to do something in the future that would cause a war?

In 1950, Rood noted, the Soviet Union signed a trade agreement with Afghanistan, a country in which Russia had traditional interests. Over the following twenty-six years, the Soviet Union provided economic and technical assistance, and kept Soviet advisers and technicians in the country to assist in Afghanistan's development. It provided weapons and training for the Afghan Army and Air Force (training some of the officers in the Soviet Union), undertook with the Afghan government a fifty-year plan for the development of Kabul, began and completed a network of highways and communications, and installed a number of military airfields along the highway system.

In 1979, Russian airborne divisions used the airfields, and Russian ground forces used the highways, to occupy Afghanistan. Did the economic, technical, and military assistance programs, and the road and airfield construction, constitute early warning that the Soviet Union was going to seize the country, or was it merely a precaution in case the country would have to be seized someday? And why should the Soviet Union wish to seize such a place anyway? Rood thought that the strategic question that must be asked here was the same as for the establishment of Soviet fortified bases in the southern Kuriles: What is it that the Soviets can do holding such places in force that they could not otherwise do? And what do they expect to happen that will require those places to be held in force?

In 1961, the Warsaw Pact held maneuvers in Central Europe. One of the exercises in that maneuver was a rehearsal of a forty-five-division-strong invasion of West Germany, and the movement forward from Poland and the Soviet Union itself of reinforcements. In the north, fourteen divisions were to move out of East Germany, with an amphibious battle group operating toward Schleswig on the Baltic Flank. On the No. 1 Central Front, seventeen divisions were used, and on the No. 2 Central Front, from Czechoslovakia, fifteen divisions were used. At the time the maneuvers were held, there were no Soviet divisions stationed in Czechoslovakia. But in 1968, as a consequence of suppressing the liberalization program led by Alexander Dubček, five Soviet divisions were introduced into the country, and the Czech Army was expanded to ten divisions. The movement of those Soviet divisions into Czechoslovakia in 1968 could be seen at the time to be necessary, because of political conditions in Czechoslovakia. But those divisions remained behind. They appeared to be configured and deployed for operations against NATO, not for internal security purposes. And five plus ten equals fifteen.[11]

Coincident with the maneuvers in 1961, East Germany began a program of construction of landing vessels for amphibious operations. Additionally, one of its motorized rifle regiments was trained and designated for amphibious operations. After these maneuvers, Poland raised and equipped an amphibious division. In September 1981, one hundred thousand Soviet troops practiced landing exercises on the Baltic Coast, during ZAPAD 81, supported by 140 ships and countless helicopters and other aircraft. Considering the interest in amphibious warfare evidenced by the Soviet Union, the intensive underwater reconnaissance that the Soviet Navy had been conducting in Swedish coastal waters over the years might not have been seen as quite so anomalous. But what events did the Soviets and their allies foresee that would require amphibious operations in the Baltic?

The Soviet Union and its allies were doing things that in past times one would have considered preparations for war, Rood reiterated. Military road reconnaissance and other intelligence activities by Eastern European truck drivers had been reported in Western Europe at least since 1976. Bulgarian trucks involved in trans-European trade were said to be conducting clandestine operations, including heroin smuggling, in support of the Palestine Liberation Organization. Operations such as Soviet submarines violating Swedish-protected harbors were done so blatantly and with so little public attention that it was tempting to neglect them as early warning indicators of what could be expected.

This, Rood argued, was the problem of early warning with respect to the Soviet Union. The warning might have come so long ago that its import had been forgotten. Or, some action that carried strategic warning might have been repeated so often in the past that it no longer carried such a warning with it. For instance, the Soviet Union moved one hundred thousand troops into East Germany by air every year, and then moved them out again. It would be strategic warning only if they had, one year, stayed for the movement westward. All one could say, Rood concluded, is that every time the Soviet Union and its allies demonstrated an increased capability to wage war, it constituted early warning. But then, perhaps, the most palpable warning consisted in the certain knowledge that the Soviet Union held the West as its enemy.

From these anomalies and other warning indicators, Rood identified the following characteristics of Soviet grand strategy:

- *Patience.* Whereas Nazi Germany acted quickly to achieve its strategic purposes, the Soviet Union, because of its enormous resources and military strength, was deliberate and almost leisurely in the application of its strategy. The prolonged time-scale permitted the Soviets to employ heavily the use of disinformation and deception, to allow the democratic strategy deficit to work in their favor.
- *Playing both ends against the middle.* In conflicts involving two other parties, such as between Germany and the West, and Japan and the West, in the 1930s, and between Iran and Iraq in the 1980s, the Soviets tried to place themselves in a position to win, no matter who lost. Whenever possible, they backed both sides in a conflict.
- *Political-strategic linkages.* The Soviet government took measures in one year that seemed to have no relation to anything immediate at the time, but that made sense in the context of some action or series of events that occurred much later. As noted above, the Soviets built roads and airports and a communications system in Afghanistan in the 1950s and 1960s, apparently to compete with the United States for political influence there. In 1979, the Soviets used this "civilian" infrastructure to support its military invasion.
- *Multiple, redundant ways to achieve the same objective.* The Soviet Union had Libya in place as a client before it prepared Egypt for war with Israel in 1973. If Egypt had been defeated, or later turned against the USSR, the Kremlin could fall back on Libya and still achieve its strategic objectives in the eastern Mediterranean.
- *Establishing the proper relationship between the main and secondary theaters.* The Soviets sought to force the United States to defend areas away from the principal theater of war, while Soviet and client forces were able to concentrate to achieve a decision in the principal theater.[12]

The Soviets practiced these principles over a period of decades to overcome what had been an inferior strategic position at the end of World War II. Despite their move into central Europe and the elimination of Germany and Japan as hostile great powers in 1945, the Soviets still needed time to recover from the enormous physical destruction of that conflict. They were also confronted with U.S. nuclear superiority, and with an American global base structure. In the classic strategic fashion of the inferior power, the Soviets worked just below the threshold of global war through a series of incremental changes. All of these changes, in Rood's assessment, added up to create a position of nascent Soviet strategic superiority by the early 1980s. Soviet strategy was underwritten by a massive quantitative and qualitative buildup in conventional and nuclear forces, in all major regions of potential conflict. Rood frequently cited the information in John M. Collins's periodically updated study, *The U.S.–Soviet Military Balance,* to buttress his case for how that balance had shifted decisively in the Soviets' favor.

The incremental development of Soviet superiority required the imaginative linkage of policy in all the major strategic theaters. For Rood, each building block of Soviet strategy was instructive not only in its own right as a threat to the West, but also as a textbook example for how to conduct grand strategy simply. Rood identified many increments of strategic advantage gained by the Soviets. We describe briefly, below, those that Rood took the greatest care to document: (1) the development of an advanced Soviet military base in Cuba; (2) the increase in Soviet military superiority opposite NATO's central front; (3) the creation of a strategic axis in the Mediterranean that undermined NATO's southern flank; (4) the emergence of a major threat to U.S. and Allied maritime lines of communication in the Pacific; and (5) the attempt to establish Soviet nuclear superiority.[13]

## AN ADVANCED SOVIET BASE IN CUBA

By the late 1970s, Cuba had unmistakably become an active ally of the Soviet Union. Rood concluded that this development was one of the most revealing of all the Soviets' strategic moves because, as noted in chapter 2, every power with ambitions to dominate Europe inevitably becomes involved in the Western Hemisphere. The creation of a Soviet naval and air base in Cuba created a strategic threat that would, at the very least, tie the United States down if war occurred elsewhere. Rood constantly stressed: "It is the very essence of strategy to force one's enemy to defend that which he has no choice to defend in areas away from the principal theater of war, while one's own forces concentrate to achieve a decision in that theater of war where the outcome of battle will decide the outcome of the war."[14]

As we have seen, Rood believed that the resolution of the Cuban missile crisis, which involved a commitment by the United States not to invade Cuba, marked a crucial turning point in the U.S.–Soviet military balance. It ought to have been a sharp warning of the shift in strategic conditions in the Gulf of Mexico, and thus in the world. For the first time since the Civil War, a major European power had sent troops into an independent country in the Western Hemisphere to establish a regime that would favor its own interests. It did this not just in any country, but in one that unmistakably revived, in full force, the problem of the Cuban-Caribbean Salient for the United States. In 1940, the mere rumor that the Nazis might attempt to support a coup in Brazil led the United States to plan for an expeditionary force to prevent the extension of German power in the Western Hemisphere. The very fact that the United States would accept that the Soviet Union had the right to establish a base in the Gulf of Mexico, so long as it contained no "offensive" weapons, was a remarkable departure from the policies implied by the Monroe Doctrine.[15]

Further, after 1962, the United States repeatedly demonstrated that it was reluctant to consider any Soviet weapons or military vehicles based in Cuba as having a "strategic" rather than a "defensive" role. This included Tu-95 bombers and the MiG-27, a ground attack variant of the MiG-23. In effect, the United States granted the Soviet Union the license to develop an advanced base from which Soviet and Cuban forces could wage war against the United States far from Europe, where the decisive battles would take place.

The strategic importance of Cuba, the Caribbean Basin, and the Gulf of Mexico had not declined since the dark days of World War II, when a handful of German submarines had inflicted horrific damage on American shipping. (These submarines, operating from bases in Europe, had nothing comparable to the facilities and infrastructure that the Soviets possessed in Cuba.) Perhaps a third of the petroleum imported by the United States in the late 1970s moved along the route through the Yucatan Channel or the Florida Straits, past Cuba to U.S. Gulf ports. More than one-half million barrels of oil a day from the Alaska North Slope Oil fields came through the Panama Canal and into Gulf ports. There were numerous oil and gas platforms in the sea off the mouth of the Mississippi alone. Almost 90 percent of the bauxite then consumed in the United States was moved through waters near Cuba from its sources in the West Indies or South America. A host of other materials were transported into Gulf ports or along the Southern Atlantic coast of the United States. All of these were obvious targets for light naval units and submarines operating from Cuba.

In any U.S.–Soviet war, therefore, among the first considerations for the United States would have been the neutralization of the island to prevent its use as a base for Soviet-Cuban operations in the area. Yet there was no assurance that Cuba could be dealt with quickly or cheaply, nor without diverting important military resources from the principal theater of war. Rood set out in some detail what this operation would involve. He compared it to the attack on Okinawa in 1945, which took two and a half months and which required three U.S. marine divisions and four army divisions, supported by at least sixteen U.S. and four British carriers, and numerous escort carriers. Rood calculated that it would take months merely to assemble the ships for an amphibious operation against Cuba. All of these forces were already committed, or over-committed, to the defense of Western Europe and the Pacific. Nuclear weapons might offer the solution, but their use would raise a host of other problems, including domestic political opposition and the fact that it might provide the Soviets with an excuse to retaliate in kind against the United States or U.S. troops in Europe (if indeed the Soviets needed such an excuse).

The bottom line for Rood: a U.S. conquest of Cuba could never compensate for an Allied defeat on the Eurasian continent; whereas Cuba's conquest by the United States would hardly have been noticed by the Soviet Union were it to have won Western Europe.

To Rood, it seemed evident that, from the Soviet perspective, Cuba was to play the same role that the Socialist Republic of Vietnam was intended to play in Indochina and the rest of Southeast Asia. That is, it would serve as the nucleus around which to organize a regional political and economic unit of the greater socialist commonwealth. The regional strategy and ambitions of the Soviets, working through Cuba but also through their other client states, was evident to those who were paying close attention to the matter. Mexico was beset by guerrillas who had been recruited in Moscow at Patrice Lumumba University, had received North Korean passports in East Berlin, and had been trained in North Korea in a camp outside Pyongyang. From North Korea, they were sent back to Mexico to begin operations against that country's government. While on a visit to Havana, the secretary of the Libyan people's bureau had declared in 1971 his country to be an ally of Cuba, while Cuba, in turn, was undertaking highway and other construction projects in Libya. The guerrilla movement in El Salvador, the FMLN, sent delegates to Libya to participate in the World Conference of Solidarity with Libya. [16]

Cuba and Mozambique expressed their fraternal relations during the course of a meeting of the Cuban-Mozambican Joint Commission in Havana in November 1981. It was as if Cuba were an African power, which of course it was, since it had armed forces stationed in a half dozen African countries, including Mozambique. Finally, in Havana that same month Dmitur Stanishev, secretary of the Bulgarian Communist Party, met with Jesus Montane Oropesa, member of the secretariat and of the politburo of the Cuban Communist Party, to celebrate Bulgarian Cultural Week. Such comings and goings between the Caribbean, Africa, the Balkans, and East Europe often included Soviet defense ministers visiting the Caribbean or the defense ministers of countries like Cuba and Nicaragua meeting with their counterparts in the Warsaw Pact.

Even more remarkably, Cuba facilitated Soviet bloc operations in Africa and the Middle East and became an instrument of Soviet policy in the world, as well as a major military power in its own right. Cuban troops played a decisive role in the Angolan campaign in 1975 and ultimately deployed between fifty and sixty thousand troops outside the Western Hemisphere. Castro supported communist movements in Nicaragua and elsewhere in Central and South America. Cuban ships dropped KGB agents in Hong Kong. Whether the Cuban dictator was a willing partner, a pliant tool, or a socialist brother-in-arms made little difference in counting the strategic consequences for the United States. It might appear incredible that the regime in Cuba would tie its fate to that of the Soviet Union in any war between that power and the United States. Rood judged that if the Soviet Union were defeated in Europe, then there seemed little doubt that Castro, if his regime had survived, would seek accommodation with the United States.[17] Were NATO to be overrun, however, then there would be equally little doubt that Castro would have claimed a Soviet reward for whatever contribution Cuba made to the Soviet victory.

Soviet and Cuban activities in the tiny Caribbean island nation of Grenada provided Rood with an additional window into the Kremlin's strategic logic and objectives in the region. He pointed specifically to Soviet and Cuban interest in an "International Airport" near Port Salines. Soviet aircraft flying from the Soviet Union via Libya could have crossed the Atlantic from Guinea-Bissau (a nation friendly to the Soviet Union and Cuba) to refuel at Grenada, and then continue on to Cuba or Nicaragua (or to El Salvador, should that country become accessible). The flights would have taken place outside the purview of the U.S. air defense warning system.[18]

An island like Grenada would have been useful, not just as a refueling base for aircraft in transit across the mid-Atlantic, but also as an arsenal where weapons could be accumulated for infiltration into countries within small-boat range. Trinidad-Tobago, Colombia, and Venezuela all had been beset by guerrilla movements, and Grenada was being used as a base for training guerrillas for deployment into Trinidad. Grenada could have been used, as well, as a base for the deployment of Soviet, Cuban, or Libyan submarines to operate in the Caribbean, beyond the ordinary patrol paths of antisubmarine patrol aircraft operating out of American bases. The submarines themselves would provide the means for infiltrating guerrillas, sabotage parties, or intelligence agents.

Rood cited numerous other uses to which Grenada could have been put under Soviet and Cuban control. An air base in Grenada would have been strategically important for the support of submarine operations throughout the Caribbean, and in the Central and South Atlantic as well. Long-range aircraft flying reconnaissance and target acquisition for Soviet and Cuban attack submarines in wartime was one possibility. The bathymetric characteristics of the Caribbean are especially good for deep-diving submarine operations. The depths of water in the Caribbean often exceed 1,500 fathoms, especially along the eastern approaches to the Panama Canal. The very deep waters and the immense number of inlets and islands render sonar detection of submarines difficult, while the thermal layers in the warm waters of the Caribbean make detection and location by sonar transponder buoys dropped from the air equally difficult.

What was clear to Rood was that the Soviet Union and its allies seemed deeply interested in contesting the United States for control of the Caribbean Basin and the Gulf of Mexico. Perhaps this was mere political gamesmanship or ideological romanticism. But Rood challenged his students to consider whether high state policy—grand strategy—was at work.

## BOLSTERING THE CENTRAL FRONT IN EUROPE

In August 1968, twenty-five divisions from various Warsaw Pact countries (the Soviet Union, East Germany, Poland, Hungary, and Bulgaria), under the command of a Soviet general, entered Czechoslovakia to suppress a liberalization movement led by Alexander Dubček. Many in the West lamented the demise of the "Prague Spring," which had seemed to promise a loosening of the Soviet grip behind the Iron Curtain, as well as the evolution of a more humane and indigenous form of socialism. The Soviet action seemed to derail an emerging East-West détente that was to include new negotiations aimed at controlling the arms race (what became known as the Strategic Arms Limitation Talks, or SALT).

Western diplomats could console themselves, however, that this unfortunate incident was managed peacefully, unlike the situation in Hungary in 1956, when thousands of Hungarians, presumably encouraged by American propaganda to believe that their liberation was at hand, had lost their lives in a futile insurrection. Furthermore, there was no real danger of an East-West war, because NATO remained restrained during the crisis. The United States and its allies signaled clearly that they saw no vital interest at stake in the settlement of an intra–Warsaw Pact political dispute. The general view in the West was that Soviet actions in Czechoslovakia, however regrettable, promoted "stability" in Eastern Europe; in the longer term, it revealed to the world the Kremlin's moral and political weakness. It was a purely political act, with no military or strategic implications.[19]

Rood argued that this conventional analysis of the 1968 Czech crisis entirely missed the fundamental strategic point. The great anomaly that should have tipped off strategic analysts that something was up was the fact that the Soviets had no need to take what they already owned, especially in such dramatic fashion. The KGB controlled the Czech intelligence service and at the very least had superb intelligence about activities in the reform movement. There was no evidence of any actual threat of organized violence against communist rule. If the Soviets truly feared the "infection" of reformist ideas, they had other ways to deal with the problem. In 1948, the Soviets managed, rather easily, to bring about a change in government in Czechoslovakia without military invasion. They did this through intimidation and through their control of the police and army. The non-communist Foreign Minister, Jan Masaryk, conveniently committed suicide by jumping out of a window. By contrast, Dubček, the Czech reformer, was later named ambassador to Turkey, a nontrivial posting.[20]

To Rood, this suggested that the entire "reform" movement had been a cover for some other project—either the movement itself had been under Soviet control all along, or the Soviets took advantage of its existence for their own purposes.

What might those purposes be? The Warsaw Pact action effectively served as a dress rehearsal for an invasion of Western Europe, without unduly alarming the United States and its NATO allies. The Warsaw Pact's preparations for entering Czechoslovakia, and the execution of the operation, mirrored what NATO intelligence services expected to see in the event of an actual attack across the border into Western Germany. In the future, Rood believed that the Soviets might use another self-generated "political" crisis in Eastern Europe to achieve strategic surprise, since the West had been conditioned to expect things to remain quiet. NATO would surely not want to take any precautionary military steps in such a situation, to ensure that the Soviets were not "provoked" while they settled communist-bloc matters in-house. The Czech operation also demonstrated the capability of the Soviet government to call upon members of the Warsaw Pact to enforce measures taken to safeguard purely Soviet interests (the Soviets, by contrast, had unilaterally invaded Hungary in 1956).

Rood believed that the Czech operation was something more than a dress rehearsal—it directly increased the military capability of the Warsaw Pact to threaten NATO's central front. After the Soviets installed what the West presumed to be a more pliant regime in Prague, many of the Warsaw Pact forces withdrew from Czechoslovakia, confirming the standard interpretation of the action as a one-off, temporary event. Many withdrew, but not all. In fact, five Soviet divisions (two tank and three motorized rifle) remained behind, even though there was no longer any serious threat to effective Soviet control of the country (if there ever had been). This was in addition to the twenty divisions in the Group of Soviet Forces in (East) Germany and other Soviet forces in Poland and Hungary, along with the armies of those nations. The Soviets showed that they could increase their forces facing NATO without any commensurate military response. In fact, after the crisis passed, the United States continued a planned draw-down of American forces from Europe.

As to the political price in goodwill that the Soviets supposedly paid for their invasion of Czechoslovakia, Rood pointed out that, within a year, Moscow and Washington had agreed to begin the SALT negotiations.

## TURNING NATO'S SOUTHERN FLANK

In the late 1970s, a superficial glance at the strategic map would have suggested that the NATO alliance held a reasonably secure position along its southern flank. The United States, presumably, could rely on its NATO allies (Turkey, Greece, and Italy), and a pro-American Israel, to block Soviet expansion—especially once Egypt (apparently) broke ties with the Kremlin and gravitated in the direction of the West. The Soviets, to be sure, had built up their naval fleet in the Mediterranean, and had secured access to ports in Syria, but otherwise their access to the region seemed limited. Austria and Malta were neutral, Yugoslavia was non-aligned, and Libya was run by an unpredictable, megalomaniac dictator apparently wedded to the quixotic idea of conquering the Arab world. [21]

Rood's analysis pointed to a rather different assessment of the strategic opportunities that the Soviets had cultivated in the region. Each step had taken place just below the threshold of Western attention. One example was Austria, whose geographic position affected both NATO's central front and its southern flank. [22] The Austrian State Treaty of 1955, hailed at the time as representing a great thaw in the Cold War, established a sovereign, democratic, and permanently neutral Austria. The World War II occupying powers, including the United States and the Soviet Union, withdrew their troops. For Rood, this seemingly happy outcome obscured a simple political truth: Austria, like Finland, remained independent at the pleasure and convenience of the Soviet Union.

If Austria were to be occupied by forces of the Warsaw Pact, NATO had no commitment to come to her defense. The occupation of Austria by the German Army in 1938 had demonstrated how quickly this small country could be seized; the point was reinforced by the Warsaw Pact's action against Czechoslovakia in 1968. By contrast, no one seriously thought that NATO might preemptively enter Austria in such a fashion. Almost every country with which Austria had to trade in order to obtain fuel resided within the political control of Moscow, or was so much under Moscow's influence as to be considered a client. Austria's leaders, whatever their political preferences, knew the truth of their position, and this affected their policies concerning trade and security.

Rood detailed the extensive commercial agreements between Austria and various members of the COMECON, the Soviet economic bloc, particularly those dealing with the supply of Soviet natural gas and other energy resources. Rood believed that those agreements were designed to place Austria at the center of a great web of commercial activity stretching north into Poland, south into Yugoslavia and Libya, east into Hungary, and beyond into Russian Siberia. Along the highways and rail lines that linked Austria with Czechoslovakia and Poland, goods from Eastern Europe flowed to Yugoslav ports on the Adriatic.

Rood acknowledged that Austrian trade with the Soviet Union and other members of COMECON need not have had political or strategic implications. Such activities might have merely been part of the natural evolution of the region's economy. After all, the Western democracies also traded with Eastern bloc countries. But this was state-directed trade, not that of the free market. Rood recalled that Nazi Germany had used trade, even during the 1930s, as a device through which to tie lesser countries into its orbit, particularly those in eastern and southern Europe. Indeed, Nazi plans for the unification of Europe were to be implemented through the purchase, by German corporations, of controlling interests in key enterprises within occupied countries. This was part of Hitler's scheme for the eventual integration of occupied Europe into the economy of the German Third Reich.[23] In this case, Soviet-directed trade with Austria created avenues through which Eastern bloc intelligence agents, terrorists, arms, and other means of Soviet policy could flow—all "laundered" (as it were) with the complicity of a democratic regime.

Austria's location and historic ties with Yugoslavia were of particular interest to Rood. In June 1948, the COMINFORM, a creature of the Communist Party of the Soviet Union and successor to the COMINTERN, announced the expulsion of the Yugoslav Communist Party. This action appeared to signal the beginning of Yugoslavia's break with the other communist powers in Europe. The United States and Great Britain soon began to offer assistance of various kinds to Belgrade, including military hardware. Although there was no expectation that Yugoslavia would become less communist, it was considered an important shift in the strategic situation, and one that favored NATO. Infiltration of communists into Greece was halted and the Soviet path to the Adriatic was blocked. This enhanced the security of Italy, Greece, and even Turkey, leaving NATO supreme in the eastern Mediterranean.

By the 1970s, however, Rood believed that something fundamental had changed. He noted that Laurence Silberman, former U.S. ambassador to Belgrade, had commented in 1977 that "Yugoslavia had consistently sided with America's enemies in the world," and suggested "that Washington should re-examine its relations according to the United States' true interests." This drew outrage from the Yugoslav government and a rebuke from the State Department, which "dissociated itself" from Silberman's views.[24]

In Rood's judgment, by the 1970s, Yugoslavia in fact had become an advanced base for Soviet military power in the eastern Mediterranean. This situation was amply demonstrated during 1973 Middle East War. Even prior to the outbreak of the war, Yugoslavia's Josip Broz Tito had already signaled his support for Soviet and Egyptian objectives, which were to bring about Israeli withdrawal from the Sinai and its reoccupation by Egypt. Rood noted various reports that Yugoslavia had served as a transit point for Soviet military equipment flowing into the region, by sea and air, before and during the war. Essentially, Tito acted like a Soviet ally in all but name, especially with respect to Moscow's policy in the Mediterranean and the Middle East. The Yugoslav Army was well armed by this time, chiefly with Warsaw Pact weapons (and with that military equipment came the need for logistical support and technicians from the Soviet Union or Eastern Europe).

How did Yugoslavia slip back into the Soviet orbit, apparently without the West noticing? Rood speculated that increased Yugoslav trade relations with the Soviet bloc, especially through Austria, may have provided one avenue of influence. Soviet willingness to take military action in Czechoslovakia against a deviationist government (whether the invasion was stage-managed or not) must have captured Tito's attention. The Soviets may have threatened Tito with a coup d'etat, a threat made credible by the activities of pro-Soviet elements among the communist parties in Croatia, Voivodina, Montenegro, and the Kosovo region, as well as an Ustashi raid carried out from Austrian territory.[25]

If the Soviet Union had simply smashed Tito's government, Rood observed, everyone would have understood instantly what was at stake (although the West might have tried to ignore it, as in the case of the introduction of additional Soviet combat forces into Czechoslovakia in 1968). And the Yugoslavs would have fought hard against a Warsaw Pact invasion. But the Yugoslav affair was handled, in Rood's judgment, with Florentine skill. There was the judicious development of economic and commercial relationships that profited Yugoslavia as much as they did the Soviet Union; the careful attention to the equipment of the Yugoslav armed forces; some rather nice demonstrations of the Soviet capability to cause Tito trouble; occasional Bulgarian reminders of disputed claims to Yugoslav Macedonia; and, withal, the seeming Soviet liberality with respect to Tito and his government that apparently left them free as the air, to outward appearances at least.

The southern end of the Soviet strategic axis across the Mediterranean extended to Libya, which by the late 1970s had become the principal bridgehead of Soviet influence in North Africa.[26] Like Yugoslavia, Libya professed to be fiercely "non-aligned" and jealous of its independence of foreign influence, yet, Rood argued, it too served as a purveyor for Soviet policy and strategy. Whereas Yugoslavia no doubt did so out of Marxist sentimentality, and because its internal circumstances rendered it too vulnerable to do otherwise, Libya apparently acted out of Muslim romanticism and the desire to gain the imperial rewards due to an active proconsul of the "Third Rome." Rood argued that, just as Fidel Castro looked to become head of a socialist federation of the Caribbean Basin, and Le Duan of Vietnam looked to become head of a socialist federation of Indochina, so too did Muammar al-Gaddafi think ahead to the day when he could lead a socialist federation of Arab states under a condition of Soviet global hegemony.

In 1974, Libya and the USSR concluded a trade agreement, apparently together with an arms deal, that granted the Soviets access to Libyan air and naval bases. Meanwhile, the 32,000-man Libyan Army and the other services somehow managed to operate and find use for two thousand Soviet tanks, two squadrons of MiG-23s, a substantial number of Tu-22 bombers, Foxtrot-class submarines, fast patrol boats, and arrays of Soviet-made antitank guns, surface-to-air missiles, and helicopters.

In 1969, before the coup that overthrew King Idris, the United States and Britain had access to the harbors at Benghazi, Tripoli, and Tobruk, and to Libyan air bases, including the Strategic Air Command (SAC) facility at Wheelus Air Base. From these facilities, Allied military power easily could reach countries then friendly to the West, like Tunisia, Morocco, Ethiopia, Chad, and Israel.[27] A decade later, Soviet aircraft operated from the old Allied bases. Soviet warships called at Libyan ports. Soviet and Cuban forces staged through Libyan airfields. Libya had become a military power in its own right, an arsenal for Soviet arms in Africa. Allied warships now had to take care to avoid minefields sown in Libyan coastal waters. In any crisis in the Mediterranean, Allied aircraft carriers could no longer safely operate within range of Libyan air or submarine bases. Libyan money went to help develop an oil pipeline through Yugoslavia to Hungary and Czechoslovakia, and Yugoslavia reportedly built an arms plant in Libya to manufacture ammunition and spare parts for the Soviet weapons in the Libyan arsenals and gun parks.

Rood noted that Libya was at once a training camp, treasury, and arsenal for terrorists. The Black September terrorists who killed the Israeli team at the Munich Olympics in 1972 were led by a Libyan and equipped with Soviet arms. Libya supplied Eastern European arms to IRA terrorists in Northern Ireland and Gaddafi openly supported the movement while boasting of support for guerrilla organizations within the United States. The "charities" to which Gaddafi subscribed, such as the Popular Front for the Liberation of Palestine, were those with which the Soviet Union materially sympathized. Libya reportedly established training camps for Palestinian terrorists inside Yugoslavia, near the Bulgarian border.[28]

Rood thought it not inconsequential for the peoples of Africa that the Soviet Union, with its Cuban and Eastern European allies, had become such an important power on the African continent. But what was of greater and more immediate consequence was the degradation of the capabilities of the Western democracies to defend Europe. The new strategic axis constructed by the USSR through Austria to Libya, in Rood's view, clearly made it easier for the Soviets to conquer Western Europe in a war. The axis opened further options for Soviet strategic progress in the Mediterranean, while reducing those of the Western alliance for the defense of Europe's southern flank.

Rood observed that the strategic importance of the Mediterranean for the defense of Western Europe could be inferred from what occurred there during World War II. The failure of the Axis powers to dominate the Mediterranean hastened their defeat. Allied success in 1942–1944 in regaining dominance of the Mediterranean exposed all of Southern Europe to Allied operations from bases themselves secure from Axis attack. Yet it was a near-run thing for the Allies, and the fact that they had to fight for three years to confirm their position in the Mediterranean delayed substantially operations into Western Europe aimed at the German heartland.

Rood observed that what the Axis had to expend in men, ships, and aircraft, to try to seize the Mediterranean during World War II, had fallen to the Soviet Union or its hirelings virtually unnoticed, through default by the West. Should war have come to Europe, the full measure of Soviet resources need not have been spent to secure the Mediterranean, but would have been available to be invested elsewhere to secure even greater strategic advantages.[29]

In any major war, Rood argued, it was almost certain that NATO would have lacked the capability to reinforce Greece and Turkey. Both countries were well aware of that fact. Rood believed that circumstances might incline them eventually toward making the best possible accommodation with the Soviet Union. Italy was also vulnerable to a variety of pressures created by the proximity of the Soviet axis—for example, by the threat of a Libyan oil embargo; by the Soviet Mediterranean Fleet and its ready access to bases on the Adriatic and in Algeria and Libya; and by the withdrawal of the Royal Navy from Malta. A future Italian government of national reconciliation might have decided that withdrawal from NATO and a declaration of neutrality and nonalignment was in its best interests.[30]

Rood concluded that, although the changes that had occurred in the Mediterranean were chiefly *political*, their effects had been *strategic*. Nowhere had the Soviet Union needed to wage war to change the strategic circumstances in its favor, although wars in the area had frequently opened opportunities for new strategic gains. Every change favorable to the Soviet Union had reduced NATO's capability to defend Western Europe. But none of those changes—strategic gains for the Soviet Union—had been paid for by a price anywhere near commensurate with its value.[31]

## VIETNAM AND THE ASIA-PACIFIC REGION

Rood believed that Vietnam was a critical location for any power that sought strategic control of Southeast Asia and the Western Pacific (for more on this point, see chapter 6). The Soviet bloc's victory in Vietnam, and the USSR's steadily increasing use of Vietnamese facilities for its air and naval forces during the 1970s and 1980s, was therefore a major blow to American security interests.

The crucial geopolitical fact affecting Soviet interests in the southern part of the Asia-Pacific region was the location of the trans-Pacific maritime routes. These are the routes along which merchant ships travel that are most economical in terms of time and fuel consumption. A maritime power capable of exercising its naval and air forces in the South Pacific can interdict the lines of communication into Australasia and the Indian Ocean, and to the Persian Gulf from North America. The newly united communist Vietnam provided a continental anchor for such a maritime interdiction strategy. The Vietnamese Army, with Soviet material support, had expanded considerably in size and capability, despite the fact that the war with the United States had ended. Its army invaded Cambodia and presented a threat to pro-Western or pro-Chinese regimes throughout the region. Vietnam thus represented a major piece in the Soviet Union's efforts to encircle China and to support communist insurgencies, for example, in the Philippines.[32]

The Soviet buildup in the South Pacific was matched to the north by Moscow's access to North Korean facilities, the development of air bases on Sakhalin, the fortification of the islands directly off northern Hokkaido, and the installation of a submarine base in the central Kuriles. These activities were intended to ensure Soviet naval access to the Northern Pacific and security for its strategic ballistic missile submarine (SSBN) force.[33] In time of war, Soviet attack submarines could deploy into a region that lay along the lines of communication between North America and Japan, the Philippines, and South Korea. The Soviets viewed the Pacific basin as a strategic whole, since Peru, El Salvador, Nicaragua, and Mexico are states on the eastern rim of the ocean. Rood believed that the Soviets were developing a maritime flank of strategic interdiction, extending from El Salvador and Nicaragua along the line of the equator to the Philippines, resting in the middle on the island nations of the South Pacific. In sum:

> If the Soviet Union exploits its wardship over Vietnam to base Soviet fleet units on the Vietnamese coast, at Cam Ranh Bay, Japanese maritime routes to the Middle East and Indonesian oil would be vulnerable to interruption. U.S. forces deployed on the West Coast and in Hawaii would have their work cut out for them in the Western Pacific were there to be a war in Europe. That is, of course, if the Soviet Union is not tempted to restore Alaska in order to prevent North Slope Oil from reaching the bunkers of American ships; or, if the Soviets do not seize islands in the Aleutians, as the Japanese did in World War II, in order to mount a naval threat to the North Pacific maritime communications. Then there is the security of the Pacific Coast of North America to be

considered, where numerous lucrative targets exist for Soviet submarine attacks.[34]

The decade of the 1970s marked the buildup of Soviet naval forces and
associated supporting air elements, to the point where they transcended
their traditional role of coastal and perimeter defense, and became a global ocean-going navy. This was especially notable in the Indian Ocean
and throughout the Pacific.[35] In Rood's opinion, the Chinese saw the
meaning of all this clear-sightedly. He frequently cited a January 19, 1978,
editorial from the *Beijing Review*:

> The Soviet strategy in Asia is to lay down a strategic cordon, stretching
> from the Mediterranean and Red Sea, the Indian Ocean, and up to
> [Vladivostok], and, using Vietnam as the "Cuba of Asia," as its hatchet
> man, seize the whole of Indo-China to dominate Southeast Asia and
> South Asia. . . . The Soviet Union started a large flanking movement to
> encircle Western Europe with the main object of seizing sources of
> strategic materials . . . [and to control] the major sea routes linking
> Western Europe and the United States and linking those two with Afri-
> ca and Asia.[36]

Soviet strategy, as always, contained a political dimension designed to
facilitate the development of this strategic cordon. In this case, it did so
by weakening U.S. ties with current or prospective allies in the Pacific.
Rood identified Moscow's efforts (1) to promote the "nonalignment" of
the newly independent nations of the South Pacific and to create a belt of
nonaligned nations from South America across the Pacific to the Indian
Ocean; (2) to foster Soviet influence in the region through commercial ties
and military assistance, and to exploit internal political factors, leading to
the formation of governments that would be pro-Soviet; (3) to dissolve
U.S. military ties with Australia and New Zealand by fostering the development of a "nuclear free zone" in the region, and by encouraging Australia and New Zealand to assume responsibility for their regional defense without the United States; and (4) to carry out the Soviet policy of
creating a "New International Economic Order" intended to isolate the
Western industrial powers from the source of supply of their raw materials and their markets abroad.[37]

## NUCLEAR SUPERIORITY AND ARMS CONTROL

As noted above, Rood argued that "nuclear weapons have not made war
impossible, they have only changed the conditions under which wars
will be fought. They have in no manner reduced the importance of strategy nor the inherent advantage of military superiority over military weakness."[38] He concluded that nuclear superiority, as a top-cover for overall
military superiority, was a feasible proposition for a determined power if
opposing states did not take adequate countermeasures. The United

States had possessed such superiority through at least the early 1960s, the time of the Cuban missile crisis. Soon after, the Kennedy-Johnson administration and its successors decided instead to abandon superiority as the criterion for U.S. nuclear forces.

> It was assumed that the Soviet Union was as interested in something called "strategic stability" as the United States. Presumably "strategic stability" was a state of being in which neither country would be able to take advantage of the other through the use of strategic nuclear weapons. The difficulty is that one had strategic stability, in a manner of speaking, at the close of World War II, after both Germany and Japan had been rendered incapable of waging war. The US was the only possessor of nuclear weapons. A monopoly of military power presents a high degree of strategic stability. The kind of strategic stability envisioned by the United States . . . however was based on some notion of parity in strategic nuclear forces. It was based also on the assumption that conflict between the US and the Soviet Union was chiefly political and not military. It was also tied up with the belief on the part of the American government that both the Soviet Union and the United States had a common interest in preserving a peaceful and stable world order.[39]

Rood did not write in detail about the strategic nuclear balance or how the Soviets might employ nuclear weapons. He relied upon and cited the research of several of his former students with particular expertise in this field.[40] He was also impressed by the work of Harvard historian and later Reagan administration official Richard Pipes; particularly "Why the Soviet Union Thinks It Could Fight and Win a Nuclear War" (*Commentary*, July 1977). One critical piece of evidence for Rood was the Soviet air, missile, and civil defense program. He noted the commonly made argument that the Soviet offensive nuclear buildup was based on a particularly robust notion of assured destruction, and mistaken fears of a U.S. first strike. The extensive Soviet strategic defenses, however, suggested something else to Rood. He was well aware that critics of Pipes's analysis—and the analysis of similar-minded students of Soviet defense policy, such as William T. Lee—argued that Soviet civil defense efforts were the modern equivalent of the Potemkin village, not to be taken seriously. In response, Rood would point to his dictum that no large expenditure of resources was ever undertaken without strategic purpose. The Soviets, without question, devoted significant resources to all kinds of strategic defense, including civil defense. If it was a Potemkin village, it was a very large and expensive one. One could draw one's own conclusion from that fact.[41]

Rood was intrigued by the Soviet approach to arms control as a supportive element in Soviet preparations for war. He had studied the failure of the arms control process in the interwar years to restrain Japanese naval power in the Pacific, beginning with the Washington Naval Disarmament Conference in 1921–1922. He regarded the SALT process as an exercise in American self-deception, a misguided effort to dissuade the Soviets from assuming the position of nuclear superiority that had been vacated by the United States over the previous decade. The Soviets cheerfully abetted this deception, when in fact they were determined to equip themselves with as great a variety and number of nuclear weapons as the traffic would bear. They would agree to whatever limitations in arms that the United States would impose on itself. "SALT I with its codicils, memoranda of understanding, interim agreements, definitions agreed upon and not agreed upon, did not halt the 'Arms Race,'" Rood argued. "It merely confirmed the withdrawal of one of the participants—the United States. . . . There was nothing in Soviet military policy that would stand as evidence of Soviet strategic restraint."[42]

For example, Rood pointed out, the Soviet Union deployed three new types of multiple-warhead ICBMs in 1975, including the SS-18, with a speed unanticipated by the United States. In that year, the Soviets spent three times more on ICBMs than it had in 1972, when the SALT I agreements were signed. The Soviets also deployed their new SS-N-8 submarine-launched ballistic missiles, whose range was such as to permit Soviet submarines to fire missiles against the United States without leaving Soviet ports. This meant that the Soviets, if they were planning an attack, would not have to surge their SSBNs out of port, beyond the number engaged in routine patrols—thus depriving the West of a key strategic indicator of possible war.[43]

Rood maintained that the Soviets cheated rather openly on SALT I, and took every opportunity to exploit loopholes in the agreement to their own advantage. For instance, in 1975, U.S. satellites, including those monitoring SALT and providing early warning of Soviet missile launches, were reportedly being blinded over the Soviet Union—because (it was blandly asserted) of large natural gas fires caused by numerous breaks in Soviet natural gas pipelines. "How burning gas from broken pipelines could blind a satellite capable of absorbing the light energy from the ignition of an ICBM rocket motor, without harm, is indeed interesting," Rood observed.[44]

He was similarly skeptical of Soviet efforts to exclude the Backfire bomber from the SALT II agreement, on the grounds that it was a theater-range aircraft capable only of one-way missions against the United States. Even assuming this to be true, Rood wrote, "the evident capability . . . can hardly be discounted as inconsiderable in the event of war. There is little reason to suppose that such one-way missions would not be flown if they could gain some military advantage during war-time. The aircraft could fly in, deliver its bombs or cruise missile against the United States and then fly on to Cuba, or some other 'neutral' country, where plane and crew might be used again for missions against the United States."[45]

As Rood saw matters, the Soviet negotiators in SALT seemed interested in who was going to be able to win a war, as though war were perfectly natural and to be expected. That attitude seemed to indicate that even in the course of disarmament talks, the Soviet Union was attempting to win some advantage that would contribute toward achieving eventual victory in war.

## DID THE SOVIETS WANT WAR OR THE FRUITS OF WAR?

To sum up Rood's view: when the strategic balance (what the Soviets called the correlation of forces) was calculated, each small increment of advantage accruing to the Soviet side would, if not somehow compensated for by the West, add to the assurance of defeat for the Western democracies. The changes that had occurred during the 1960s and 1970s were chiefly *political*, although their effects had been *strategic*. Nowhere did the Soviet Union have to wage war in order to change the strategic circumstances in its favor, although wars in regions such as the Middle East frequently opened opportunities for new strategic gains.[46] Every change favorable to the Soviet Union had reduced NATO's capability to defend Western Europe. But none of these changes were paid for by Moscow with a price anywhere near commensurate with the value to be gained.

> Every strategic, technical or tactical advantage gained by the Soviet Union, if not nullified or compensated for by the West, reduces the freedom of action of the West to wage effective war, while increasing the Soviet capability to do so. The more the balance tilts towards the Soviet Union, the less likely it is that the West can take advantage of whatever weaknesses or vulnerabilities the Russians may have. When the sum of assets on one side outweigh that on the other, the defects and mistakes of the weaker side are compounded while those on the stronger side lose strategic significance.[47]

Rood said he did not suppose that the Soviets were ten feet tall or that Warsaw Pact forces would make no errors in judgment or tactics. But he believed it was sheer illusion to suppose that NATO forces, as they existed in the late 1970s and early 1980s, would have been able to exploit Soviet errors to obtain a decisive tactical or strategic advantage. The ability to exploit an enemy's errors requires freedom of action and the material resources to do so.

> Given what appear to be grossly unfavorable ratios of forces between NATO and its adversary on the Central Front [as of 1980], the most optimistic assessment of NATO's chances would seem to fall within the following characterization: if the forces of the Warsaw Pact make all possible mistakes they could sensibly be expected to make; if the forces of NATO responded perfectly to the situation presented by the attack and do not make any mistakes, then, NATO will have its work cut out

for itself just to hold the Warsaw Pact forces somewhere before they
reach the Rhine.[48]

When Soviet military craftsmen detected a weakness or vulnerability
in their forces, Rood observed, they seemed to take every possible opportunity to correct it. If correction was not possible, then the vulnerability
or weakness was compensated for elsewhere, in such a fashion as to
render it unimportant. If a significant objective needed to be gained, the
Soviet Union was rarely satisfied to set in hand only one measure for its
accomplishment, when three or four different measures would render its
accomplishment more certain.[49]

How was this all to end? What was the culminating point of Soviet
strategy? In Rood's analysis, everything seemed to point toward Soviet
preparations for war. But were Soviet leaders actually determined upon
war, especially a world war with the United States and its allies, no
matter what? Or did they believe that they could achieve their objectives
short of war through, for example, the "Finlandization" of Europe?

In *Kingdoms of the Blind*, Rood wrote that "presumably the hawks or
hardliners in the Soviet regime are those who would go all out and smash
the West at whatever cost. The moderates are those who would wait until
the West is powerless and then do it."[50] By rendering the West powerless, however, was it possible that the Soviets would then be satisfied
with peaceful accession to their writ? Churchill, after all, had said in the
Iron Curtain speech that what the Soviets desired was not war, but the
fruits of war. (He added that they respected nothing so much as military
power.)

Rood himself, as we have seen, liked to cite Sun Tzu: "attack by stratagems . . . supreme excellence [in war] consists in breaking the enemy's
resistance without fighting."[51] Rood wrote, in his own name: "If the enemy faces the realization that resorting to war will lead to his certain
defeat, he may eschew war in order to avoid the possibility of having to
live with the fruits of his defeat."[52] In chess above the beginners' level, it
is typically unnecessary for players to capture the opponent's king, once
they have achieved a decisively superior position. The other player rec-
ognizes the hopelessness of his or her position and resigns, making it
unnecessary to play the game out to its completion.

Rood, on balance, seems to have doubted that the Soviets aimed merely at the peaceful surrender of the West. Given their ruthlessness and the
scope of their ambition, things would come to the point where even
surrender would not be enough for the Kremlin. Patience had its point of
diminishing returns. In his view, the Soviets gave every indication that
they intended to fight a real war, if for no other reason than to impress
upon the democracies and their allies, especially the United States, that
they had lost, just as Germany had done with France in 1940. On the
other hand, as noted above, Rood sketched out ways in which the nations

of NATO's southern flank (Greece, Turkey, and Italy) could be pried away from the West and into the Soviet orbit by means short of war. His analysis allowed that much the same might be done for nations of the Pacific basin.

Rood certainly believed that the Soviets were developing the *capacity* to go to war successfully, and that their military forces and plans were the absolute foundation of their political strategy. Even if the Soviets preferred a peaceful outcome—that is, a peaceful transition to a global socialist commonwealth—the Soviets had to convince the West that they were prepared to resort to force, and that they could make that force stick. They certainly would play upon Western fears about the destructiveness of war. The Soviets also had to take into account the possibility that, if a communist or Findlandized Eurasia came over to the Soviet bloc through intimidation rather than military occupation, the United States would resort to nuclear weapons to destroy the USSR's newly acquired industrial-economic base outside the Soviet Union proper. Although it is hard to imagine the United States using nuclear weapons in this fashion, the Soviets at a minimum would have wanted the capacity to preempt such a development.[53]

What impressed Rood was the Soviet attention to detail when it came to grand strategy, and military planning and preparations. If the Kremlin's aim was merely to intimidate the West into submission, it would have been relatively straightforward just to keep building ever-bigger armies, navies, and air and missile forces, thus playing on the democracies' general fear of war. But the Soviets always sweated the small stuff, such as gathering in-place intelligence about the roads of Europe and the coastal waterways of Scandinavia. Few in the West noticed such matters and so the Soviets seemingly gained no political advantage from the resources devoted to these activities—unless there was going to be a war, when such things would matter, a great deal.

Rood's students would sometimes ask whether the United States was innocent in all this. After all, it deployed thousands of strategic and tactical nuclear weapons, controlled the air and sea lines of communications to Eurasia, and maintained hundreds of thousands of troops overseas. American officials spoke of the eventual triumph of democracy. Would it not be reasonable for Soviet leaders to conclude that the Western alliance had cleverly encircled the Soviet bloc and that it was the United States that was preparing for war? If so, could not the Kremlin's political and military activities be understood merely as a defensive reaction to perceived American provocations, and not the indication of an aggressive strategy or intention to attack? What we were arguably witnessing was a classic case of the security dilemma, in which efforts by one side to increase its security threatened the other side, which then led to a response that decreased the security of both, even though neither intended to attack in the first place. Soviet efforts to increase their perceived security by no means indicated that the Soviets intended war. Brezhnev, so the argument went, was certainly no Hitler.

Rood would respond, of course the Soviets think we are preparing for war, or think that we should be preparing for war if we are at all rational. It would hardly be a shock to a communist—or to any hardened practitioner of politics—that one has enemies and that they might attempt to use force as a means to advance their interests. Soviet leaders were hardly surprised that the United States had engaged in limited wars, such as Korea and Vietnam, to preserve its Eurasian strategic perimeter and contest Soviet expansion. As both communists and hardened practitioners of politics, however, the Soviets had made a careful examination of the West's intentions and capabilities. First, at a time when the United States was in the best position to wage offensive war against the Soviet Union—while it possessed a nuclear monopoly and then nuclear superiority—it had not done so, for whatever reason. Perhaps American leaders had been intimidated by Soviet blustering and bluff, designed to frighten them with the specter of nuclear destruction. Whatever the reason, after having lost its nuclear superiority—partly as a matter of American policy, partly as a result of Soviet counteractions—why would the United States now resort to major war by attacking the USSR?

Second, Rood argued, the Soviets could easily evaluate the military situation in Europe, which would be the prize and likely the most important theater in any major conflict. It was clear to see that the balance of forces, certainly conventional forces, favored the Soviet Union; and that this balance (as of the early 1980s) continued to be shifting in favor of the Eastern bloc. It seemed only a matter of how many days NATO could hold out against a Soviet assault, not whether NATO was capable of conquering territory in Eastern Europe, much less of invading Soviet territory. NATO's nuclear weapons did not fundamentally change this military equation.[54]

Rood thought that if the West acted upon the belief that the Soviets were not really serious about going to war, that they were only interested in security, the West would fall victim to the self-deception that characterized the democratic strategy deficit. The comfortable assumption that there would be no war, paradoxically, made war more likely. The same was true of the misguided notion that war, if it occurred, would be the result of nations blundering into an unwanted conflict during a crisis because they misunderstood each other's intentions and actions—the (distorted) World War I model. Either of these typical Western interpretations of the risks of war played perfectly into Soviet hands, especially if the USSR intended to attack. The West's psychological condition was such that it increased the likelihood of strategic surprise—and thus the likelihood that the Soviets would find it feasible to attack.

Rood posited two possible Soviet paths to strategic victory.[55] The first was a multi-theater military campaign designed to conquer Eurasia, and to isolate the United States in the Western Hemisphere. This would involve the defeat of U.S. forces abroad, but not necessarily their destruction, the destruction of their dependents, or of those who had allied themselves with the United States. The Soviet Union would hold a considerable number of hostages, as well as control the dominating resource base of what the British geographer Halford J. Mackinder called the World Island. This path made sense for a great power with a continental outlook. In this case, Soviet operations in the Gulf of Mexico, the Caribbean, and Central America would constitute the erection of a secondary theater of operations to pin U.S. forces down, while the Soviet Union and its allies sought decisive operations elsewhere.

What sort of political demands would the Soviets try to exact in this circumstance? Certainly they would want guarantees that the United States would not challenge the new socialist world order (for instance, through limitations on the size and deployment of the remaining U.S. armed forces). Perhaps the settlement would involve changes in the U.S. political order, such as the exclusion of "anti-Soviet" elements from government. Rood believed there would be no shortage of American friends of peace to step forward to be certain that legitimate Soviet demands were met. Rood would point to the example of "unoccupied" France in World War II, and of the French Empire overseas, where German writ effectively ran even though no German troops were present. Meanwhile, democratic government would be extinguished throughout the rest of the world.[56]

The second Soviet option was to aim at the defeat of the United States *directly*, not only through nuclear strikes against the American homeland, but with military operations from adjacent waters and lands in the Western Hemisphere. Once that had been accomplished, the non-communist nations of Eurasia would fall into Soviet hands like ripe fruit. "If Soviet strategists have done their homework, they understand that if the United States is rendered powerless, all else will fall by the wayside," Rood wrote. "That is because the United States is the center of power of the Western Alliance."[57]

If the Soviets had decided to "go for the jugular" rather than to engage in a Eurasia-first approach, then their global strategic dispositions after the Cuban missile crisis made sense. These dispositions gave the Soviets the option of waging war on four fronts against the continental United States: the Atlantic, the Pacific, the Gulf, and the Caribbean, as well as that to be mounted against the American homeland by Soviet nuclear forces. It was inconceivable to Rood that the Soviets would not have had active agents in place to support their campaign. Perhaps Soviet tanks would not have rolled down the Los Angeles freeways but Rood assumed that the Soviets would have sought to fracture the nation by combining military and psychological actions. They would have used in-place operatives or agents of influence and special operations forces to break the nation apart, perhaps into distinct regional confederacies, or to agitate it into a state of more or less permanent revolution.[58]

For Rood, the beauty of Soviet strategic preparations was that they provided Moscow with choices, as well as the initiative—and that made the defense of the West that much more difficult.

The most common argument against Rood's position at the time was that the Soviets would be deterred from such actions—they would never dare go to war, because of the devastation that would be caused by American nuclear retaliation. Rood would rejoin that deterrence had depended upon the ability and willingness of the United States to retaliate in a strategically meaningful fashion, and to convince the Soviets of this point. The military balance, broadly considered, was tipping rapidly against the United States in the late 1970s and early 1980s, and the psychology of appeasement appeared to be growing correspondingly. America had not toughed it out in Vietnam—why should it be any different in Western Europe, when the costs would be so much higher? Was the United States really prepared to sacrifice New York for Bonn or Paris?—the contemporary equivalent problem of "why die for Danzig?" in 1939. Were the European and Asian allies prepared to follow the United States off the nuclear cliff when Washington could offer no confident assurance of victory? When the balloon went up (as Rood put it), would not sensible voices counsel nuclear restraint, even if the Soviets went first?[59]

In addition, Rood asked, would not the Soviets have planned carefully to maximize their chances to negate American nuclear forces through various means, besides the canonical first strike? For instance, Rood said, each time a new American strategic nuclear submarine went under construction, the Soviets undoubtedly opened a book on it. The book grew as the submarine was completed, commissioned, underwent trials, and deployed. The U.S. Navy said it was confident that its strategic nuclear submarine force was secure and undetectable. The truth of the matter, Rood would point out, was that the navy was confident that it had never detected that the Soviets had detected our SSBNs, which was not quite saying the same thing. But even if the navy's judgment was accurate, we could not be completely sure that other unconventional means had not been put into place by the Soviets to deal with the problem. The book, after all, had been growing for twenty-some years, and there was no reason to believe it would not continue to grow.[60]

When it came to the ultimate war warning, Rood wrote this in 1980: "The two principal dictatorships in the world, the Soviet and the People's Republic of China, are totalitarian in the extreme. For the moment they remain sworn enemies of one another as well as of liberal democracy. Their conjunction in the fashion of the Hitler-Stalin Pact would—as in 1939—shift the balance of power almost irretrievably against the democ-

racies and make war a virtual certainty rather than merely a strong probability."[61]

## THE END OF THE SOVIET UNION AND THE
## CONTINUITY OF THE RUSSIAN PROBLEM

Of course, things have changed since Rood wrote those words, often in
unexpected and dramatic ways. In chapter 7, we explore the possible
reasons that war with the Soviet Union did not come, and consider if
Rood was mistaken in his analysis. For the moment, we might ask whether the withdrawal of Soviet forces from Eastern Europe in 1989–1990, and
the dissolution of the Soviet Union itself in 1991, constituted a major
change in the Russian/Soviet Problem as defined by Rood. The original
problem, simply formulated, was characterized by the persistent Russian
imperial drive to obtain access to open waters and to control exclusively
the approaches to those waters. If successfully accomplished, this strategy would have left Russia the dominant Eurasian power, given Russia's
long-standing ability to control or influence events in Eastern and Central
Europe and Central Asia.

There were several possible answers to the question of whether the
Russian Problem had changed fundamentally. The first was that the Russian Problem would be resolved in the context of a Europe whole and
free, in much the same as the German Problem was resolved (at least in a
military sense) by integrating West Germany, and later a united Germany, into a larger Euro-Atlantic community, consisting of NATO and what
became the European Union. The second possibility was that Russia
would become the equivalent of China from the mid-nineteenth to the
mid-twentieth century; that is, a one-time empire that was no longer a
going concern. The Russian Problem would then have become one of
dealing with lands that had no central authority, but in which nuclear
weapons, and nuclear materials, went unsecured. It would also become
one in which warlords and criminals would struggle for regional power.
Foreign nations would try to establish spheres of influence to contain the
situation, and to obtain access to Russia's material riches. A third possibility was that Russia would become a more-or-less normal nation, reduced in power and aware of its limits, but still a major player on the
international scene. Moscow would resist what it regarded as the imposition of an American-led world order in the name of the balance of power,
and would defend its own prestige and interests, but it would not become a fully revisionist state.

The fourth alternative would be something like the recovery that Germany experienced between 1919 and 1939, in which the Russian government, whether democratic or autocratic, would refuse to abandon its
maximum historic ambitions. The Kremlin would seek to cover its politi-

cal and military preparations to restore the Russian Empire, and to revive its larger imperial ambitions, through diplomacy and subterfuge. This project would go well beyond merely reincorporating Russian peoples left outside the Federation by the breakup of the USSR, although the claim of ethnic solidarity might be the leading edge of the enterprise.

Rood, as we shall see, did not believe that the Russian Problem had changed fundamentally by what was termed "the end of the Cold War." He went even further, arguing that the dissolution of the Soviet Union, and the apparent retreat of Russian power, in certain respects actually served to weaken the long-term ability of the United States to deal with the new Russia. Whether an accident of history or the result of deliberate policy, this was one of those anomalies that Rood liked to point out. In particular, he wondered if objective conditions now rendered an alliance between Moscow and Beijing, based on their common anti-Western perspective, much more viable than it had been in 1980.

## NOTES

1. The scholarly debate over the origins and course of modern Russian/Soviet politics, and of the Cold War, is immense. Rood's own views were perhaps closest to those set out in Richard Pipes's trilogy, *Russia under the Old Regime* (New York: Scribner, 1974), *The Russian Revolution* (New York: Knopf, 1990), and *Russia under the Bolshevik Regime* (New York: Knopf, 1994). For authorities who offer a range of perspectives, see, for example, Adam Ulam's *Expansion and Coexistence: Soviet Foreign Policy, 1917–1973*, 2nd ed. (New York: Praeger, 1974); Raymond Garthoff, *Detente and Confrontation: American-Soviet Relations from Nixon to Reagan*, rev. ed. (Washington, D.C.: Brookings Institution, 1994), and Garthoff, *The Great Transition: American-Soviet Relations and the End of the Cold War* (Washington, D.C.: Brookings Institution, 1994); John Lewis Gaddis, *The Cold War: A New History* (New York: Penguin, 2005); and Melvyn Leffler, *For the Soul of Mankind: The United States, the Soviet Union, and the Cold War* (New York: Hill and Wang, 2007).

2. Harold W. Rood, "The Eastern Question: 'Peace in Our Times'" (unpublished manuscript, 1989), Print, 31–35.

3. Harold W. Rood, "Early Warning, Part IV," *Grand Strategy: Countercurrents*, June 15, 1983, 5.

4. Harold W. Rood, *Kingdoms of the Blind: How the Great Democracies Have Resumed the Follies that So Nearly Cost Them Their Life* (Durham: Carolina Academic Press, 1980), 234. Rood compared the Soviet *nomenklatura* with that of Nazi Germany, which was "run by a collection of assorted ruffians, street hoodlums, pretentious intellectuals, and compliant bureaucrats who disappeared from the scene almost as quickly as they had come upon it, once the *Wehrmacht* was destroyed." Rood, "Early Warning, Part IV," 5.

5. Ibid., 6.

6. Quoted in ibid.

7. Rood discussion with the authors.

8. Rood, "Early Warning, Part IV," 8.

9. The following analysis of Soviet strategy in the Pacific and Central Asia is taken from ibid., 8–10, and Harold W. Rood, "The Increasing Soviet Presence in the Pacific" (Claremont Institute, 1988).

10. Quote in Rood, "Early Warning, Part IV," 9.

11. The Central European case study is taken from ibid., 10–11.

12. These characteristics of Soviet grand strategy are taken from ibid., 6–11; Harold W. Rood, "Soviet Strategy and the Defense of the West," *Global Affairs* 2 (Summer 1987): 10–11; and Rood discussion with the authors.

13. In addition to these, Rood noted the growing Warsaw Pact superiority in manpower, tactical aircraft, tanks, and artillery opposite NATO's central front, which went beyond the addition of Soviet forces in Czechoslovakia; Warsaw Pact civil defense preparations, along with the training and equipment of Warsaw Pact forces to employ and withstand nuclear, chemical, and biological attack; and the increase in Soviet capabilities to move troops by air and to support Soviet and Cuban forces at long distances. "And there are a hundred more that through ignorance or neglect are neither compensated for nor even considered." Rood, *Kingdoms of the Blind*, 147.

14. As Rood saw matters, Soviet and Cuban forces on the island resembled the *Afrika Korps* under Rommel in the Western desert. If the Allies did not defend Egypt and the Suez Canal from German attack, those places would ultimately fall to the Axis. This would bring about the loss of the Middle East and inflict upon the Allies an enormous handicap that might well have led to the defeat of an important ally, the Soviet Union. Yet when the British and the Americans defeated the *Afrika Korps*, as they did in 1942–1943, that victory did not automatically lead to the defeat of Germany. In the same way, during a war for NATO Europe, the United States could not ignore Cuba as a Soviet base. Rood discussion with the authors.

15. Rood discussed the Cuban situation in great detail in *Kingdoms of the Blind*, 111–34; and Harold W. Rood, "Cuba: Payment Deferred," *National Review*, November 27, 1981, 1401–17. This case study is taken from those sources.

16. The information about Cuba's relations with the Soviet Union and its client states is taken from Harold W. Rood, "Grenada: The Strategic Dimension," *Claremont Review of Books* 2, no. 4 (Winter 1983), accessed July 18, 2014, http://claremontinstitute. org/index.php?act=crbArticle&id=1452#.U8bdQLEUp2A. The conclusion about Cuba's role in a greater socialist commonwealth is from Rood, *Kingdoms of the Blind*, 137.

17. To which it might be objected that Castro did not seek accommodation with the United States when the Cold War ended. Rood undoubtedly would have rejoined that the Soviet Union was never actually *defeated* in Europe, but only pulled back of its own volition—and that post-Soviet Russia's political ties with Castro, after a period of apparent public estrangement, never really wavered.

18. The following analysis is taken from Rood, "Grenada: The Strategic Dimension."

19. This account of Czechoslovakia and Soviet strategy is drawn from Rood, *Kingdoms of the Blind*, 83–95.

20. In *Kingdoms of the Blind*, Rood did not develop the thesis that the Soviets had been behind the Czech "reform" movement all along, in order to provide the USSR with a convenient political pretext to strengthen its military position in Central Europe. He did make this argument in his classroom lectures and public talks.

21. This case study of NATO's southern flank is taken from Rood, *Kingdoms of the Blind*, 149–200.

22. Rood also pointed out that a Warsaw Pact attack through Austria toward Munich and NATO's rear area meant that NATO forces would have been required to defend an additional two hundred miles of frontier while they were engaged against Warsaw Pact forces coming from East Germany and Czechoslovakia. Meanwhile, on the southern flank, U.S. carriers could no longer be expected to provide support and disrupt Soviet advances toward Munich through Austria. This was because Soviet naval forces were by the late 1970s operating in the Adriatic, and Soviet air forces could be expected to operate from Yugoslav airfields. Ibid., 211, 225.

23. Ibid., 156–57.

24. Quoted in ibid., 163.

25. The Ustashi was a fascist and terrorist organization devoted to the creation of a Greater Croatia, and hence the breakup of Yugoslavia, before and during World War

II. During the war it was patronized by Nazi Germany and Italy, in opposition to Tito's communist movement. Rood concluded that the Ustashi's postwar incarnation, or at least some groups operating under that name, were under Soviet control. Ibid., 167; and Rood discussion with the authors.

26. Rood concluded that Malta—the "unsinkable aircraft carrier" in the Mediterranean during World War II, unmistakably showed signs that it had become a virtual dependent of Libya by 1980. "If Libya and Yugoslavia find it useful or necessary to serve Soviet strategic purposes in the Mediterranean, the Middle East and Africa, it seems unlikely that tiny Malta will be permitted to find otherwise." Ibid., 186–89.

27. Rood wrote in ibid., 110n37, that he had suggested to a civilian official in the Pentagon at the time of the coup, that U.S. withdrawal from the bases in Libya would alter the strategic circumstances of the United States in the eastern Mediterranean. "The reply was that Wheelus had only been used by the Air Force to base fighter bombers for bombing practice in the desert and that could be carried out as easily at airfields in Spain." In Rood's mind, this argument neglected to account for the use to which the Soviets could now avail themselves, as well as to the lost opportunities for the United States to use Libyan facilities for something other than bombing practice, if indeed that had been the primary use of the facilities.

28. Ibid., 181.

29. Ibid., 199–200.

30. Ibid., 192–94.

31. Ibid., 195.

32. Rood, "The Increasing Soviet Presence in the Pacific," 11.

33. Ibid., 9–10.

34. Rood, *Kingdoms of the Blind*, 144.

35. Rood, "The Increasing Soviet Presence in the Pacific," 3, 6–8.

36. Ibid., 7.

37. Ibid., 13.

38. Rood, *Kingdoms of the Blind*, xiv.

39. Ibid., 255.

40. William Van Cleave, Ronald F. Lehman II, and Steven Maaranen, among others.

41. Rood discussion with the authors.

42. Rood, *Kingdoms of the Blind*, 256.

43. Ibid., 261.

44. Ibid., 258.

45. Ibid., 264.

46. Rood apparently did not characterize the Soviet military invasion of Afghanistan in 1979 as "waging war," in this sense. He probably concluded that they already "owned it," like Czechoslovakia in 1968.

47. Rood, *Kingdoms of the Blind*, 272.

48. Ibid., 209.

49. Ibid., 226.

50. Ibid., 268.

51. Quoted in ibid., 83.

52. Harold W. Rood, "Why Fight in Vietnam," *Infantry Magazine*, November–December 1967, 11.

53. Rood discussion with the authors.

54. Rood discussion with the authors.

55. These two Soviet strategic options were outlined in Rood, "Soviet Strategy and the Defense of the West," 16. Rood discussion with the authors.

56. Rood discussion with the authors.

57. Rood, "Soviet Strategy and the Defense of the West," 16.

58. Rood discussion with the authors.

59. Rood discussion with the authors.

60. Rood discussion with the authors.

61. Rood, *Kingdoms of the Blind*, 4. "Can one expect China to tie its fortunes to the side which it believes will be defeated in a war?" Rood asked. "Will China not instead, prefer another version of the Hitler-Stalin Pact with which to buy time to get ready?" Ibid., 284–85.

# SIX

# America and the Distant Ramparts

*Understanding the particular strategic conditions of the United States was, for Professor Rood, the essential prerequisite to dealing successfully with America's foreign policy challenges. Absent this understanding, no amount of study of any real or potential enemy of the United States was likely to lead to successful strategy. This chapter describes his views on America's strategic conditions, and relates his powerful examples of what those conditions mean and why they matter.*

*In one sense, the debate over American foreign policy has always been about differing views of our specific strategic situation. Can our survival be sustained solely through hemispheric defense? Can we thrive under such circumstances? Is an America active in the world a matter of choice, or a necessity to which we must attend? Our political leadership, scholars, and statesmen have differed widely on these questions.[1]*

*Rood 's analysis here is useful again because it is rooted in thinking about the "small c" constitutional character of the United States, its geographical resources and position relative to other powers, and how it is viewed by others who have sought (and might seek) to reorganize the world. Rood looked out through the eyes of would-be adversaries and perceived the "America Problem" that they must solve. Rood focused on those elements of America's condition that change little and change slowly. Understanding America's particular circumstances helps the student and statesman avoid the pitfalls and weaknesses that those circumstances suggest, and exploit the opportunities they present.*

The Soviet Union's main protagonist in the Cold War emerged from a very different geopolitical setting and historical experience. Rood thought that the United States was part of the mainstream of constitutional development in the West, in which peace, justice, and defense were the objects of a free society. He quoted from the first draft of President Washington's farewell address:

> That we may be always prepared for War, but never unsheathe the sword except in self defense so long as Justice and our *essential* rights, and national respectability can be preserved without it. . . . That our Union may be as lasting as time.—For while we are encircled in one hand we shall possess the strength of a Giant and there will be none who can make us afraid—Divide and we shall become weak: a prey to foreign Intrigues and internal discords:—and we shall be as miserable and contemptible as we are now enviable and happy—[2]

The preservation of the community from internal disintegration compels certain kinds of actions, appropriate to the particular circumstances of the community and of the times. The same is true, Rood wrote, of the defense of the community from threats to it from abroad. The nature of these defensive actions is dictated partly by geography, partly by the nature of the threat, and finally by the manner in which a nation's wars must be fought.[3]

In light of the particular circumstances of the community and of the times for the United States, Rood concluded that the principal American strategic objective is, as it has always been, the prevention of direct attack upon the United States. The goal of U.S. foreign and military policy is to secure the Western Hemisphere, in order to defend the United States. The preferred military strategy of the United States is to secure the Western Hemisphere forward. In short, if there is to be a war, Americans will want to fight it abroad.

Rood set out some key assumptions, or guidelines, that formed the foundations of American strategy, broadly defined:

- It is preferable to defend the United States by fighting the initial defensive battles of any war as close to the enemy's homeland as possible, or, at least as far away from the continental United States as possible. America's wars with transoceanic powers should not be fought on America's soil.
- The initial strategic defense in any war is only the prelude, which will make possible the assumption of the strategic offensive necessary to achieve U.S. political objectives.
- It is preferable to undertake military action at a time and place where the least military power will be the most effective in maintaining the country's strategic position. A concomitant to this assumption is that U.S. influence ought to be exerted so that strategic threats to the United States may be contained or canceled without recourse to full-scale or general war. If you want to avoid fighting a big war, be prepared to fight a lot of little ones.
- To execute this strategy, the United States must have bases and allies abroad, from which to conduct military operations. Wars

with European powers almost invariably require America to have allies in Europe, if the war is to be waged successfully.[4]

Some of these guidelines simply reflect the basic commonsense strategy that would guide any great power. But Rood also derived them from his study of U.S. history, particularly from the American experience in wartime. Rood thought there were characteristics peculiar to the American regime, and to its position in the world, that recommended strongly that these general guidelines always be followed. The particular manner in which the United States has acted in the world, and the particular places in which it has been engaged, have necessarily changed, due to the circumstances prevailing at the time. But for Rood, the essentials of American strategy have remained constant.

## THE AMERICAN STRATEGIC EXPERIENCE

For Americans, the imperatives of peace, justice, and defense have been conditioned historically by the geographic position of the Union. Their homeland—North America—and South America are little more than continent-sized islands off the west coast of Europe and off the east coast of Asia. Military threats to the United States originate from the Eurasian land-mass, because that enormous area—the largest in the world—is home to all the other great world powers. For a majority of the past four centuries, one great power after another has sought to dominate its region, the oceans, or the entire Eurasian landmass, and to organize those things to its liking. Other great powers have resisted these efforts, whether to prevent that hegemony or to seek their own. The result has been a series of wars that have spilled over into the far reaches of the globe. The Western Hemisphere has been one of the regions affected by the wars of Eurasia, at first because the great European powers had colonies or commercial interests there, and more recently because of the power potential of the most important hemispheric nation, the United States.[5]

The balance of power in Eurasia has thus always been of intense interest to Americans, according to Rood. If a hostile nation or coalition of nations actually came to dominate Eurasia and was able to organize its economic and military resources, the United States would be faced with an overwhelming material threat to its existence. That worst-case scenario aside, any war among the great powers, fought to overthrow or maintain the Eurasian balance of power, affects American security. The United States has always had a rich global commerce that contending Eurasian powers have wanted to bring to their side during a war. Certainly they wanted to deny that commerce to their enemy. During the twentieth century, the United States also developed the latent and then the actual military capability to decide the outcome of wars abroad. As a result, the contending Eurasian great powers have actively sought to entice or intrigue the United States into war on their behalf, or at least to dissuade it from supporting their adversaries. When great powers feel that the United States may be inclined to go to war against them, they will take measures to deter American intervention, or else take preventive military action to see that U.S. intervention cannot be decisive. They will also try to league together with America's enemies in the hemisphere and with disaffected elements in the United States itself.

The American people must concern themselves with a Eurasian balance of power favorable to the United States, Rood argued, not merely as a matter of national defense, but of domestic justice and peace. Americans have always been a commercial people, with far-flung interests and the desire for open markets. The pursuit of private interest serves the public good; commerce not only enriches the people, it provides resources to the government. (As Rood noted, the first congressionally authorized uses of force, in the Quasi-War against France and later against the Barbary regency of Tripoli, were intended to protect U.S. commerce.) Some wars abroad have created opportunities directly to enhance American prosperity. But for the most part, by closing markets and otherwise truncating American commerce, Eurasian wars threaten the general prosperity that underpins our domestic peace. Some groups will want to take measures to defend and extend that commerce. Those who are not directly benefited by trade, or who would be placed most at risk during a war, sometimes resist those measures, as did Federalist New England during the War of 1812.

Rood contended that these potential domestic divisions, which are a threat to internal peace, are compounded further by the character of the American people and their constitutional arrangements. The U.S. Constitution established a federation that guarantees equal rights and protections to all its members, whether states or citizens. The United States cannot barter away the territory of its constituents in a peace settlement. Nor can the federal government place less emphasis on the security of some citizens in favor of others, even as a matter of strategic prudence. Hawaii and Alaska are no less important than New York or California. Many loyal Americans trace their ethnic and religious roots to other lands. Whenever foreign wars occur, this creates passion and a desire for justice for their kinsmen. Americans also have a notable passion for justice at home, to see that they receive their due, even at the expense of peace and defense. The deliberately divided nature of the American system of government, and the willingness to allow a multiplicity of factions and sects to compete in an open political system, adds to the fractious character of the regime.

Internally, Rood found much of this to be admirable, that of a worthy and highly successful experiment in self-government, one certainly worth preserving. The peculiar American character, however, when facing the rest of the world, exhibits certain weaknesses that go beyond the strategic deficit that is characteristic of all democracies. Its fractiousness leaves the country vulnerable to foreign meddling and intrigue, and, in the event that things start to go very bad in a war, to fundamental division. Americans have always managed to deal with these challenges. At their wisest, they have followed a strategic course that minimized the risks to domestic peace and maximized their freedom to pursue justice. But that course has never been easy or straightforward.

In the wars that befell the British Colonies in North America between 1689 and 1762, European powers contested control of the continent in the interest of the balance of power in Europe. These wars brought down on the Anglo-American colonists the scourge of French and Indian alliance, the depredations of the Spaniards, and, in the end, the intolerable acts (literally and figuratively) of the British government. These conflicts were settled on the basis of European, not American, interests. The colonists suffered the consequences of fighting and settling wars without their consent because they had no choice; their security depended on the protecting hand of the mother country. New Englanders fought to take the French fortress of Louisburg in 1745, only to have Britain return it to France during peace negotiations, in exchange for French concessions elsewhere. But once the most serious external threat, that of the French, was removed, without any corresponding indication that their British rulers would henceforth take the peace and justice of the colonists into account (indeed, quite the opposite), the Americans launched their revolution.

The Declaration of Independence accused the English king, both in Parliament and out, of a failure to fulfill the obligations of government with respect to English subjects residing in the North American colonies. Among the bill of particulars:

> He has abdicated Government here, by declaring us out of his Protection and waging War against us. . . .
> He has constrained our fellow Citizens taken Captive on the high Seas to bear Arms against their Country, to become the executioners of their friends and Brethren, or to fall themselves by their Hands.
> He has excited domestic insurrections amongst us, and has endeavoured to bring on the inhabitants of our frontiers, the merciless Indian Savages, whose known rule of warfare, is an undistinguished destruction of all ages, sexes and conditions.

Thus, and in other ways, did the English king and his parliament lose the political right to rule over the English colonies in North America. But the argument in the Declaration did not suffice to secure liberty for the Americans. It was necessary to wage war against the English, until the claims of Americans to be free were recognized by that government. This required the Americans to take advantage of the European balance of power, particularly the long-standing Anglo-French antagonism.

It would have been nearly impossible for the United States to have waged a successful war against Britain without an alliance with France. The French Army fought alongside the Continental Army, and the French Fleet helped to defend the coast of the United States. This occurred while the French threat against England from the continent of Europe tied down those British naval forces and British troops that otherwise could have been deployed to defeat the Americans. Afterward, although the Anglo-French antagonism caused many complications for the United States, it still could be taken advantage of in America's interest. It made the Louisiana Purchase possible. And although the United States did not ally itself with Napoleon during the War of 1812, the fact that Britain was engaged in war with France at the same time that the Americans were at war with Britain prevented the United States from losing that war—this, despite the defeats inflicted on the American Army during the British invasion.

Rood thought, however, that the United States could not expect that the European balance of power would always work in its favor, especially if the struggle over that balance played out solely in the Western Hemisphere. Even in the course of the Revolutionary War, despite the necessity that most of the fighting be done in the American theater of operations, Americans began to apply the principle that, when compelled to defend their interests, they should fight abroad and not at home. The Continental Navy and American privateers operated in the Bay of Biscay, the Irish Sea, and the English Channel. The reason for this is evident from the consequences of such operations. In 1777, Captain Lambert Wickes in the Continental ship *Reprisal*, eighteen guns, in company with *Lexington* and *Dolphin*, raided English shipping from the Bay of Biscay to the waters about the British Isles. English maritime insurance rates increased by 23 percent as a consequence. On April 22, 1778, John Paul Jones in the ship *Ranger* landed a force of marines and seamen at the English port of Whitehaven, to spike the guns of the forts and burn English vessels in the harbor.

Rood saw this as simply sound strategy. Every English ship captured by Continental naval vessels or American privateers was one less that could carry supplies to the British Army in America. Every vessel of the Royal Navy compelled to guard British shipping in European waters was one Royal Navy vessel that could not be employed to prosecute the war off the coast of the United States. Every solider who had to be detailed to guard English harbors was one fewer who could fight against Continental and French armies in North America.

The imperative to fight America's wars abroad to the extent possible had a strategic corollary—that of disengaging the European powers from the Western Hemisphere. The Monroe Doctrine became the canonical statement of this purpose. Such a strategy not only permitted American expansion, but also insulated the new republic from the wars and quarrels of Europe—quarrels that would otherwise spill over into the New World and agitate the domestic peace of the still-settling American regime.

This was not merely a theoretical concern, Rood pointed out. The original party system was founded on close and competing attachments with foreign nations—Britain and Revolutionary France—and those great powers meddled in U.S. domestic affairs and presidential elections. The War of 1812, fought to protect American commercial rights and the rights of U.S. citizens, as well as to remove the British threat from Canada, resulted in the burning of Washington, D.C., savage frontier warfare, and British attempts to set up an Indian buffer state in the Northwest. New England Federalists, who felt disenfranchised and impoverished by the pro-French policies of the Republican South and West, toyed with secession under the protection of Britain.

The American Civil War, whatever its economic and political origins, turned on the determination of Lincoln and the North to prevent the splitting of the United States into two separate nations. Such a split, had the Confederacy won, would have faced the North with endless coalitions between the Confederacy and any European powers with territorial ambitions in North America. One consequence of the Civil War was the French attempt to make an Austrian prince the ruler of Mexico. Had the South won, Rood noted, Maximilian and his French master might have succeeded in Mexico, and the possession of the American West might have become subject to European arbitration rather than American determination. After the Union won the war, this was no longer an issue. In 1898, the United States took the occasion of the latest revolt against Spanish rule in Cuba to eject the last remaining European colonial power from the hemisphere.[6]

Exclusion of the great European powers from North America permitted the growth of population and the expansion of the territory of the United States, leaving it free to industrialize and prosper without European interference. It was the good fortune of the United States not to be required to engage in wars with the European powers between the end of the War of 1812 and beginning of the Spanish-American War in 1898. The balance of power in both Europe and Asia remained in such a state that the United States had no compelling interest to wage such a war.[7] Although the European powers were engaged in a competitive scramble for colonies in Africa and Asia, they largely stayed out of the Western Hemisphere, after the French foray in Mexico failed. This was partly the result of not wanting to provoke the United States, but also because of the development of a tacit U.S. strategic rapprochement with Great Britain. Rood emphasized the fact that the British North America Act of 1867, which granted federal dominion status to Canada, and other actions (e.g., the settlement of the *Alabama* claims), marked the final acceptance by London of the viability of the United States. The Royal Navy excluded

European adventurers from South America and permitted the long-existing U.S. commercial interests in the Far East to flourish.

The progressive development of an Anglo-American rapprochement in part reflected the fact that new threats to the Eurasian balance of power were beginning to emerge, and with them new risks to American commerce abroad, and to security in the Western Hemisphere. While it was England and France that compelled American attention in the eighteenth and nineteenth centuries, it was Germany, after its unification in 1870 and its consequent rapid industrialization, that began to develop the capability to impinge on American interests. Similarly, the industrialization of Japan following the overthrow of the Tokagawa Shogunate lent Japan the ability to impinge upon American interests in the Pacific. To counteract these changes and the emerging challenge to the balance of power in continental Europe, Britain shifted its naval assets from the Asian theater to focus on the North Sea and the Mediterranean. As a result, the United States now had primary responsibility for the defensive approaches to the Western Hemisphere, and it became even more involved in Asia and the Pacific due to its acquisition of Hawaii, Alaska, and the Philippines, and the threat to those interests by the ambitions of Japan.[8]

The twentieth century was marked by a return of the cycle of European wars and crises. This cycle of conflict was played out on a global stage given advancements in technology, the interconnectivity of the European colonial empires, and the rise of Japan. The outbreak of the Great War in Europe was an occasion that, for the first time in generations, presented the United States with the prospect of a shift in the balance of power in Europe. While American concern for the impact of such a shift was hardly apparent at the time, there was a concern once removed: that the United States might, against its will, become involved in the Great War. Yet, Rood observed, it was in the nature of such things that the United States would become involved in a European war, just as Americans had been, against their will, involved in all the great European wars through 1815. North America, before American independence, had been the arena within which the European powers endeavored to influence the balance of power in Europe. Now, the increasingly powerful United States, however reluctantly, served as the makeweight to restore the balance in Europe, whenever the balance was threatened by those who were determined to overset it. The imperatives of strategy would eventually overcome the American notion of political and military isolation from Europe.

Such was the case with Germany and the Great War (World War I). Germany's war aims in 1914 clearly included domination of the European continent, which meant controlling the maritime approaches to Europe and dictating the terms of peacetime commerce with powers like the United States. The United States attempted to remain neutral, as it had tried to do in the great European wars from 1792 to 1815—but, as in the earlier cases, to no avail. American neutrality policy led to complaints against restrictive British naval practices, as well against as those of Germany, but the latter soon became the dominant concern. President Wilson ran for reelection in 1916 on the slogan, "He kept us out of war." But Wilson's persistent efforts to mediate the conflict and bring peace demonstrated his concern over the effects of the war on American security. Wilson's policy, intentionally or not, conveyed the message that the United States, if it so chose, could play a decisive role in the construction of a new European balance.

That Germany was aware of such a thing, Rood observed, seemed apparent in its efforts to keep America talking peace, while taking such measures as would prevent the United States from making any effective contribution to the Allied cause. In 1917, Germany embarked on a submarine campaign that was designed to sever the United States from Europe. Even the Wilson administration could not accept this, especially when it became clear that without direct American military support to the Allies, German arms would eventually win the day on the continent.

The course of World War I, and Germany's strategic objectives that involved overthrowing the balance of power inevitably meant that the United States would face threats to its commerce and security in the Western Hemisphere, and to its own territory. Rood put it this way:

> One of the invariable indications that the United States is in for trouble with a foreign power is when that power begins open or clandestine operations in the Western Hemisphere. It is the very essence of strategy to force one's enemy to defend that which has no choice to defend in areas away from the principal theater of war, while one's own forces concentrate to achieve a decision in that theater of war where the outcome of battle will decide the outcome of war. Since the beginning of the twentieth century it has been almost a corollary of American strategy that the U.S. can decide the outcome of any European war if it chooses to. But it is equally clear to Europeans that any power wishing to dominate Europe will have to attempt to force the United States to fight in the Western Hemisphere to tie down American military power there so it cannot be fully deployed to Europe.[9]

Not surprisingly, Rood noted, this basic concept of strategy was demonstrated by Germany's attempt to open the Caribbean-Cuban Salient. In 1914, during a civil war in Mexico, Germany dispatched shiploads of arms to Mexico (as Japan had done a year earlier). The arms were intended to buy influence and encourage anti-American sentiment while keeping the conflagration hot. In 1916, perhaps not by coincidence, the leader of one faction in that civil war, Pancho Villa, sent his forces on a raid across the border into New Mexico. This led to the dispatch of an American punitive expedition into Mexico, consisting of a good part of the U.S. Army. German agents were sent to encourage Cuban rebels to disrupt the production of sugar, which forced the deployment of the 7th Marine Regiment into Cuba to protect sugar production. And in 1917, Germany attempted to foster a treaty between Germany, Mexico, and Japan to keep the United States out of the war in Europe. Germany promised funds and military assistance to allow Mexico to recover the "lost provinces" of Arizona, Texas, and New Mexico.[10]

The United States concluded that the best way to deal with these interrelated threats—those of German hegemony in Europe and the challenge to American security in the Western Hemisphere—was to "defend forward." This was done by forcibly maintaining the lines of maritime communication to the British Isles and the European continent, and by dispatching an expeditionary force to France to ensure German defeat in the decisive theater. The key point for Rood, to repeat, was that the United States could not "isolate" itself from the war in Europe. Its massive economic and financial weight, combined with its military assistance and manpower, would tip the scales decisively in the Allies' favor—if the United States chose to intervene. If the United States decided not to provide that assistance, or did not do so in a timely fashion, then Germany would probably win. Germany, as would any great power with similar ambitions, did its best to influence the American decision through a combination of diplomacy (which meant obfuscating the long-term threat), and of military activities aimed at pinning the United States down in the Western Hemisphere.

It took three years, until 1917, for the United States to figure out this strategic equation and to make its choice. The delay meant it had to scramble to organize and deploy the immense resources required to defend forward in the midst of an ongoing European war. It was a near-run thing: with the collapse of Russia, American assistance on the Western front arrived barely in time. The delay was costly for the United States, but cheap relative to the enormous price that the Allies paid.

After the war, American political leaders failed to create a domestic political consensus in favor an internationalist foreign policy, and the United States decided, in effect, that it would reset the clock. America would not help to organize and support a system of alliances that might deter or defeat another attempt at European hegemony. Such a preventive strategy might have deployed forward some American military units in Europe, but at a minimum the United States would have made preparations to reconstitute a sizable expeditionary force in time to meet any emerging threat. Instead, the United States treated its wartime experience from 1914 to 1918 as an aberration. At the outset of World War II, the United States once more attempted to maintain its neutrality while it lagged in its military preparations, in the hope that the great powers resisting the German and now the Japanese drives for hegemony would succeed on their own. America's assistance was to be limited to the economic and moral realms.

The United States again recognized, belatedly, that German (and now Japanese) war aims would result in the Axis powers' control of the Atlantic and the Pacific. That meant the strategic encirclement of the Western Hemisphere and its economic domination by a hostile coalition. Not surprisingly, Rood noted, German agents were once more active in the Western Hemisphere. Nor was Tokyo idle in this respect. In 1941, when it had become clear to the Japanese government that war with the United States was likely, the Japanese undertook the establishment of intelligence and communications networks in Central and South America. Efforts were made to set up centers of pro-Japanese and anti-American sentiment in Mexico, Nicaragua, and Guatemala. A coded dispatch from the Japanese embassy in Mexico read, in part:

> Military Attaché NISI . . . has a great deal of confidence in the possibility of planning a rebellion in Guatemala. . . . On the other hand, is it not a good plan to get Marshall URUT-TADO of Nicaragua . . . to lead a rebellion. . . . Such a plot might not necessarily be a success in every respect; however, even if it fails, it would have to be quieted by the United States with its armed forces.[11]

Such indications of Japanese subversion in the Western Hemisphere, and also in Hawaii, formed the background for FDR's decision to intern large numbers of Japanese-Americans after the outbreak of war. The Roosevelt administration's policy of indiscriminate internment was unjustified. But the fact that President Roosevelt had to make such a decision demonstrated the strains on the American sense of justice that emerge when wars abroad are allowed to get too close. FDR, Rood pointed out, made that decision when Hawaii, and even the waters of the West Coast, seemed to be in jeopardy.[12]

When the United States finally entered the war in December 1941—because American territory had been directly attacked—it first had to secure the lines of communication to Europe and the Pacific, in order to deploy large expeditionary forces to bring about the defeat of Germany and Japan in their homelands. This task was made harder than necessary, not only because the United States was late in preparing for war and producing the means of victory, but also because it had not adequately secured the locations it would need to deploy an expeditionary force in Europe. In 1917–1918, members of the American Expeditionary Force could disembark at their leisure in ports in France and march through Paris en route to the front. In 1943–1944, however, the United States would need to fight its way onto the European continent, and that only after it secured North Africa.

In the Pacific, the United States lost the Philippines and other island possessions that, properly fortified and protected by large and forward-based naval and air forces, might have formed a defensive barrier to Japanese aggression much closer to the Japanese home islands. This would have saved much American time, treasure, and casualties, and perhaps deterred war in the first place. As it was, the protracted defense of the Philippines tied down Japanese air, naval, and ground units that otherwise would have been available to strengthen the Japanese drive toward Australia. The Japanese defeat on Guadalcanal left Australia as a secure base from which to begin the Allied counteroffensive. Fortunately, as noted in chapter 4, the U.S. armed services had prepared the operational concepts, and developed many of the weapons systems, that would support large expeditionary operations (if given time to put the plans and forces into effect). America once more had fought its wars abroad, as strategy dictated, although again relatively late in the process.

Ironically, as Rood commented, from one perspective America's delay in entering World War II might seem to have been a stroke of strategic genius. It meant that the other great powers, including the Soviets, would absorb the bulk of the cost, in manpower and material, of defeating the main enemy, Germany. The United States ended the war with a bourgeoning industrial base, roughly 50 percent of the world's gross domestic product (GDP), cutting-edge military technology, and access to or claims upon military bases and strategic locations around the perimeter of Eurasia. Rood observed that if one were conspiratorially minded, one might think that the American prewar foreign policy of isolationism, pacifism, and neutrality, coupled with a military policy designed to prepare for the contingency planning of transoceanic war, was actually a clever plan for American aggrandizement, for one result of the war was to leave both enemy and allied nations economically and militarily dependent upon the United States.[13]

Whether this favorable result was obtained by cleverness or accident—Rood did not think it was the former—the natural inclination of the United States immediately after World War II was to return to its preferred national security policy, that of distancing itself strategically from Eurasia. America would not exactly revert to full-scale isolationism, but it would withdraw militarily to the Western Hemisphere and rely on the wartime Allies (through the agency of the United Nations) to man America's forward line of defense against future threats to the Eurasian balance of power. The United States would remain over the horizon to buttress the Allies as necessary, largely with naval and air power (including nuclear weapons, assuming these were not banned by international agreement). The U.S. Army was demobilized as rapidly as practical, and then some. If it became necessary to redeploy overseas, the American armed forces would do so using the strategic locations that its wartime allies would continue to hold. From this perspective, the United States in 1945 enjoyed a surplus of resources and near-complete strategic freedom of action—the very definition of strategic superiority.[14]

The real cost of America's late entry into World Wars I and II soon became clear, however. The British and other West European empires, which were natural allies of the United States and which occupied critical strategic locations along the Eurasian periphery, essentially collapsed. None of these American allies was able to step into the power vacuum created by the complete defeat of Germany and Japan—save the Soviet Union, which immediately manifested signs that it was determined upon not merely Eurasian, but global dominance (see chapter 5). In Rood's opinion, had the United States understood and acted upon its best interests in 1914–1915, and certainly during the 1920s and 1930s, and had it intervened in Europe and the Pacific much earlier and with greater mass, Britain and France would have emerged from the World Wars in a much stronger position. Germany and Japan might have been deterred in 1939 and 1941 or, if they had gone to war, their defeat would have been brought about much more quickly, and with fewer gains for the Soviet Union. The European powers might have been able to maintain key strategic locations in their overseas possessions, if not political control of the colonies themselves.[15]

Although Rood did not make the point explicitly in his writings, it is reasonable to assume he believed that, had the World Wars been deterred or fought more expeditiously by the democracies and their allies, the decolonization process might have resulted in imperial (or federal) relationships more friendly to the West. The home countries would have been much stronger and better able to manage their own defense as well. This relatively happy outcome would have depended on a more forward-looking American national security policy and greater near-term expenditures, but in the long term the United States would have acquired fewer enduring overseas commitments than it was eventually forced to assume. As Rood put it, "our failure to influence the developments in Central Europe and the Far East in the 1920s and 1930s meant the exhaustion of British power, the breakup of the British, French and Dutch Empires in the Far East and the end of any substantial hope of a China unified under any regime other than the Communists."[16] The price of America's illusion that it need not concern itself with events in Europe during peacetime was the recession of British power, the defeat and eventual alienation of France, and the subjugation of Eastern Europe by the Soviet Union.

By contrast, had Washington concerned itself with the inner workings of Europe and Asia in the 1920s and 1930s, the United States might have sensibly followed its preferred strategy, letting others man the ramparts of Eurasia, backed up at a distance by the military power and diplomatic support of the United States. As it was, the post–World War II erosion of the balance of power began with the accommodation of the Soviet Union in the matter of Eastern Europe. Rood did not quarrel with the necessity of a wartime alliance with the Soviet Union. If Britain and the United States had not helped the Soviet peoples to fight on against the Nazis, he acknowledged, Germany could not have been defeated by 1945. The full power of the German Army and Air Force would have been waiting in France to contest the entry of British and American armies onto the continent, with the attendant price of much higher casualties. The price for the early liberation of Western Europe, however, was the Soviet occupation of Eastern Europe.[17]

## DEFENDING THE RIMLAND

As a consequence of the weakening of U.S. democratic allies during World War II, the relative strength of the Soviet Union, and the victory of the communists in China, the United States found itself compelled to man the distant ramparts itself. America's forward line of defense, which was necessary to keep foreign wars out of the Western Hemisphere and away from America's shores, eventually became that of the North Cape, the western Baltic, the inner-German border, the eastern Mediterranean, the Persian Gulf, Southeast Asia, Korea, and Japan. In Rood's view, the United States no longer had the luxury of being half-ready, while others fought to hold the line until America became sufficiently ready. It would have to engage fully and directly along the entire Eurasian periphery, which meant assuming control of many old European colonial bases, or creating new ones, and cultivating regional allies in areas wracked by colonial and postcolonial wars.

Rood extrapolated here from the strategic ideas of Yale University social scientist Nicholas Spykman.[18] In the early 1940s, Spykman argued that a properly structured forward defense in Eurasia was militarily feasible, despite the apparently revolutionary changes in military technology—particularly, airpower and the use of road and railroad transportation, which seemed to advantage large continental states over the maritime powers.

According to Spykman, America's principal security concerns were located in the "Rimland" of Eurasia. The Rimland, broadly speaking, included Western Europe, the Maghreb, the Middle East, and continental South, Southeast, and East Asia. This region contained (and still contains) the majority of the world's population and natural resources. The Rimland is connected by a series of marginal seas, such as the Mediterranean and the South China Sea. The gravest threat to the global balance of power would occur if a single power or coalition of powers hostile to the United States dominated the Rimland, whether those hostile powers came from the Rimland itself, such as Germany; from an offshore island in the marginal seas, such as Japan; or from a continental power, such as the Soviet Union.

Spykman's key proposition was that American security depended on ensuring that the states of the Rimland remain independent from a would-be hegemon. Modern technology and communications were such that threats to the Rimland could emerge very rapidly. The United States could no longer afford to wait at a distance and see how events developed before deciding whether it should intervene in a Eurasian conflict. The United States needed to become actively engaged across the oceans during peacetime, through alliances and military bases that maintained air and maritime access to the Rimland, and that preserved the security of the marginal seas. The United States need not be solely responsible for the security of the entire Rimland, Spykman argued, because other powers would naturally align with it against any hegemonic threat, irrespective of their political orientation. Spykman, like many other prominent analysts at the time, including Walter Lippmann, thought that the most likely threat to Eurasian security after World War II would be a revival of the German and Japanese threat, and that the natural anti-hegemonic combination would be that of the major wartime allies, Britain, the United States, and the Soviet Union. But Spykman (who died in 1943) allowed for the possibility that the Soviet Union would become the next great threat to the Rimland.

When that threat did emerge, Rood, following Spykman's logic, favored a strategy of containing the Soviet Union and preventing it from dominating the Rimland (although Rood never explicitly referred to his preferred strategy as one of "containment"). For Rood, this strategy had to be based on the ability and willingness of the United States to wage war abroad successfully. By establishing itself along the Eurasian Rimland, by supporting local allies, and by waging small wars whenever necessary to maintain its strategic position and to keep great power threats in check, the United States could preserve its security without having to fight another global war.

Rood's approach to containment, unlike that advocated by George Kennan, did not aim to deal with purely "political" challenges to the Rimland. Nor did Rood rely on the ability to inflict "unacceptable damage" on the enemy to deter war, and thus make ordinary military actions unnecessary. He argued that forward bases and secure strategic lines of communication in and around Eurasia were more than a distant shield to keep the war far away from the Western Hemisphere. They were necessary to wage war against any Eurasian power that might seek to overthrow the balance of power. Passive defense of the Rimland perimeter was not enough; the United States and its allies must demonstrate the ability to take the war to the enemy and its proxies. As Rood wrote in 1967:

> The capacity to carry the war to the enemy is essential to the national strategy in war, the possession of such a capability may deter the outbreak of war entirely. If the enemy faces the realization that resorting to war will lead to his certain defeat, he may eschew war in order to avoid the possibility of having to live with the fruits of his defeat. If war comes in any case, American bases on the enemy's periphery force him

to deploy forces to reduce those bases, thereby limiting his freedom of action in the initial stages of war. Even in a strategic nuclear war, those bases overseas from which U.S. forces may launch nuclear strikes are targets with the highest priority. Thus, tactical aircraft in forward positions, aircraft carriers, medium bombers, and Polaris submarines are capable of launching devastating nuclear strikes against any country without U.S. ICBMs being engaged. If an enemy chooses to strike the United States first, he does so at the risk of receiving a devastating attack from U.S. nuclear power based overseas. If an enemy chooses to employ his strategic forces, in part, to take out U.S. nuclear forces overseas, then he has fewer missiles to fire at the strategic striking forces based in the United States.[19]

Rood did not propose to take the war to the main enemy—the Soviet Union—proactively, but rather to defeat probes or aggression by the communist bloc in the Rimland; to threaten to escalate the conflict locally if circumstances warranted; and to roll back marginal communist gains in the Rimland whenever the opportunity presented itself.

Rood acknowledged that preparing to fight, and actually fighting, relatively small wars to maintain forward bases and allies would be burdensome in lives and treasure. But this would be nothing like the cost of fighting a global war, especially a global nuclear war. The importance of far-off places was not always self-evident, unfortunately.

> At what point the strategic defense of the United States should compel intervention abroad remains, as it has been since 1898, the baffling question for those Americans concerned with the safety of the Republic. Should the United States wait until circumstances abroad have so far deteriorated that the safety of the United States is in obvious jeopardy or take measures that will forestall that deterioration? Which course of action is the most economical in terms of the expenditures of American lives and American resources, for in the end it is the general citizenry who bear the cost in lives lost or disrupted and in the resources that those citizens generate through their labor, industry and ingenuity.[20]

Rood, as we shall see, believed in early and active measures, including military operations, that would forestall a deteriorating geopolitical situation. He thought it strategically sound and economically wise to anticipate and preempt threats, but he understood that his fellow citizens, imbued with the democratic distrust of strategy, often differed on that point. He judged that the real pressures for U.S. retrenchment from the Rimland of Eurasia were political, not fiscal or military. Our sympathies (anticolonialism and self-determination) often ran up against the strategic imperative to maintain our position of influence in Eurasia. The United States frequently found itself allied with characters deemed less than savory by editorial columnists and university professors. The practical alternatives, however, were either to lose a key strategic position or ally—which meant that the overall costs and risks of maintaining the security perimeter would rise correspondingly—or to go in and run these places ourselves. Americans were unprepared to do the latter, as a rule. The only other way out of this messy business of manning the distant ramparts and fighting small wars would have been (as Rood put it) "to go for the jugular in Moscow," that is, to wage global war as a matter of choice.[21] Rood never advocated such a course.

Rood's preferred strategy was not anti-Soviet in the strict sense. He concluded that, in strategic terms, the United States after 1945 had to expand its "peacetime" (prewar) defensive perimeter much farther forward than it had previously, because the power vacuum after World War II so dictated. Even if the Soviet Union had not immediately shown signs of challenging American efforts to organize the peace along liberal lines, great power politics were bound to resume at some point, quite possibly on very short notice. Someone, if not the Soviets, would have made a play for the large prize, even if only to preempt another suspect. Rood wrote:

> There are . . . areas in the world where the U.S. may exert influence over events but where there are other powers whose influence may be significant and whose interests if they are pursued may conflict with the interests of the United States. . . . In an area such as this, where the U.S. may have vital interests but where U.S. influence is opposed by that of other powers, the U.S. may actually have to deploy its military power in order to exert influence over events which if permitted to develop unimpeded would raise a costly and dangerous threat to the U.S.[22]

American control of overseas bases and strategic locations, and its use of military power in regional conflicts, did more than serve immediate operational or strategic purposes. The United States, unlike Russia or Germany, is a great power in, not of, Eurasia. If it wishes to affect the great power competition there, it has to establish itself through presence, work, and organization. Direct U.S. engagement in a particular region of Eurasia serves to clarify the nature of the great power conflict that is taking place at any given time, by forcing adversaries (and allies) to declare themselves by their actions.[23] Political clarity of this sort gives the United States the opportunity to identify and deal with problems while they are relatively manageable, and to avoid strategic surprise. At one time the United States could have expected other nations, Britain, in particular, to serve as the strategic catalyst in key regions of Eurasia, so the United States could hang back. But no longer.

## WHY FIGHT IN VIETNAM

For several decades after the end of World War II, the United States enjoyed workable strategic advantages over the Soviet Union and its ally,

China. In Rood's judgment, America had established a manageable line of defense in key locations in and along the Eurasian periphery, backed by the credible threat to employ nuclear weapons effectively. The United States was in a position to fight small defensive wars if necessary, or to use coercion to improve its strategic position and to deny or roll back marginal communist gains. If there was a limited or even general war against the communist bloc, the United States held a winning position (or at least the communists did not hold such a position, and they and the world knew they did not). Rood acknowledged that it was impossible to be certain that the Soviets and Chinese were, in fact, deterred from general war during this period. But the fact was, they did not wage it, and it made no strategic sense for them to do so. They allowed proxies to fight small wars on their behalf—and even precipitated a limited war (Korea)—but this was to be expected, and it was a manageable situation for the United States.[24]

This strategic situation, to be sure, was not as strong as the one France held with respect to Germany from 1918 through the early 1930s, and Rood undoubtedly would have preferred an even greater margin of safety. In any event, the political-military trends eventually started to turn against the United States and its allies, as they had done for France and Britain in the 1930s. Rood believed that the democratic strategy deficit, so dominant in the West before World War II, still existed in large segments of the academy and public opinion. Communist diplomats and agents of influence played upon fears of nuclear war, and on the hopes of "peaceful coexistence." Those in power in the West who knew better were often reluctant to speak the hard truth about the imperatives of strategy. Khrushchev's successful gambit in Cuba should have demonstrated that the Soviets were playing for keeps and had achieved a major strategic success, yet it was generally treated as quite the opposite.[25]

Rood thought that the successful defense of one particular outpost of the American-led security perimeter—South Vietnam—constituted a critical test of American resolve and of the long-term viability of its Cold War strategy. Rood viewed the war in Vietnam through the strategic prism outlined above. He offered his most comprehensive analysis of American strategy there in two essays, "Distant Rampart" (the 1967 Gold Medal–winning prize essay in the U.S. Naval Institute *Proceedings*) and "Why Fight in Vietnam" (*Infantry Magazine*, November–December 1967).

Rood's fundamental judgment on Vietnam was this: "It was an absolutely crucial war, unless you were going to go for the jugular in Moscow. If deterrence was to mean anything, then deterrence required that we meet the Soviets at any place on the perimeter where they crossed over, whether through their minions or themselves."[26] The United States, Rood argued, needed actively to prevent the Soviets and Chinese from acquiring those marginal strategic advantages that, taken cumulatively, would provide them with strategic superiority. That meant fighting difficult little wars in places like Vietnam (little, that is, compared with what a general war, especially a general nuclear war, would involve).

To be sure, Rood acknowledged that not all places were of equal value and that, for political as well as strategic reasons, policy makers would value some regions more highly than others. For Rood, however, Vietnam was not just "any place." It held particular significance for an offshore power like the United States—a power that needed to ensure strategic access to the Asian mainland, in order to protect the sea lines of communication from the Indian Ocean into the Western Pacific, and to secure the island perimeter that lay off the coast of Asia. The area composed by South Vietnam,[27] Rood argued, bears a particular importance to the defense of the Gulf of Siam, and of Thailand, Laos, Cambodia, and Malaysia. Malaysia, in turn, has a vital strategic relationship to Indonesia, the Bay of Bengal, and the Indian Ocean. A hostile power based in Indonesia would pose a direct strategic threat to Australia, New Zealand, and the Philippines. The Southeast Asian mainland and offshore islands together lay astride the maritime trade routes, north and south, along which Japan receives its oil supply from Indonesia and from the Persian Gulf. Japan must import nearly all of its petroleum and coal. Any interruption of those supplies for more than a month would dislocate Japanese industry. Post–World War II Japan lacked the means to defend those maritime trade routes and depended on the United States to do so.[28]

Rood illustrated Vietnam's significance by recounting the sequence of events that led to the loss of Singapore in 1942. In 1939, Japan, then engaged in the conquest of China, occupied the island of Hainan in the Gulf of Tonkin and the Spratly Islands off the coast of Indochina. Following the surrender of France in June 1940, Japan forced France to accede to a Japanese share in the administration of Indochina, as well as the right to use Saigon as an airbase. In the following year, Japan progressively occupied the remainder of Indochina and began to bring pressure on Thailand. On December 8, 1941, from bases at Saigon, Camranh Bay, and Hainan, attacks were launched by sea and air across the Gulf of Siam against the Siamese coast and Kota Bharu in Malaya. With about sixty thousand combat troops, supported by air and naval forces, the Japanese were able to seize Thailand, Malaya, and Singapore within seventy days. By the middle of 1942, the Japanese were in a position to make raids into the Bay of Bengal, and to secure their hold on Burma, having conquered the Philippines and the Netherlands East Indies as well.

According to Rood, the strategic position of China in the 1960s with respect to Southeast Asia was similar to that of the Japanese in 1939, albeit with some interesting differences. China already bordered some of those countries, and had subversive means, through guerrilla movements or the Chinese diaspora, to influence politics in India, Nepal, Sikkim, Malaysia, and Indonesia. China penetrated north Burma through support for the communist insurgency there, and equipped the Pakistani Army and Air Force in several Indo-Pakistani wars. The Chinese had air and naval bases on Hainan, the firm possession of the Chinese coast from North Vietnam to North Korea, and access at its pleasure to Laos, Cambodia, and North Vietnam. China was now unified, save for Taiwan, had a respectable and sizable army and submarine force, and showed a capacity to manufacture and deliver nuclear weapons.[29]

Mainland Southeast Asia, Rood argued, must always be subject to the exercise of influence of the two great Asian powers between which the region lies. Whenever India and China are unified and at all expanding, the region will fall into their zone of contention. During the 1960s, Southeast Asia became a transit area through which Chinese policy toward India could be implemented. Rood cited the Indian minister for home affairs, who, in Parliament in 1963, observed that the *Brief History of Modern China* (published by the PRC's Yi-Chang State Publishing House) contained a map showing Chinese claims to Assam, the North-East Frontier Agency (as it was then known) and Nagaland areas, and also Sikkim, Bhutan, Malaya, Singapore, Thailand, North and South Vietnam, Laos, Cambodia, and North and South Korea.[30]

The war in Vietnam should have been seen in this broader geopolitical context, Rood argued. The North Vietnamese and their instruments in the South, the Viet Cong, were fighting a so-called war of national liberation to establish a unified, communist regime. The consequence of a communist victory would be the defeat of the United States, the expulsion of its ground, naval, and air forces, and the loss of the military facilities in South Vietnam to which it had access. The idea that Ho Chi Minh might be an Asian Tito was nonsense, in Rood's opinion. Ho may have been a dedicated patriot, but he was able to wage war against the United States only with the material and diplomatic support of China and the Soviet Union. North Vietnam, or a unified Vietnam, remained independent only at the pleasure of China. Chinese forces were in a position to dominate completely the northern borders of North Vietnam and the waters of the Gulf of Tonkin. A few changes in the North Vietnamese leadership, engineered by pro-Chinese elements or party leaders intimidated by the proximity of Chinese armed forces, would have made Vietnam even more of a creature of China than it presently was. The strategic consequences would have been to place Chinese armed forces in those very bases from which Japanese armed forces launched an invasion of Malaya, Thailand, Indonesia, and Burma.[31]

Those countries of Southeast Asia might have chosen to fight, in which case, after a desperate resistance, Rood thought they would have been defeated. What was more likely than outright invasion was the Chinese sponsorship of armies of national liberation within each of those countries. Pro-Chinese insurgents would have overthrown the existing governments, and new governments—clients of China—would have been installed. The Chinese military and political presence would be so potent that it probably would have been unnecessary for China to cross a single frontier with its forces in order to secure the submission of those countries. The strategic position of those countries would be dramatically altered by the American defeat in Vietnam, Rood wrote in 1967. Thailand, like Cambodia, would have been forced to accept an accommodation advantageous to China. Northern Malaysia would have been exposed to the same kind of attack to which it was exposed in World War II. There were already guerrilla bands operating in the border areas between south Thailand and Malaysia.

It was not just that the dominoes of Southeast Asia might fall if the United States were to withdraw from Vietnam without defeating the Viet Cong and North Vietnamese forces. Such a withdrawal, in Rood's opinion, would signal the general withdrawal of U.S. forces from the island shield of Asia. Guam was the only base on U.S. territory that was close to China, and that island managed to hold out for all of twenty minutes against Japan in 1941. Bases in the Philippines, South Korea, South Vietnam, Japan, and Taiwan remained accessible to the United States only so long as it suited the interests of countries upon whose territories the bases were located. Those nations had to make a political calculation based on their assessment of whether the United States was capable of defending them, and whether it had the staying power to do so, because none possessed the resources for self-defense. That political calculation, in turn, depended upon the chances that the United States would remain a significant force in Asia and the Pacific.

If the United States withdrew from Vietnam, Rood thought that the Philippines would be forced to reconsider its attitude toward China and at best seek an alliance with Japan, if it were not subject to a massive revival of Huk guerrilla operations. Indonesia might dissolve into civil war or become a stepping-stone for the extension of Chinese influence. From the Japanese perspective, if the United States could not defeat a minor Asian power like North Vietnam, could one really assume that it could defeat China? Therefore, Japan would have to consider its own interest, which might require the development of a large nuclear arsenal to meet the threat from China, and possibly an alliance between Japan and the Soviet Union. Those nations in the region that might prefer to work with the United States as part of a broader Asian anti-communist coalition—Indonesia, Australia, India, and Pakistan—would be exposed to increasing pressure from China, at first from the threat posed by Chinese subsidies to armies of national liberation, and ultimately by Chinese military and naval power, backed by nuclear weapons.

In Rood's judgment, American overseas bases and allies, such as those in South Vietnam, were critical means of reducing the probability that a major war would be fought on U.S. territory, while contributing to the possibility that major war might be avoided entirely.

American bases in the Far East are a promise to our allies and to the Red Chinese as well that there is an American military commitment in the area that the Red Chinese may ignore only at their peril. Prosecution of the war in Vietnam is a means to measure the determination behind the American commitment in the Far East. The fact that the war is a difficult one to fight in an unpromising area under far from advantageous conditions only lends credibility to U.S. determination. For it is an indication to our allies and to other free countries in the area, as well as to China, that the U.S. will not permit Asia to become an exclusively Chinese pasture.[32]

What would be the strategic result of general withdrawal of U.S. forces from the island shield of Asia, and the collapse of the anti-communist strategic coalition that had been bound together by American power? The defense of the Pacific Coast would then rest on Hawaii and Alaska — both states of the Union (which had not been the case in 1941) and thus constitutionally guaranteed the same level of defense and security as the other states. The initiative in any Pacific war under those conditions would rest with the Asiatic power that might, in Rood's judgment (writing in the late 1960s), be Japan and the Soviet Union as easily as it might be China.

Rood recalled that during World War II, the Japanese attacked Midway to provide an advanced base from which to operate against Hawaii — either to neutralize or seize it. They also attacked the Aleutians as part of an effort to secure the North Pacific area. With the seizure of further positions in Alaska, the Japanese would have been in a position to challenge American control of the coastal waters of the west coast of the United States. So Alaska and Hawaii were vital, not only for the prosecution of the war against Japan, but also for the actual defense of the continental United States. The counteroffensive in the South Pacific would have been delayed months while the United States dealt with this threat, providing the Japanese with the time and forces to extend their defensive perimeter into Australia, and to establish themselves in strength in New Caledonia, Fiji, and Samoa. The U.S. counteroffensive in the Pacific would have had to have been conducted from California.

Events in Asia, Rood noted, influence events in Europe and those events, in turn, bear directly on U.S. interests. If the United States were to have become involved in a war of this sort with China, Rood argued, the Soviet Union could have used the occasion to solve some of its outstanding problems in Europe. In return for a pledge of Soviet neutrality in a Sino-American war, the Soviets might have attempted to extract concessions from the United States in Europe and the Middle East. Berlin would have been the most obvious concession. Soviet neutrality, spelled out in terms of the best interests of the Soviet Union, would have meant that Moscow could continue to supply materials to China. The United States would have been in no position to object, or even interfere. Such developments might have led to an isolated America, whose only recourse for resisting Soviet interference in Western Europe and Chinese occupation of the island shield of Asia would have been a transoceanic nuclear war. That would have meant war on the soil of the United States, the very eventuality that generations of Americans had sacrificed to avoid.

The key to American strategy was to make such a war decidedly unattractive to a great power adversary—unattractive, because the United States had the means to defeat the adversary within the theater in question without resort to transoceanic nuclear war. To that end, Rood asserted, success in Vietnam was important to maintain a war-winning capability against China in Asia. (Success, as Rood defined it, meant an independent South Vietnam—one that could defend itself sufficiently to force any attacker to mount a major offensive, which would trigger a U.S. response in the form of a military redeployment.) The strategic defense of the United States in any war with China would be eased considerably if the United States had bases from which to deploy close to the coast of China. From bases in South Vietnam, U.S. air power would cover the operations of carrier task forces and antisubmarine warfare (ASW) elements, which would close the South China Sea to Chinese use. A strategic threat could be posed against the Chinese base in Hainan and in the waters of the Gulf of Tonkin. From bases in the Philippines, South Korea, Taiwan, and Okinawa, Chinese access to that sea would be severely restricted. The Chinese would have to deploy forces along their entire coast from the Gulf of Chihli to North Vietnam, to meet the possibility of attacks that might be launched anywhere along the coast at the convenience of a sea power that controlled Chinese coastal waters. Meanwhile, Chinese forces deployed to meet this threat would not be available for attacks on Burma, Malaysia, and Thailand. The Chinese would have been confronted by a war in which the United States could levy damage on the Chinese homeland at will, while China itself possessed (at the time) only nominal power to attack the United States directly.

The choice confronting the United States, in Rood's judgment, was either (1) to continue to fight in Vietnam with the hope that a military defeat administered to South Vietnam's attackers would promote the stability of that country, and provide deterrence to any Chinese thought of war with the United States; or else (2) to abandon South Vietnam and risk a later war with China when it had developed a full-sized nuclear arsenal, backed by the capacity to command the sea areas around the island shield of Asia. "Resolution where others waver is the mark of leadership among nations," Rood wrote. "The discriminate application of military power to serve the strategic interests of the United States is a warning to those who wish the nation ill and a reassurance to those whose alliance lends us strength. Is it better to wait until something really bad happens, then, perhaps, to act? Or should we act now whatever sentiment may be ranged against us?"[33]

Those who opposed the war in Vietnam, in addition to voicing their moral and political objections, argued that the war was essentially unwinnable and therefore that the United States should cut its losses. According to the common wisdom, the conventional forces of a foreign power can never defeat locally based guerrillas animated by the desire for national liberation. Rood argued, to the contrary, that such wars not only could be won, but that the war essentially had been won when the United States chose to withdraw from Vietnam. He pointed, for instance, to the maps used by commercial aviators in the region, which were marked in red for places to avoid because they were controlled by the Viet Cong. If one looked at those maps in 1967–1968, most of South Vietnam was red. By 1970, there were only a few spots that were red.[34]

In his published writings, Rood did not lay out a detailed plan to win the war in Vietnam. He did not take a position in the "search and destroy" versus "clear and hold" debate, for instance. He concluded that the proper U.S. operational object was to make the insurgents fight a conventional war, where the United States had the upper hand—something that Rood believed had been accomplished by the late 1960s.

> Air bases were a kind of lure. The more the perimeters were probed, the more we extended them, and the more the V.C. had to have better and better ordnance to attack them. This made them more dependent on logistics, and they became more structured. And thus they become more predictable. The guerrilla now has to come to you. Similarly, the Tet Offensive meant the guerrillas had to come out of the brush, which is the worst thing to do as a guerrilla. Newspapers made Tet look good for the V.C. but a lot were killed or captured, which is precisely what guerrillas aren't supposed to do; they're supposed to survive each engagement to fight another day.[35]

Rood often pointed out that, when Saigon fell in 1975, it was not to pajama-clad guerrillas but to the tanks of the North Vietnamese Army.

In wars such as Vietnam, Rood remarked, the most important step for the guerrilla or the national liberator is to establish moral superiority over the enemy. If the fight is being carried on against a modern enemy, the guerrilla will never be able to gain anything but temporary fire or equipment superiority. So the guerrilla strives to achieve moral superiority by tiring his enemy, stretching and breaking his logistical support, and diverting his strength from more decisive theaters of operation. The guerrillas hope to convince the enemy that they (the guerrillas) are too clever, too crafty, too dedicated, too highly mobile, and too difficult to detect until too late; and that they do not really need very much in the way of logistical support while the conventional army is tied to a huge logistical tail. Rood turned that argument on its head:

> As it turns out, of course, the guerrilla—in this case the Viet Cong—is about as fragile as other human beings; he is just as subject to anxiety,

hunger, illness and small arms fire as another man would be under similar circumstances. At the same, time, the guerrilla has discovered that U.S. soldiers and Marines can be tough, cagey, highly mobile, difficult to detect and, in addition, are well fed and equipped and indeed well cared for. In short, the gigantic logistical tail behind U.S. forces has given to the Americans the same kind of advantage that the Viet Cong were supposed to enjoy from not having logistical support. . . . If you are a Viet Cong sitting in ambush for a U.S. patrol, and if every time you fire off your imported rifle at a likely target some impetuous American calls down a battery, four rounds of high explosive on your position, or whistles up a fighter bomber strike, the time can begin to drag a bit; indeed, one's whole day can be spoiled. So while the Viet Cong might enjoy a certain sense of moral superiority, it has become clear that a 105 round on the way can alter one's moral perspective rather decisively.[36]

Rood challenged the argument that the local population was bound to be sympathetic to the guerrillas, who were, after all, supposedly trying to liberate them. "The local South Vietnamese population will give you information, if you treat them right. What they won't do is give you much information if they think you are going to lose. If they think you're going to win, they'll give you a lot of help."[37]

Once the United States established its military superiority on the battlefield in Southeast Asia, in Rood's opinion, the North Vietnamese and their supporters were left with one major strategic option, of which they took full advantage: to expand the "moral battlefield" to the American homeland. They appealed to the American sense of fairness, love of freedom, and dedication to humanitarian principles. They accused the United States of fighting without quarter in Vietnam, and thus (according to the war's critics), debasing America's moral character. The North Vietnamese, for instance, waged a worldwide propaganda campaign to protect their dikes, insisting that if they were destroyed, the result would be widespread destruction and loss of agriculture and civilian life. The North Vietnamese then proceeded to build supply depots and antiaircraft batteries on the dikes—"having established that we weren't bombing dikes, that's a marvelous place to store things—it's better than building a bomb shelter."[38]

As to the matter of allegations that the United States fought without quarter in Vietnam, Rood noted that guerrilla or partisan wars have generally been vicious, barbaric, and thoroughly inhumane, on both sides. That has certainly been the case when the regular formations fighting guerrillas were fielded by non-democratic regimes.[39] In the case of Vietnam, Rood argued that the United States, compared to the standards of World War II (for instance), had been remarkably careful in protecting civilians.[40]

## DID DEFEAT IN VIETNAM MATTER?

When Saigon fell, why did the dominoes throughout Asia (outside of Indochina) not fall to the communists? Critics of American involvement in Vietnam, and of Rood, often argued that the United States failed to appreciate the significance of the Sino-Soviet split, which meant that there was no monolithic "communist bloc" of which the North could be a part. There was no great communist conspiracy to dominate Southeast Asia. Even if there had been, Sino-Soviet hostility guaranteed that the dominoes of Southeast Asia would not fall, because the two communist great powers, and their clients, would negate each other. A united Vietnam, so the argument went, would be more nationalist than communist, and it would retain its independence by playing its former allies off against the other. In any case, Southeast Asia was a strategic backwater in the nuclear age. Defeat in Vietnam had no material effect on vital U.S. national interests.

Rood would counter the critics by arguing that the objective fact was that the Soviet Union and China, both of which supported Vietnam militarily and diplomatically, were the chief agents in bringing about the American withdrawal from the South, using the military forces controlled by North Vietnam as their proxy. The fate of Southeast Asia, henceforth, would essentially be outside of the influence of the United States. China and the Soviet Union might balance one another for a time, but this balance would be unstable—one side or the other would win, or (more likely) they would settle their differences against a common enemy, the United States.

For those who had supported the war, one could take solace in the argument, which was made widely in the region by leaders such as Lee Kuan Yew of Singapore, that by fighting in Vietnam, the United States had bought enough time for the non-communist, postcolonial governments and societies of Southeast Asia to survive (and, in many cases, prosper). In this sense, although the United States lost South Vietnam, it did accrue important strategic benefits throughout the region—and thus its sacrifices were not in vain. Rood agreed, to a point, but he did not think that this was necessarily a stable situation. The countries in the region outside of the communist orbit have fragile economies. Their administrative structure and governments are hardly less fragile, confronted by political divisions along class, ethnic, linguistic, and religious lines. To some degree, each country was, and still is, beset by insurgent groups led by disciplined communist parties. Those on the mainland are directly susceptible to land invasion. They are capable of a modicum of self-defense against minor military threats, but powerless, without outside help, against any strong and determined military power.[41]

Rood believed that a tenuous balance of power in Asia had emerged after 1975, not because of the growing strength of non-communist Southeast Asia, but principally because of Sino-Soviet differences that could well be transitory. This situation could not be relied upon to protect American interests over the long term. However nationalist and independent its government might seem to be, Vietnam still required a great-power patron if it was threatened by another great power. As ancient Vietnamese-Chinese differences emerged, it was Moscow, rather than Beijing, that became Vietnam's patron, for the time being. The Soviets moved to make Vietnam their naval and air base of operations in the region, only eight hundred miles from the Philippines. The Vietnamese Army, which expanded considerably after the end of the war with Soviet assistance, was now in a position to play the role of regional policeman.

Rood also pointed to the strategic patience of the Soviets as a reason that greater Southeast Asia had not collapsed after the Vietnamese communists took control of Indochina—although, as Rood documented, there was every indication that the Soviets were getting rather impatient by the late 1970s and early 1980s. With Vietnam safely in their pocket, the Soviets could take their time, and wait on other events, to exploit the strategic advantages they were developing throughout the Pacific (see chapter 5).

By the turn of the millennium, it appeared to Rood that the Chinese had once again supplanted the Soviets (now the Russians) as the most probable great power threat to dominate the Asian shield and its offshore islands. Or, perhaps they would do so in conjunction with the Russians. Whatever the case, the United States, by losing in Vietnam, had ceded strategic control of the situation in Southeast Asia to other great powers. At the very least, it was no longer running the show itself. It had also lost the flexibility to deal with situations elsewhere by shifting forces from the Asia-Pacific region, which hitherto had been a secure flank of America's defense perimeter. The United States was no longer in a position to require enemies and allies to declare themselves, or otherwise to clarify the strategic situation on the Asian mainland. As a result, Southeast Asia and the offshore waters today no longer seem like a strategic backwater.[42]

## WHAT WAS TO BE DONE?

Rood believed that the communist victory in Vietnam, along with the other Soviet gains cited in chapter 5, meant that by the mid to late 1970s, the margins of safety for the West were minimal or nonexistent. "The strategic interests of the United States are in more serious jeopardy now than they have been since the surrender of France in 1940 and Allied defeats in the Far East in the early spring of 1942," Rood judged in 1979.[43] Each particular setback for American national security policy—the establishment of a Soviet base in Cuba, the defeat in Vietnam, the fall of the Shah, and so on—did not seem disastrous in and of itself. But each loss limited American freedom of action in the world, and made the next crisis that much more difficult to resolve to the advantage of the United States and its allies. Rood judged that America's weakened position meant that if war came with the Soviet bloc, it was much more likely to be global in scope and nuclear in character, neither of which suited U.S. strategic objectives.[44]

What was to be done? Rood offered many thoughts on this subject in conversation with his students—and in off-the-record discussions with those who had responsibility for U.S. defense policy—but he put few of them on paper. He certainly believed that the road back required ordinary Americans, as well as their leaders, to begin thinking strategically again. This was the purpose of his book, *Kingdoms of the Blind*.

> It seems the only way in which those who live in a free society can continue to reap the blessings of freedom, in a world that is rapidly becoming unfree, is to develop the same instincts about defense that they now have for justice and right. . . . While ordinary Americans might choose to ignore such imperatives of strategy in peacetime, it is only because they expect that those who have the constitutional responsibility to defend the United States will not ignore them. One of the good reasons for having a republican form of government is to permit ordinary citizens to pursue their own interests while the government concerns itself with those that require constant attention. It may be that in today's world such a division of labor is an indulgence that the nation cannot afford.[45]

If the first step was to reacquire basic strategic wisdom, the next step was to rearm, quickly and massively. "There are two things which appear to bear consideration in the long run: (1) A large increase in defense spending; [or] (2) a general and extremely devastating war."[46] According to Rood, the U.S. military force structure must be of sufficient size and quality to fight major wars in multiple theaters. This meant a substantial increase, as rapidly as feasible, in the size of the U.S. Navy (especially its carrier task forces) and the U.S. Army.[47]

Rood emphasized the need for an effective homeland defense. Defense of the homeland, including civil defense, was made more, rather than less, essential by the immense power and range of nuclear weapons. The United States should also deploy a vigorous air defense. This would involve a force of interceptor aircraft to deal with bombers, as well as antiaircraft missiles on the ground to deal with those bombers that evaded the interceptors. (The Soviet Union, Rood noted, deployed over 2600 aircraft and twelve thousand antiaircraft missiles to defend its territory.) The air defense of the United States would not be complete until it extended over the North Pacific and the North Atlantic, so that the United States could safely reinforce and support its forces overseas in South Korea, Japan, and Western Europe.[48]

The extended air defense of the United States must include weapons capable of intercepting ballistic and cruise missiles, Rood thought. "Such weapons have not been fully developed and they require to be so," he wrote in 1980, three years before President Reagan announced plans for the Strategic Defense Initiative. "The most advanced technology must be applied to the problem and that as quickly as possible." [49]

The United States, of course, should also strengthen its power projection forces and the military assets that were forward deployed in Europe and Asia. They represented the first lines of American defense. But, in Rood's view, it was not to be expected that successful war could be waged abroad if the people at home were not given some measure of protection against attack. The purpose of such defenses would be "to prevent the development of attacks on the territory of the United States which would compel diversion of American and allied forces from their strategic objective: the destruction of the enemy's armed forces." [50]

Rood recognized that dramatic improvements of this sort could not be brought about immediately. The American people, however, deserved honesty from their elected officials, and from those who studied such things, about what would be required materially to deal with the Soviet threat. This was the beginning of strategic wisdom. Rearmament, in turn, would have to be guided by military policy and concepts of operation developed by defense planners who had sound ideas of the basic nature of war, and the particular character of war in the future. Defense planners had succeeded in this task during the 1920s and 1930s, and their efforts should serve as a model. Rood argued that the contemporary U.S. military must be reconstituted in line with the strategic imperatives of the United States, the current state of military technology, and the need to defend or acquire essential overseas bases and allies.

Rood urged the United States to do what it could to acquire those essential bases before war occurred, when the costs and risks of doing so were much less. American strategic policy should also aim to whittle down the marginal advantages that the Soviets had acquired over the previous decades. The United States should take advantage of opportunities to improve its own strategic position. The invasion of Grenada in 1983 exemplified for Rood what might be accomplished: the Reagan administration's rescue of American medical students on the island—an action that was highly popular with the American public—had the effect of removing what was rapidly becoming a significant Soviet-Cuban base of operations. When the United States bombed Libya in 1986, in retaliation for Libya's involvement in terrorist operations in Europe, Rood believed that American military action should have been much stronger, aimed at the removal of Gaddafi's regime. [51]

Vietnam was not likely to be retrieved soon, but Rood advocated doing what was possible to shore up the remaining U.S. base structure in the Western Pacific. The greatest assets the United States had in the Pacific region were its friends and allies there, especially Japan, South Korea, the Philippines, and Taiwan. Rood concluded that the rapid development toward democratic government in many of those nations, despite the difficulties that accompanied that development, promised to make their ties to the United States even stronger. The United States possessed many means to nurture these ties, but in Rood's opinion few were of more immediate importance than the maintenance of a policy of free trade. Protectionism needed to be resisted on both sides of the Pacific.[52]

Because America's naval presence is the only means for ensuring freedom of passage in the Pacific, Rood argued that the U.S. Navy must be kept adequate to the task of patrolling the expanses of that ocean. It was especially urgent that these forces be maintained to secure the strategically vital Straits of Malacca and the South China Sea, the waterways through which fuel and raw materials are borne for the economies of the region. The navy's mission in the Pacific requires bases for docking, ship repair, and resupply, so existing locations needed to be held and new locations investigated.

Rood agreed with most experts that the United States should take advantage of whatever strategic opportunities might be presented as a result of Sino-Soviet hostility. He believed that there were clear limits to this strategy, however, because mainland China has a long-term agenda in the region that is opposed to that of the United States. Rood thought that Taiwan was a much more reliable ally.

Rood's most elaborate discussion of shoring up the U.S. global defense posture concerned Western Europe, which he believed to be the decisive theater in a Soviet-American war. He advocated taking steps to ensure that the United States would be able to hold a lodgment on the continent in the event of a Soviet offensive. That lodgment would consist of Norway, the British Isles, and Spain.

The United States, in his judgment, could not afford to abandon critical allies and bases in Europe. These were the key to ultimate victory, because they tied down Soviet forces and because they allowed NATO to strike and enter Soviet territory. If the United States were forced, through strategic short-sightedness, to abandon all of Europe, the Europeans would lose hope of eventual liberation—and therefore the will to resist. That would render easy the consolidation of Western Europe into the Soviet Empire. The expulsion of American forces from European territory would also raise the temptation in the United States to await America's fate in the Western Hemisphere, rather than carrying the war to the heart of Russia, which was the only means for avoiding the ultimate defeat of the West. The ability to carry the fight to the heart of Russia, in turn, increased the chances that the Soviets might be deterred from a general war.[53]

Rood noted that the loss of Western Europe would have confronted the United States with a decision harder and more deadly than ever before. The Soviet Union, already formidable in military power, would enjoy the fruits of Western Europe as it made that territory part of the Socialist Commonwealth of nations. Western Europe's addition to Soviet industrial and military capability would permit the USSR literally to dominate the world by decoupling the American economy and military capability from Europe, even if the United States itself would remain unscathed. (There was, of course, no reason to suppose that the United States *would* have emerged unscathed.) The United States would then have had to decide whether it were possible to liberate Europe with forces projected from the continental United States, something that would take enormous military power and was probably unfeasible. If the United States could not bring itself to mobilize the strength to reenter Europe and wrest it from communism, then it would have had to consider using nuclear weapons to destroy Europe—its population and industry—to prevent Europe's assets from being used against the United States.[54]

We stress that Rood did not advocate such a horrible action. He felt compelled, however, to point out the consequences of failing to deter general war with the Soviet Union, and of losing that war. This meant that if the United States were to avoid expulsion from the continent of Europe during wartime, it must take those measures in peacetime that would permit America to defend its European allies and ultimately itself. In terms of tactical disposition, combat power, and reinforcement capability, as Rood judged matters in 1981, there was simply no way that the forces of NATO, assigned to the defense of the front from Norway to the Austrian border with Germany, could expect to do more than delay a Soviet advance from the east. All they could do was buy time and inflict casualties, as the American defenders had done in the Philippines from December 1941 to May 1942.[55] "For every soldier killed is one fewer than will be available to carry on the war, and to resist the eventual assault on the Soviet homeland," Rood wrote.[56]

In one of his unpublished papers, Rood outlined a "firebase" concept—the development of heavily defended positions that could deliver long-range artillery fire against the enemy's formations on the march, especially south of Hannover, where the terrain favored the defense. Warsaw Pact forces would be required to seize and hold such positions before they could advance. Rood did not favor a linear defense of NATO but, applying the principle of economy of force, he advocated this as a relatively cheap way to slow and attrit Soviet maneuver elements, as well as to conserve NATO's mobile forces.[57] He saw this not as an end in itself but as a means to an end—as a holding action to buy time to implement the "lodgment" strategy.

"Given the present inability of NATO to hold Germany if the Soviet Union is determined to have that country," he wrote, "there are three countries that absolutely must be held in order to deny the Soviet Union the fruits of a victory in Europe. Those places are the British Isles, Norway and Spain. If they are lost to the West, all will be lost. If they are held by the West, the Soviet Union cannot win."[58] These bastions would have played a role similar to that of Australia in the Pacific theater in World War II. Rood certainly favored defending the territory of other NATO allies, particularly West Germany. In time, if the West continued to rearm, such a comprehensive territorial defense might be possible as well as desirable. But he was working with the realities of the military balance as it appeared to him in the early 1980s.

Of the three places, Rood believed that Britain would have been particularly crucial in deciding the outcome of a war with the Soviet Union. So long as Britain stood free, and as stubborn in defense as it had been in the past, the resources of the Warsaw Pact would have been burdened by the price that military, naval, and air operations from Britain could exact. This price would be in the form of resources that could not be employed elsewhere to further Soviet purposes. So long as Britain controlled the "narrow seas," the Soviet Union could not have a free run in Europe. Nor could it have hoped to command the approaches to North America.[59]

Norway's defense was vital, not just to frustrate Soviet strategic operations, but to hold open Allied opportunities to pin Warsaw Pact forces behind Scandinavia, to pose a threat to Soviet control of the Baltic, and to threaten a descent on Warsaw Pact forces in Central Europe. Free of such a threat, Warsaw Pact forces could deploy where necessary to carry out their own strategy against the West. Any Warsaw Pact forces required for the defense of the Baltic and for the seizure of Norway would be compelled to fight on Allied terms. This would not have constituted a victory for the Allies, but only an opportunity to inflict casualties on Warsaw Pact forces, while depriving them of some of their capability to exercise strategic initiative. Beyond that, holding Norway forced the Soviet Union to conform to the possibility that Allied operations would be launched against north Russia, for the Soviet Union must also have known that war on its own soil could lead to its eventual defeat. A lodgment in Spain held similar benefits in southern Europe and the Mediterranean.[60]

Holding these three critical lodgments would have bought the time and the strategic opportunity necessary to carry the war to the Soviet homeland. To be successful, such an assault required allied forces in every category to be superior to those of the Warsaw Pact, in the arena where the final decision was to be sought. Accumulation of that superiority required time and immense effort, as had been the case in World War II. It also required a clear conception among those who felt obligated to understand such things, about how the United States must conduct such a war.

For most American leaders and citizens at the time, the notion of actually fighting a transoceanic war on such a massive and destructive scale would have seemed fantastic, a greatest generation nostalgia for the long-gone days of World War II. Surely nuclear weapons would quickly have put an end to things, one way or the other, before the Soviets had driven the United States off the continent (or before NATO actually counterattacked Russia proper). Thus, there could be no such war. Yet Rood's careful and detailed analysis of Soviet strategy revealed clear signs of Soviet preparations for war. Something was up. Fortunately, we did not have to see how everything would have played out—at least, not then. We must ask ourselves why that was the case and what lessons we can learn from the experience.

## NOTES

1. The following authors, for example, have analyzed the traditions of American foreign policy and have reached very different conclusions about what Americans have done, and should do, in the world: Walter LaFeber, *Liberty & Power: U. S. Diplomatic History, 1750–1945* (Washington, D.C.: American Historical Association, 1990), and LaFeber, *America, Russia, and the Cold War, 1945–1990*, 9th ed. (Boston: McGraw-Hill, 2002) ; Walter A. McDougall, *Promised Land, Crusader State: The American Encounter with the World Since 1776* (New York: Houghton Mifflin, 1997); Walter Russell Mead, *Special Providence: American Foreign Policy and How It Changed the World* (New York: Knopf, 2001); Robert Kagan, *Of Paradise and Power: America and Europe in the New World Order* (New York, Knopf, 2003).

2. Quoted in Harold W. Rood, "A Free Society in an Unfree World: Peace, Justice and Defense" (unpublished manuscript), Print, 45.

3. Ibid., 52.

4. These rules are taken from Harold W. Rood, "Distant Rampart," U.S. Naval Institute *Proceedings* 93 (March 1967): 30–37; Harold W. Rood, "Why Fight in Vietnam," *Infantry Magazine*, November–December 1967, 8–9; and Rood discussion with the authors.

5. The following discussion of the American strategic experience, unless otherwise noted, is taken from Rood, "A Free Society in an Unfree World," 52–66; Rood, "Distant Rampart," 31–32; and discussion with the authors.

6. Rood noted that war with Spain over Cuba required neutralization of the Spanish Fleet in the Far East. Not to have defeated that fleet would have left the Pacific Coast exposed to Spanish naval operations. Rood, "A Free Society in an Unfree World," 55–56.

7. Those occasions between 1815 and 1914, during which American ships and American marines were in combat outside of North America, arose out of what was then considered the obligation of the government to protect American lives and property abroad. Such occasions arose often enough in the Far East and in the Mediterranean so that it was necessary to maintain U.S. naval squadrons in both areas. Ibid., 55.

8. The fact that statehood for Washington, Oregon, and California had already forced the United States to interest itself in the balance of power in Asia to the same extent as the state of the balance of power in Europe compelled American interest in Europe. Ibid., 56. See also Harold W. Rood, "Traditions of American Strategy," in "Notable Statements by Harold Rood," ed. Christopher Harmon (unpublished manuscript), Print, 9–10.

9. Harold W. Rood, "Early Warning, Part IV," *Grand Strategy: Countercurrents*, June 15, 1983, 11.

10. Ibid. Harold W. Rood, *Kingdoms of the Blind: How the Great Democracies Have Resumed the Follies that So Nearly Cost Them Their Life* (Durham: Carolina Academic Press, 1980), 107–8.

11. Quoted in Rood, "Early Warning, Part IV," 11.

12. Rood discussion with the authors.

13. Harold W. Rood, "Strategy Out of Silence: American Military Policy and the Preparations for War, 1919–1940" (PhD diss., University of California, 1960), 22.

14. Rood discussion with the authors.

15. Rood discussion with the authors. Rood argued that there were three things that made colonial status rather than independence barely acceptable to a colony: the provision of good order based on a consistent justice, a flourishing and protected commerce, and the surety of defense against foreign invasion. When any of these things was weakened by external circumstances, independence became less unattractive to the mass of indigenous colonial peoples. The easy and comfortable commerce that had characterized the relationships of the European colonial powers in regions such as Southeast Asia suffered as a result of the war in Europe between 1914 and 1918. The colonial economies faced the headwinds of inflation and debt. The United States and Japan entered the market with manufactured goods and increasingly assumed the carrying trade. The European great powers suffered catastrophic losses of their "best and brightest"—many of them future colonial leaders—on the battlefield. The intellectual phenomena that had been unleashed in Europe—nationalism, self-determination, and independence—became strongly manifest in much of the colonial world. Taken together, those factors disrupted the colonial administration and imposed social changes in traditional societies. This process was accelerated by World War II, especially with the demonstrated inability of the colonial powers to fight in Europe and defend the colonies at the same time. This destroyed whatever prestige those powers once enjoyed in Asia and lent force to the notion that the welfare of the colonial peoples would be readily sacrificed when circumstances in the mother countries demanded it. Harold W. Rood, "Southeast Asia" (unpublished manuscript), Print, 16–17.

16. Rood, "Distant Rampart," 34.

17. Rood, *Kingdoms of the Blind*, 83.

18. This summary is based on Nicholas Spykman, *America's Strategy in World Politics: The United States and the Balance of Power* (New York: Harcourt, Brace, 1942), and *The Geography of the Peace* (New York: Harcourt, Brace, 1944). Rood did not use the term "Rimland" in his classes or writing but he clearly drew on a similar geopolitical assessment of Eurasia.

19. Rood, "Distant Rampart," 35.

20. Harold W. Rood, "AVOT—Harold W. Rood on the War in Iraq," Claremont Institute, October 2007, http://www.claremont.org/projects/pageid.2501/default.asp.

21. "Remarks on the War in Vietnam: Reflections from a listener's notes at a talk in Claremont, CA, July 7, 1980," in Harmon, "Notable Statements by Harold Rood," 5.

22. Rood, "Why Fight in Vietnam," 9.

23. See Rood's argument about the strategic purpose behind the 2003 Iraq War, in chapter 7.

24. Rood discussion with the authors. As late as 1967, for example, Rood did not seem to regard the strategic threat posed by Cuba to be urgent. "There are areas of the world where the US may exercise a dominant influence on the outcome of events," he wrote. "Such an area is the Caribbean Basin, where, if the US chooses and where if its interests dictate, US power may be deployed to exclude significant opposition to its policies. In such an area the US may choose not to act at all, since it may serve its interests not to act; or it may postpone action until the situation has become clarified or until a propitious opportunity presents itself. Thus, while Cuba remains hostile to the US and its interests, no direct military action against Cuba is necessarily desirable under the present circumstances. Cuba can, under some circumstances, contribute a major strategic threat to CONUS [the Continental United States], but it is clear that Cuba pursues an independent course of action only so long as it suits the pleasure of the US to permit her to do so. On the other hand, an invasion of Cuba by US forces would be extremely expensive in lives and property on both sides, might unnecessarily provoke Latin American sensibilities, and would leave the US to develop a responsible government in Cuba. . . . In weighing the advantages or disadvantages of direct

US military intervention in Cuba, the US has the freedom of choice to act only when it appears absolutely necessary to do so in terms of its own convenience and interests." Rood, "Why Fight in Vietnam," 9.

25. Rood discussion with the authors.

26. "Remarks on the War in Vietnam," in Harmon, "Notable Statements by Harold Rood," 5. The typical contrary argument held that containment ceded the strategic initiative to the Soviets, contrary to sound strategy, because they could pick and choose where they wanted to cross the perimeter. Rood might agree with this, to a point, but the alternative, as he put it, was "to go for the jugular in Moscow," a course that Americans were not likely to support in the interests of fair play and their desire for peace. At some point it also exceeded the military capacity of the United States. Rood did not explore, in writing, the other alternative, which arguably proved fruitful in the Reagan administration—that of finding ways to weaken the Soviet perimeter at places of our choosing, without resorting to or provoking general war.

27. In his writings, Rood did not advocate the occupation of all or part of North Vietnam, or a change of the regime in Hanoi. That might have been the consequence of U.S. military operations in the theater, but Rood apparently thought that the strategic locations in the South would suffice for American strategic purposes.

28. Rood, "Southeast Asia," 47–48.

29. This analysis of Japanese and Chinese strategy in Indochina is taken from Rood, "Distant Rampart," 34.

30. Rood, "Southeast Asia," 39–40.

31. The following section on American strategy and Asia, unless otherwise indicated, is drawn from Rood, "Distant Rampart," 35–37, and Rood, "Why Fight in Vietnam," 10–12.

32. Rood, "Why Fight in Vietnam," 10.

33. Ibid., 12.

34. "Remarks on the War in Vietnam," in Harmon, "Notable Statements by Harold Rood," 7.

35. Ibid.

36. Rood, "Why Fight in Vietnam," 6.

37. "Remarks on the War in Vietnam," in Harmon, "Notable Statements by Harold Rood," 7.

38. Ibid., 6.

39. Rood, "Why Fight in Vietnam," 6.

40. In this, Rood compared civilian casualties inflicted by the strategic bombing campaign against Germany, which were much less than those that Hanoi claimed to have been killed or wounded in airstrikes against the North. "Remarks on the War in Vietnam," in Harmon, "Notable Statements by Harold Rood," 5–6.

41. Rood, "Southeast Asia," 45–46.

42. Rood discussion with the authors.

43. Harold W. Rood, remarks at the CEI Conference, Claremont McKenna College, Claremont, CA, April 20, 1979, 2.

44. See, for example, Harold W. Rood, "The Strategy of Freedom," *Grand Strategy: Countercurrents*, July 1, 1981, 17. Rood discussion with the authors.

45. Rood, "A Free Society in an Unfree World," 51–52, 59.

46. Rood, Remarks at the CEI Conference, 7. Here, the authors have inserted "or" for "and." Rood would sometimes incline to the view that a large increase in the U.S. defense budget, if guided by proper strategy, would restore a situation where the Soviets ceased to believe they could win a war. At other times, he seemed to believe that the Rubicon had already been crossed, and that massive investments in defense would be necessary to wage a general war.

47. Rood discussion with the authors.

48. This discussion of homeland defense is taken from Harold W. Rood, "Naked to our Enemies" (Claremont, CA: Public Research, Syndicated, 1980). Rood was certainly familiar with the arguments about the destructiveness of nuclear weapons, and the

difficulty (many would say impossibility) of effective means of civil defense. Rood would counter that this end-of-the-world view of nuclear weapons assumed that reasonably effective active defenses against nuclear weapons and their delivery systems, complementing civil defenses, would never exist; and that the Soviets (or other adversaries) would necessarily launch a nuclear attack with the sole purpose of killing as many Americans as possible. He also pointed out that other nations, such as Finland, Switzerland, and the PRC, to say nothing of the USSR, had constructed underground shelters against the possibility of nuclear war.

49. Ibid.

50. Rood, "A Free Society in an Unfree World," 66; Rood discussion with the authors.

51. Harold W. Rood, "Grenada: The Strategic Dimension," *Claremont Review of Books* 2, no. 4 (Winter 1983), accessed July 18, 2014, http://claremontinstitute.org/index.php?act=crbArticle&id=1452#.U8bdQLEUp2A; Harold W. Rood, "The War for Iraq," Claremont Institute, April 2003, http://www.claremont.org/publications/pubid.285/pub_detail.asp. Rood discussion with the authors.

52. The discussion of America's Pacific strategy is taken from Harold W. Rood, "The Increasing Soviet Presence in the Pacific" (Claremont Institute, 1988).

53. Harold W. Rood, "Toward a Defense of the West: Spain," *Grand Strategy: Countercurrents*, August 1, 1981, 1.

54. Rood, *Kingdoms of the Blind*, 281. Nor would the Soviets have confined their operations to Europe, Rood noted. Soviet occupation of Japan would have been nearly as serious a blow to the West as the occupation of Europe. Japanese industrial capacity in Soviet hands, and the use of the Japanese Home Islands as a base for deploying Soviet military, naval, and air power, would make the Western Pacific untenable for U.S. forces. The United States would face the same decision about whether it would have to destroy the Japanese industrial base to prevent its exploitation by the USSR. Ibid., 284.

55. "The fact that the Philippine and American forces held out until May 1942 tied down Japanese sea, air and ground units that would otherwise have been used to seize territory in Australia before the Allies were prepared to defend the country. The cost to the Japanese lay in the men, ships and planes lost to take the Philippines and in the delay to the development of strategic operations, a delay that permitted the Allies to meet and stop the Japanese at Guadalcanal." Ibid., 195n93.

56. Rood, "A Free Society in an Unfree World," 68.

57. Harold W. Rood, "Economy of Force" (unpublished manuscript), Print.

58. Rood, "Toward a Defense of the West: Spain," 1; Rood discussion with the authors.

59. Harold W. Rood, "'Masters of the Narrow See': The British Isles in the Defense of the West," *Grand Strategy: Countercurrents*, October 1, 1981, 1–6.

60. Harold W. Rood, "Norway: Bastion of the North," *Grand Strategy: Countercurrents*, March 1, 1982, 13–17.

# SEVEN

# The "End" of the Cold War

*Professor Rood was uncomfortable with the term "Cold War." The term suggests that the Soviet-American conflict had something of a unique character, that it was political not military, and that it had a beginning and an end. Thus Rood's startling view that the Cold War never ended is really not so startling when put in this context. Whatever one might think of the Cold War, for Rood the Russian Problem remained.*

*We try to frame Rood's perspective on the "end" of the Cold War in a way that points to the enduring strategic problems America will face in the future. Because Rood's approach was specifically focused on the actions of the great powers to serve their strategic purposes, much of Rood's analysis of this period — from the first Gulf War through the Global War on Terrorism — stands apart from more accepted expositions. The student should already be familiar with these standard accounts to appreciate fully Rood's completely different perspective on this period.*[1]

*Rood ended where he began: war is coming — little ones for sure and a big one if we are not careful. This conviction informed his understanding of why and how the United States should act to protect and promote its strategic interests in the twenty-first century. His conclusion that it was necessary to fight in Iraq in 2003, in order to anchor the United States in a strategically vital region — not principally to eliminate weapons of mass destruction (WMD) or a terror-supporting state or spread democracy in the heart of Islam — is instructive beyond the case. His conclusion flowed from his central premise that international politics is about the struggle for strategic advantage in both peace and war, and that the nation that best sustains its advantages will be best suited to prosper in peacetime, avoid war in crisis, and win wars if necessary.*

One September day in 1978, Rood addressed the Winston Churchill Society at the American Political Science Association's annual convention in

Washington, D.C. He listed a host of indicators that the Soviets might not have peace and international comity first and foremost on their minds. Present at the speech from the Soviet Embassy was a close-cropped gentleman in a gray suit and shiny shoes. After the speech he rose, introduced himself, and asked, "If we are as powerful as you say we are, why haven't we crushed you long ago?"

"I don't know, sir," said Rood, backing up a step or two and giving the close-cropped man a quizzical look. "Perhaps you can tell us."[2]

As we know now, the West remained uncrushed. War did not occur. A little more than a decade after that exchange, the Berlin Wall fell, and shortly thereafter the Soviet empire in Eastern Europe disintegrated. Within a few years the Soviet Union itself was gone. The Fulda Gap, now deep inside a united Germany, remained peaceful.

So was Rood wrong? He wrote in *Kingdoms of the Blind* that "if the West prepares for war and no war comes, we may enjoy the freedom of criticizing ourselves for our foolishness." Were Rood and his students therefore foolish?[3]

The case can be made that Rood was right in the essentials. In concluding *Kingdoms of the Blind*, he wrote: "It is far cheaper to win an arms race than lose a war."[4] That is a reasonable point of departure, or working hypothesis, to begin to understand "the end of the Cold War."

Let us explore that hypothesis, which follows the general perspective on history and strategy taught by Rood. By the early 1980s, the Soviets had reached a point of diminishing marginal returns in their efforts to reorganize the international system to their liking. Perhaps they had even reached a point of no return in preparing for war. During the later stages of the Carter administration and throughout the Reagan administration, the United States itself took the possibility of war much more seriously, and began to follow the general outlines of the strategy called for by Rood. This strategy included a major rearmament program (although not as much as Rood would have preferred); the development of a military policy and corresponding force posture designed explicitly to defeat Soviet strategy; and the use of public and private indicators signaling that the United States was prepared to take the geopolitical initiative against the Soviet empire and even the Russian homeland (for example, the Reagan Doctrine, the Maritime Strategy, AirLand Battle, and Samuel Huntington's notion of conventional retaliation into Eastern Europe).[5]

The United States, meanwhile, took steps to secure its position in the Western Hemisphere through operations in Grenada and Nicaragua. American strategic planners conceptualized a revolution in military affairs in which U.S. technological superiority would negate the Soviet quantitative military buildup of the previous few decades (for example, the Strategic Defense Initiative), and otherwise place stresses on the Soviet military modernization programs and infrastructure. NATO did not buckle under Soviet intimidation, and the European allies permitted the deployment of U.S. intermediate-range nuclear force systems (which the Soviets evidently took very seriously on military, not just political grounds).

The United States, in the spirit of the Reagan Doctrine, actively began to roll back Soviet incremental gains and to achieve some marginal advantages of its own, by striking through proxies at exposed salients in the Soviet Eurasian cordon (for example, in Afghanistan); by supporting political resistance in Eastern Europe (notably, in Poland); by putting pressure on the Soviet economy (for example, by encouraging the Saudis and others to push down the price of oil); and by closing off the transfer of vital technology, through overt and covert means. The strategic recovery of the United States gave the Chinese and others a powerful incentive to shift to the Western side, or at least to remain neutral, rather than cutting the best deal they could with Moscow. Rood's critical war-warning signal—that of an open PRC-USSR rapprochement—never occurred, due in large part to astute U.S. diplomacy, coupled with an advantageous shift in the balance of military power toward the West.

The Soviets, according to this strategic hypothesis, faced a fundamental choice in the early 1980s. Their command economy could not long continue to sustain the overwhelming strain that massive military spending (relative to GDP) placed on the system. The Kremlin could have tried to cash in on its rapidly diminishing strategic advantages by going to war—that had been Hitler's choice in the late 1930s, when Germany was faced with a similar situation (of course, Hitler had planned on war all along; the only question was one of timing). Or, with trends moving against them, the Soviets might have sought to "reboot" the game in order to regain the strategic initiative later, after a period of foreign retrenchment and domestic reform. This shift of Soviet tactics, although not of strategic ambitions, would be covered up by a charm offensive and disinformation.

During this period, the Soviets also went through a change of generational leadership. It was not foreordained who would come out on top and what position they would take concerning this monumental choice about the future of the communist world. In the end, those leaders who found themselves in power in the Kremlin collectively chose the course of foreign retrenchment and domestic reform. Some apparently believed sincerely that socialism with a human face was possible, and that their "new thinking" in international relations could lead to an era of peace and cooperation. Other Soviet leaders, more cynically, perhaps thought they could maneuver rather than fight their way to socialist victory.

As Rood would have told either camp in the Kremlin, the world doesn't work that way. Soviet leaders of both stripes either forgot the essential role of force in maintaining the Soviet regime (as well as its external empire), or they lacked the stomach to employ it, or they simply lost faith in the Soviet project entirely. In particular, they lacked the stom-

ach for war with the West, which another set of leaders might have employed in order to try to resolve the contradictions and weaknesses of the
Soviet project. Things in the Soviet bloc spiraled out of control, and what
was left of the regime had no choice but to settle the Cold War on Western terms, including the reunification of a Germany that remained in
NATO. The United States, partly by chance, but perhaps with more design than Rood would have credited, had found a way to impose strategic defeat on the Soviets. America, with its improved military posture,
did not have to go to war, because its goal—containment of the communist threat—did not require defeating the Soviets on their own soil. At
this point, diplomacy played a critical role, by allowing both sides peacefully to ratify changes in their strategic relationship that reflected the
basic shift in the balance of power.

Of course, there were, and are, many other interpretations of the end
of the Cold War, many of which give far more credit to chance, diplomacy, and the sincerity and moderation of the Soviet leadership, than to
Western strength and resolve. Clearly, a remarkable juxtaposition of
leaders (Reagan, Thatcher, François Mitterrand, Helmut Kohl, Gorbachev, and Eduard Shevardnadze, among others ) played a critical role.

Rood's own particular take, predictably, went entirely against the
grain of all the conventional explanations. The demise of the Soviet Union, understood as an "objective" phenomenon, could be explained as a
gigantic strategic deception, or self-deception on the part of the West. The
Soviet Union, now Russia, arguably continued its pattern of making political gains by means short of war, which ultimately would have the
effect of improving its capacity to go to war at a time and place of its own
choosing.

For instance, Soviet/Russian policy had consistently aimed to weaken
or eliminate the U.S. military presence in Europe. As a result of the apparent collapse of the Soviet threat, Rood pointed out, the bulk of U.S.
ground and air forces devoted to NATO's defense, especially the combat
elements, were disbanded or were deployed elsewhere, because the
threat seemed to have disappeared. Russian forces, of course, are no
longer stationed in what was once called Eastern Europe, but geography
has not changed. Even a diminished Russia is still only a few hundred
miles from the German border, while the United States will always be
thousands of miles away. The likelihood of U.S. forces returning to Europe in any substantial numbers is now essentially nil, as is the possibility
of a meaningful increase in European defense capability to make up the
difference. The American military assets best suited to project power outside of Europe, those based on the territory of its most reliable and democratic allies, are fewer and may soon be gone.[6]

Rood was one of the few strategic analysts, if any, who maintained
that the Soviets/Russians did not face a true systemic crisis, and that the
USSR/Russia's position as a dominant power was never truly in jeopar-

dy. For instance, he criticized the journalist William Pfaff, who wrote in August 1988 that "the real struggle for the Soviet Union is simply to survive as a serious nation."[7]

Pfaff's analysis would soon seem to be vindicated, as the Soviet Union ceased to exist a few years later. But as time has passed, Rood noted, the centuries-long Russian Problem evidently has not been solved; nor is there a new era of peace and harmony between Russia and its neighbors. "[O]ne may believe that Communism was ended with a stroke of the pen in East Germany, Czechoslovakia, Hungary, Romania, Bulgaria, Albania and the Soviet Union," Rood wrote, but "the organization remains."[8] And, as Rood pointed out, the character of the people at the top has not changed, either. He thought that it was no accident that the president of the Russian Federation—the man who spoke of the demise of the Soviet Union as the greatest geopolitical tragedy of the twentieth century—was a former KGB apparatchik. Russian planes still occasionally fly mock bombing runs against North America and fly in and out of Cuba. Russia opposes any sort of U.S. military presence in Central Europe, such as ballistic missile defenses (BMD), that might serve as a significant barrier to the extension of Russia's strategic influence.

Moscow still acts as if it wants to disrupt the U.S. strategic perimeter elsewhere in Eurasia, such as the Mediterranean. The Kremlin treats Syria as a client state, the anchor of Russian influence in the Middle East. (In 2014, we would note that the Russian Defense Minister announced that Russia was seeking to negotiate air and naval access rights to facilities in Cuba, Venezuela, Nicaragua, Algeria, Cyprus, the Seychelles, Vietnam, and Singapore.) The Russians, Rood pointed out, maintain a significant strategic and tactical nuclear arsenal, which they continue to modernize, along with an improved missile defense capability.[9]

Perhaps all this is pure nostalgia on the part of the Russians, or merely the resumption of "ordinary" great power jostling—the search for prestige and political advantage—in which the possibility of major war is no longer a salient issue. Those convenient explanations struck Rood, however, as precisely one of those deceptions that Russian (and Chinese) leaders would want to promote, and that Western officials and intellectuals would be eager to hear. Surely, we are reassured, there can be no return to the Cold War; Russian assertiveness on the international scene, we are told, cannot cover up the fact that it has grave internal problems and limited external power, which will prevent it from challenging the Western-led liberal order.

Rood would entertain, at least for the sake of discussion, the argument that the Russians had indeed suffered a major strategic setback at the end of the 1980s, something akin to defeat. Even if that were the case, however, he argued that Russia, like Germany after the First World War, had not accepted any diminution in its basic geopolitical goals. The enduring Russian Problem, Rood believed, cannot be considered "solved" for the same reason that the German Problem had not been solved in 1918. Germany had not been defeated on German soil, just as Russia has not been defeated on Russian soil. The German Problem, as it manifested itself from 1871 to 1945, was only solved when the Allies met in Berlin and dictated a peace that included the division of Germany and the change of regime. Rood, as we noted above, did not argue for the defeat of Russia (the Soviet Union) on Russian soil, unless that became necessary as the result of a war begun by Moscow. But the fact that Russia, like Germany after 1918, had not been occupied meant that, in the mind of its leaders and people, it had not truly been defeated. It had been cheated out of its rightful place in the sun by traitors and scheming foreign enemies. [10]

If that were the case, then the Kremlin most likely began to take covert steps to recover its position almost immediately after the fall of the Berlin Wall and the dissolution of the Soviet Union, just as democratic Germany had done after signing the Armistice in 1918. If so, Russia has been on the path to strategic recovery for over two decades now. "In 1918, Germany avoided decisive defeat by accepting an armistice, withdrawing its armies from France and Belgium, and by conforming, more or less, to the conditions imposed by the Treaty of Versailles," Rood observed. "But the outcome of the war gave Germany no reason to abandon its aims of reorganizing Europe, nor did the victorious allies put into force those measures that would prevent Germany's accumulating the material means and strategic position with which to try again." [11]

Or, to take an even more relevant case from history: post-czarist Russia signed the Treaty of Brest Litovsk with Germany as a temporary expedient, to allow it to exit a war that it was losing, while expecting that the territory it had to sacrifice (and more) would be recovered when circumstances permitted. This was indeed what happened. During the 1920s and 1930s, Germany turned to its former enemy, the Soviet Union, for covert assistance, and later for an open alliance, in order to break down the Versailles settlement. Post-1989, in Rood's opinion, Russia and China have had the same set of incentives to work together, at least for a time. [12]

If Rood's judgment about the continuity of the Russian Problem is correct, at some point it will become irrelevant as a matter of policy whether Russia engaged in a vast strategic deception to fool the West about its purported weakness, or whether it actually had been weak but then recovered. The end state for American strategy would be the same. Rood pointed out that Germany's path to Paris was much easier in 1940 than it had been in 1914, when Germany had been defeated. Rood might ask whether Russia's path to the English Channel would be even easier and safer in the future than it would have been at the height of the Cold War. If that is the operative analogy, then, in Rood's view, the United States should now actively be seeking to "put into force those measures that would prevent [Russia] accumulating the material means and strategic position with which to try again." [13]

## WHY FIGHT IN IRAQ

"Why should one believe that the great struggle between and amongst the powers of the world, ended with the self-disintegration of the Soviet Union?" Rood asked in 2003.

> Those struggles had gone on from before Rome became an empire, continued after the end of the Roman Empire right through the formation of England, France, Russia, the Ottoman Empire, and the unification of Germany and the founding of the United States through the 20th century. Did such struggles cease with Gorbachev? Yeltsin? and, Putin? Will, in the new era, after the "Cold War," the rise of India as a potential power with nuclear weapons be acceptable to the folks who rule in Beijing and Moscow? Will they wait and see if India makes it to the top, or prudently act to prevent it along the way? Is that the way things go? For 800 years French policy aimed at preventing the unification of Germany. Did France wait until Germany was unified to see if it would be bad for France? No, they acted where they could to prevent it, even though the policy failed: . . . Did Japan wait until China was unified to act against China? No . . . there was a concept at work having to do with the defense of Japan against the rise of a great land power on the mainland of Asia. [14]

Rood thus anticipated that, among other things, a rising India would become part of the larger Problems of Asia (which turn fundamentally, as we have seen, on the political condition of China). China, once weak and divided and occupied by foreign powers, has undergone a process of reunification and economic and strategic modernization (a process not yet fully complete). It now clearly thinks of itself as a rising power, determined to regain its place in the sun. The People's Liberation Army is pursuing an anti-access military strategy designed to prevent the United States from operating within its sphere of Asian maritime influence—essentially rolling back the American strategic perimeter in the Pacific. (Seen in this light, the geopolitical analysis in Rood's "Distant Rampart" essay, which might have seemed quaint a few decades ago, now seems quite insightful.) Rood noted that China is also out and about in the broader world, taking a more active role in the Middle East, investing and deploying personnel in South America and Africa, and, together with Russia, aligning itself with despots such as (the late) Hugo Chavez.

Meanwhile, Rood pointed out, Russia and China have declared their opposition to any measure that would increase the capability of the United States to defend itself. Declaring it "a milestone in the development of Russia-Chinese relations," the leaders of Russia and China "sealed a strategic partnership" on July 16, 2001, and in doing so condemned the American plan for a missile defense of the United States. Considering that Russia remains the strongest military power in Europe (in Rood's opinion), armed with strategic nuclear weapons, and that China is the strongest military power in Asia, also armed with strategic nuclear weapons, such a *"strategic* partnership" is a formidable one. Rood quoted a professor at the Institute of Asian and African Studies at Moscow State University, who said, "The treaty has one purpose—to show the United States that there are two countries that can be together against the United States." [15]

Rood concluded, therefore, that the United States still faces challenges by a coalition of hostile powers that seeks to reorganize the international system to their individual likings. That reorganization will require the ejection of the United States from Eurasia. The United States, to counter this pressure, should be seeking to assure itself the necessary strategic depth and allies in Europe, Asia, and the Middle East, so that its future wars will be fought overseas; and to guarantee that it can still decide the outcome of Eurasian wars when it finds it in its interest to do so.

Rood's most detailed reflections on how to think about future American grand strategy might be summed up as, "Why Fight in Iraq," the updated counterpart of "Why Fight in Vietnam." [16] Rood pointed to the ongoing Middle Eastern Question as evidence that the struggle for Eurasian supremacy did not cease with the so-called end of the Cold War. The Middle Eastern Question, as we recall, could be summarized: "when some great struggle is underway in Europe, the adversaries, whenever capable of doing so, will seek whatever strategic advantage that can be gained through alliance with a Middle Eastern power, or intervention in a Middle Eastern dispute." [17] The Middle Eastern Question has now clearly taken on a global dimension, not merely limited to its impact on Europe.

As we have seen, the Middle Eastern Question manifested itself forcefully with the Iraqi invasion of Kuwait in August 1990. Rood regarded Iraq as a Soviet client state despite Gorbachev's diplomatic support for the coalition. (Rood thought this a typical Soviet/Russian ploy of trying to be on both sides in a war, so as to win either way.) At the time, however, Saddam Hussein's aggression created an enormous strategic opportunity for the United States. By his threat to the Saudi oil fields and his possession of WMD, Rood believed that Saddam gave legitimate domestic and international cause for the United States to remove a major Soviet (Russian) client state. The United States had the luxury of cashing in on the (supposed) end of the Cold War to achieve a real strategic gain, thereby strengthening its position in Eurasia.

The United States did not immediately remove Saddam, however. Rood believed that this led to unfortunate side-effects in the region, which perhaps had been anticipated by the Soviets/Russians. The continuation of air operations by Britain and the United States against Iraq for thirteen years did not persuade the regime in Iraq to become any less of a threat in the Middle East than it was in 1990, as Rood saw matters. The dithering of the international community and the divisions created in the Western Alliance were all the result of failing to remove the Iraq regime in 1991. Rood noted that the incomplete outcome of Operation Desert Storm left American military forces deployed near the holy places in Saudi Arabia, providing a pretext for radical Muslims to stir things up, including plotting terrorist attacks directed specifically against the United States.

Rood noted that radical Muslim sentiment, objectively speaking, served Russian interests, insofar as both parties sought to eject the United States from the Middle East. (The possibility that such cooperation might be active and that the Russians might be behind certain "Muslim" acts of terrorism should have been a matter of further research, in Rood's view.) "The attack on USS *Cole* in Yemen, the attack on U.S. embassies in Africa, the two attacks on the World Trade Center, one in 1993, and the second in September 2001 that included a coordinated attack on the Pentagon were carried out by organizations having roots in the Middle East. Those can be seen as strategic attacks for they were aimed at changing U.S. policy toward the Middle East," Rood wrote. "Whose interests would be served were the United States to renounce Israel and give up on disarming Iraq?"[18] Cui bono?

Rood concluded that when the airplanes hit the twin towers on 9/11:

> It should have been without hesitation a principle of strategic policy that a devastating attack on the United States—such as that of September 11, 2001—would call forth measures by the U.S. government to gain some strategic advantage in a struggle for which that attack gave ample evidence. The United States should have, within a week of that attack, moved swiftly against Libya to remove its dictator from power. That would have changed the resolution of forces in the Mediterranean and Middle East. Spain, Italy, France and Germany would have had reason to applaud, if only in the recesses of their government houses. It would have lent assurance to Morocco and Tunisia that alliance to the West was worth something to their internal stability. Algeria, caught between the Islamic fundamentalists and its ties to France, would have been free to settle its own affairs without interference from the regime in Tripoli.[19]

Rood did not take seriously the idea that Al-Qaeda, as such, represented a *strategic* threat to the United States. He thought the United States missed a major opportunity to gain a tangible strategic advantage by not taking out an enduring strategic liability such as Libya, "but instead began the pursuit of a bearded figure and his fellows in far away Afghanistan. As the French might say, 'They seek him here, they seek him there, they seek him everywhere, the elusive Pimpernel.'" Rood acknowledged that "pursuing terrorists to bring them to justice is a necessary part of life in the 21st century," but "it is not a substitute for measures aimed at gaining strategic advantage for the United States and the Western Alliance. For strategic advantage increases the freedom to act effectively, even against terrorists."[20]

The basic strategic problem for American national security policy, according to Rood, remained the need to deal with the coalition of hostile powers that aimed to push the United States out of the Middle East; a coalition that was taking advantage of—or possibly even directing—terrorist activities to that end. The 9/11 attacks should have reminded Americans of the price to be paid for fighting wars on their own territory. Rood may have focused on Libya because of its close ties with international terrorism, as well as its strategic importance in the Mediterranean and its long-standing relationship with the Soviets/Russians. That connection with terrorism, in Rood's mind, would have provided the United States with a convincing public justification, in the aftermath of 9/11, to deal with a lingering and very real strategic weakness.

Having neglected that particular opportunity, Rood thought it even more important to finish the job in Iraq after a decade of strategic drift with respect to the Middle Eastern Question. Rood supported the U.S. decision to go to war in 2003 as a necessary means to put an end, finally, to the Persian Gulf War that had begun in 1990. He concluded that this should be done for reasons of basic strategy, not to overthrow a tyrant who was oppressing his own people or to bring democracy to the Middle East.[21] "Removing a dictator from power is, no doubt, a laudable enterprise for civilized people to undertake, but evidently a never-ending task," Rood argued. "Waging war to do so is bloody and expensive. But if the dictator poses a threat to the safety of the United States and that of those countries upon which that safety in part depends, war is the only reasonable course of action when all else fails."[22]

Exactly what threat did Saddam pose to the safety of the United States? Iraq's seizure of Kuwait in August 1990 opened the possibility that Saddam would overrun Saudi Arabia, the Emirates, Qatar, and Bahrain. At the very least, these states could be cowed into an Iraqi orbit. For Rood, this mattered primarily because he still regarded Iraq as a Russian proxy in the ongoing conflict to resolve the latest round of the Middle Eastern Question. The Kremlin was the primary beneficiary of the continued existence of Iraq's regime, and of any future military progress it might make in changing the balance of power on the Arabian Peninsula. As to the threat posed by Iraq's presumed possession of WMD, Rood wrote:

> It should not be forgotten that the impetus of the current conflict—the continued possession and development of weapons of mass destruction—cannot today be stopped by any other means. The United States

does not possess a ballistic missile defense that would render Iraq's weapons useless. Today the United States must suffer an attack and retaliate, presumably, with our own weapons of mass destruction. Such a missile defense should be built with all speed. Absent such a defense we are faced now with the only reasonable alternative.[23]

This was a rather general judgment on Rood's part about the WMD and ballistic missile threats, which could have been applied to various adversaries of the United States besides Iraq. Rood spoke of Iraq's WMD as the "impetus" of the current conflict, but not its underlying cause; and he certainly did not base his case for war on that ground. He argued, instead, that the United Nations' sanctions and inspections regime could not be relied upon to control Iraq's military posture writ large. Rood also expected that Saddam would continue to receive help from abroad by those whose interests dictated the survival of his regime.

In Rood's judgment, the United States would be prudent to take the necessary occasion of removing this particular dictator and disarming his regime, to anchor itself strategically more firmly in a key region (as it should have done in Vietnam), while disrupting the hostile campaign to diminish the American presence in Eurasia. The American-led war in Iraq should serve as a "reconnaissance in force" to determine who was friend and who was foe; and to determine whether the great struggle of the last half of the twentieth century was over, as declared, or merely in recess. The United States should determine whether Moscow and Beijing were still seriously engaged in a conflict with the West, and whether the Middle East was but one theater of that conflict. Rood himself had few if any doubts on that score, but he hoped that the war would clarify things before the United States suffered a devastating loss there, or elsewhere. Americans, he said, should know that for their own safety.[24]

Rood believed that Russian (and Chinese) activities before and after Operation Iraqi Freedom amply demonstrated their hostile strategic intentions, and their view of Iraq as a strategic asset. In April 2003, while the second war for Iraq was under way, elements of the Russian Fleet from the Black Sea and the Pacific began deployment from Sebastopol and Vladivostok. They joined together off the Yemeni island of Socotra in the Gulf of Aden, whence they were to proceed together to join in exercises with the Indian Navy.

How was one to explain this activity, so far away from the Russian heartland? Rood noted that the waters of the Gulf of Aden are an extension of the Indian Ocean, which washes the shores of Yemen and Oman and extends into the Red Sea toward the Suez Canal; the waters of the Persian Gulf enter via the Gulf of Oman into the Arabian Sea that is part of the Indian Ocean. Such maritime routes have been, and remain, fundamental to the movement of commercial goods among the ports of the world. But these routes are equally fundamental to the movement of naval forces in support of the strategic interests of maritime powers and their allies. Rood noted that the two Iraq wars demonstrated the ability of naval power to support the operation of land forces in a country where a military decision is being sought by powers not resident in the region.

> The recognition by those who rule in Moscow, as well as those who think of such things in India, that strategic matters are at stake in the Indian Ocean and adjacent waters, should suggest that such matters are still at stake for the United States as well. The fact that Australia, lying in the Indian Ocean, should see its interest to be engaged enough to deploy forces to fight in Iraq implies that what happens in the Middle East has some strategic importance to Australia. But then the region of the Middle East, even before oil became important, has been a place where distant powers, capable of doing so, have felt compelled to intervene to support their endeavors elsewhere.[25]

Four years later, in 2007, Rood offered a considered assessment of the war in Iraq. He judged that it certainly had accrued strategic advantages to the United States. Iraq had been removed as a protégé of Russia and was no longer as disruptive force in the Middle East. For the moment at least, there was one less frontline state aligned against Israel; an anti-American Iraq could no longer exercise influence over its neighbor, Jordan; and Yemen had lost a possible ally against Saudi Arabia. The vigor and resolution of the coalition led by the United States in the prosecution of the war in Iraq made the United States appear to be a formidable enemy to those in the Middle East who had hostile intentions. It did not remove those enemies, but it made them wary of pursuing policies that might call down upon themselves the kind of intervention that had liberated Iraq from its dictatorship. Of course, Rood acknowledged, a consistent American policy in the region could be subject to the erosion inflicted by the shifting political climate in the United States. No Middle Eastern country, or its mentors, would be unaware of that fact.[26]

Rood, then writing at the height of the insurgency in Iraq, reflected on the difficulties faced by the United States and its coalition partners in the reconstruction and pacification of that land. We recall his argument in 2003 that the United States had not gone, or should not have gone, to war in Iraq to overthrow a tyrant or foster democracy, but for reasons of strategy. Still, if the United States failed to stabilize Iraqi politics, then it would fail to achieve its overall strategic objective as well. He saw no reason for despair or throwing in the towel in the face of what seemed, to many experts and the media, to be an intractable insurgency—any more than he despaired of success against the guerrillas in Vietnam.

Rood postulated that the establishment of good order in Iraq depended on the judicious exercise of military power to suppress violent resistance, the restoration of the public services, and ultimately the will of the Iraqi people. What seemed like liberation to the coalition looked like a war of conquest to some, or even most, Iraqis. Those Iraqis not aligned with Saddam realized that they had not been freed of despotism through their own endeavors but by foreigners with numerous tanks, aircraft, and high explosives. Hostility and resistance to what many Iraqis saw as a foreign infidel occupying force was to be expected. They could hardly appreciate that the war fought within their land was a discriminating one, aimed not at the destruction of their country but only at the regime's ability to resist its overthrow.

Iraq has never before been a place where political freedom has flourished, Rood observed. Political turbulence is the principal tradition that Iraqis have had to look back upon since the country's independence from four centuries of rule by the Ottoman Empire (which suppressed turbulence by force). Saddam's dictatorship used terror and force as the basis of civil government. Access to the reins of government by the citizens of Iraq has not been, since 1918, a characteristic of the Iraqi constitution. Iraq has the people and resources to become a prosperous state. But, as Rood wrote, miracles cannot be expected, nor should it have been expected that Iraq would quickly evolve into a stable democracy. Like the conduct of the war, the restoration of order in Iraq required resolution, determination, patience, and the deliberate and discriminating application of force where necessary. Whatever resentments the Iraqi people might harbor against their liberators could be set against concern for the safety of person, family, and community, and the promise of prosperity.

Establishing order and encouraging the construction of administration and government serviceable to the Iraqi people are noble enterprises, Rood observed. Iraq can be made a decent and comfortable place for its ordinary citizens to live and prosper. But Rood cautioned that such an expectation, with its hope and promise, is subject to political passions, deeply rooted animosities, and resistance to foreign intervention. Its success would ultimately be up to the Iraqi people themselves.

As to the broader strategic picture, Rood wrote that removing Iraq from the ranks of militant Arab states, for the time being anyway, still left the rest to be dealt with. Decoupling Iraq from its Moscow connections rendered other radical states even more valuable as strategic assets for Moscow if it still conceived that, despite "the ending of the Cold War," the struggle with the Western democracies continued. If that is still the case, in Rood's judgment, the militant Arab states remain as strategic outriders in that struggle, and ought to be dealt with in that light by a comprehensive Western strategy aimed at defanging them. Otherwise, they are nuisances to be handled as occasion demands with the appropriate applications of diplomacy and military power.

Whether the American advantage gained in Iraq was to endure, Rood concluded, would depend not just on the run of politics within the United States; it would also depend on the ability of unfriendly countries to exploit international hostility toward American intervention, and to find other means to counter these U.S. advantages. Rood did not suppose that Syria and Iran would accept the neutralization of Iraq by the coalition as a reason to moderate their hostility to the Western alliance, and especially to the leader of that alliance. "It is well to remember that Syria's army, navy, and air force were equipped and trained by the Soviet Union," Rood wrote, "and after the Soviet Union was dissolved, by Moscow."[27] Nor could one expect Moscow to encourage such moderation, or to dismiss its own interests in the region. Nations that see future benefits from the pursuit of strategic competition do not easily abandon such competition because of a setback; they seek means to turn the setback to advantage.

Rood concluded that the United States had neutralized Iraq, but had not dealt with other hostile nations claiming leadership of the Arab world. Nor had it resolved the terrible weakness of the Saudi regime in the face of Arab-Islamic terrorism; that weakness was and is the logical strategic point to be exploited by the enemies of the United States. Thus Rood concluded: "It doesn't take a higher degree in social studies for those hostile to the West to understand the vulnerability of Saudi Arabia, or the value to the militant Arab cause of possession of the holy places of Islam by a new regime in Saudi Arabia—one constituted to carry on the struggle that Syria, Libya, Yemen, and Iran seem dedicated to, and that Iraq has been forced to abandon, at least for a time."[28]

## NOTES

1. For an argument that war among great powers has become obsolete, see John Mueller, *Retreat from Doomsday: The Obsolescence of Major War* (New York: Basic Books, 1989). Among those who emphasize threats and challenges outside of the great-power conflict model, see Samantha Power, *"A Problem from Hell": America and the Age of Genocide* (New York: HarperCollins, 2002); and Graham Allison, *Nuclear Terrorism: The Ultimate Preventable Catastrophe* (New York: Holt, 2004).

2. Ward Elliot and Dennis Teti, in *Memories of Professor Bill Rood, Scholar and Gentleman, from his Students, Colleagues, and Friends*, ed. Patrick J. Garrity, Christopher Harmon, and Colleen Sheehan (unpublished manuscript, January 2012), Print, 18–19, 73.

3. Harold W. Rood, *Kingdoms of the Blind: How the Great Democracies Have Resumed the Follies that So Nearly Cost Them Their Life* (Durham: Carolina Academic Press, 1980), 285.

4. Ibid.

5. For more detailed treatments of the argument that the Reagan administration had a grand strategy that followed the general lines that we set out, and that it was by and large successful, see, for instance, John Lewis Gaddis, *Strategies of Containment: A Critical Appraisal of American National Security Policy During the Cold War* (New York: Oxford University Press, 2005), 342–79; Hal Brands, *What Good Is Grand Strategy? Power and Purpose in American Statecraft from Harry S. Truman to George W. Bush* (Ithaca: Cornell University Press, 2014), 102–43; John Arquilla, *The Reagan Imprint: Ideas in American Foreign Policy from the Collapse of Communism to the War on Terror* (Chicago: Ivan R. Dee, 2006); Steven F. Hayward, *The Age of Reagan: The Conservative Counterrevolution* (New York: Random House, 2009); and Peter Schweizer, *Victory: The Reagan Administration's Secret Strategy That Hastened the Collapse of the Soviet Union* (New York:

Atlantic Monthly Press, 1994). Not all of these authors would necessarily agree fully with this strategic hypothesis (or with each other), but they provide useful points of departure to consider how the Cold War ended.

6. Rood discussion with the authors; Harold W. Rood, "AVOT—Harold W. Rood on the War in Iraq," Claremont Institute, October 2007, http://www.claremont.org/projects/pageid.2501/default.asp.

7. Quoted in Harold W. Rood, "Handwritten Notes on Gorbachev and Reform" (unpublished manuscript, 1988), Print.

8. Harold W. Rood, "The War for Iraq," Claremont Institute, April 2003, http://www.claremont.org/publications/pubid.285/pub_detail.asp.

9. The following analysis of the continuities of Russian strategy are based on Rood discussion with the authors; Rood, "The War for Iraq," and Rood, "AVOT—Harold W. Rood on the War in Iraq."

10. Rood discussion with the authors. We stress that this was a contingent argument by Rood, who preferred the case that there was greater design and continuity in Russian policy from 1989 to the present than most would allow.

11. Harold W. Rood, "Soviet Strategy and the Defense of the West," *Global Affairs* 2 (Summer 1987): 4.

12. On this point Rood recommended that his students read John W. Wheeler-Bennett, *Brest-Litovsk: The Forgotten Peace, March 1918* (1938; repr., New York: St. Martin's, 1966).

13. Rood, "Soviet Strategy and the Defense of the West," 4.

14. Harold W. Rood, letter to Christopher Harmon (July 19, 2003), Print.

15. Quoted in Rood, "The War for Iraq."

16. Unless otherwise noted, the following argument about Iraq and American strategy is taken from Rood, "The War for Iraq" and Harold W. Rood, "The Long View: Democracy and Strategy in Iraq," *Claremont Review of Books* 3, no. 4 (Fall 2003), accessed July 18, 2014, http://www.claremont.org/article/the-long-view-democracy-and-strategy-in-iraq/#.VAsGtfldUpg.

17. Rood, "The Eastern Question: 'Peace in Our Times'" (unpublished manuscript, last modified 1989), Print, 13.

18. Rood, "The War for Iraq."

19. Ibid.

20. Ibid.

21. As we noted above, Rood did not dismiss the possibility that democracy might come to Iraq, but only as the result of a war that was fought for strategic reasons, and only after a very long time.

22. Rood, "The War for Iraq."

23. Ibid.

24. Even if the conflict between democracy and its enemies no longer defines international politics—if the Russians and Chinese have limited aims and were merely acting to protect their own interests—then reducing the number of Middle Eastern powers actively hostile to the United States was still important, in Rood's judgment. Iraq was worth taking out in its own right because it was at the center of those Middle Eastern countries whose hostility was directed at the United States: Libya, Yemen, Sudan, Syria, Iraq, and Iran. Ibid.

25. Quoted in Ibid.

26. The following analysis is taken from Rood, "AVOT—Harold W. Rood on the War in Iraq."

27. Ibid.

28. Ibid.

# Conclusion

## Rood's Challenges

We began this book with the observation that Professor Rood's teachings and scholarship challenged his students and colleagues to *think* for themselves about strategy. In doing so, history, observation, and common sense should be our guide. He made his arguments in the most provocative fashion to overcome the intellectual straitjacket of received wisdom, and he encouraged us to do the same. Rood believed that we should study strategy in this manner not merely because it is a pleasurable intellectual exercise, but mainly because the most important things rest upon it.

Thinking for oneself includes not accepting Rood's arguments uncritically. Serious and informed men and women, including those who studied with Rood, disagreed with his judgments about Vietnam or Tiananmen Square or Iraq. We have pointed out such criticisms at the appropriate point in the narrative. We offered some ourselves. The reader may decide who had the better of the particular arguments.

But setting aside his provocations, Rood offered a powerful template for understanding international politics as they have been carried on "since time immemorial," as he liked to say. If we apply that template to the future, what does strategy, rightly understood, have to teach us about long-terms issues and challenges to American security? What issues should we be thinking about and which strategic indicators should we be looking for? "In a world that can promise neither peace nor safety to sovereign nations," Rood challenged us, "it is the burden of statesmanship to look ahead to distant dangers that are today obscured by more immediate concerns, only visible, perhaps to the informed, thoughtful and far-sighted."[1] We should accept that challenge in the spirit with which it was issued, with the appropriate modesty for just how far-sighted it is possible to be.

Let us begin, first, with Rood's argument that human beings are *strategic* animals. They systematically employ power, in the form of politics and technology, to organize their physical and social environment to suit their sense of order and justice. This involves constant struggle within and among human communities. In the context of this struggle in the international realm, Rood believed that "you run the show or the show runs you." The essence of strategy is to array the proper military, diplomatic, economic, geographic, and psychological resources in optimum fashion, so as to be able to run the show, whether in peacetime or war-time. Rood contended that strategy, so defined, was possible and neces-sary—and ubiquitous. It is going on all around us, whether we choose to recognize it or not.

It strikes us that that there are two significant contrasting ways of looking at politics and strategy that run counter to Rood's position. We draw them here with a very broad brush to help clarify the fundamental issues at hand, and to put in context the challenges that Rood's strategic thought puts before us. We understand that individual policy makers and scholars have more nuanced views,[2] but these alternative perspec-tives have had, and continue to have, considerable influence in the for-mulation of U.S national security policy. They are worthy of serious con-sideration.

One viewpoint, or pole of thought, posits the essential harmony of human interests and rejects the notion of zero-sum, win-lose outcomes. Cooperation, not conflict, is, or should be, the natural state of affairs. International norms, not power, and certainly not hard power, should govern relations among communities. From a rational perspective, the human, economic, and environmental costs of modern wars vastly out-weigh the benefits. The mere existence of nuclear weapons reinforces the imperative of peace, certainly for the great powers. The proper end of policy is to expand the existing zone of peace, cooperation, and democra-cy, and to contain and ameliorate those remaining atavistic forces that have not yet gotten the message. Military force, in extremis, may be nec-essary to deal with such outliers, but for the most part, the U.S. military should be configured and deployed largely for political purposes—for example, to maintain existential deterrence, reassure allies, build cooper-ation, and signal diplomatic resolve. From this perspective, Rood's con-cept of strategy could lead to policies that interfere with the progressive evolution of the international system.

The other position, or pole of thought, accepts the fact that war and conflict will always be with us, but it emphasizes the limits of traditional notions of strategy, and perhaps the impossibility of strategy altogether. As recent developments in the Middle East and elsewhere have con-firmed, it is impossible to run the show with any sort of confidence. Those who try to do so are doomed to suffer the effects of imperial overstretch, unintended consequences, "blowback," the nonlinearity of human affairs, the intractability of culture, asymmetrical warfare, and the tyranny of the culminating point of victory. The world resists organiza-tion, whether by international norms, democratic governance, or tradi-tional instruments of power. One must proceed modestly, adopt low-regret policies, avoid binding commitments, and be exceptionally cau-tious of military solutions. Let others overextend themselves and suffer the consequences, while the United States husbands its resources to deal with truly critical threats.

The authors recognize that both major poles of thought—painted here, we emphasize again, with a very broad brush—have something important to say. There is indeed a liberal community of nations and peoples, call it the West if you will, that embraces the precepts of world order and democracy and that provides a zone of peace. This community is substantially the creation of the United States, but many others embrace it and still others will adhere to it if circumstances allow. It is by and large a good thing and worthy of strong support.

That said, Rood challenges us with the reminder that there are those who do not share these ideals. They regard them as threatening. They believe the United States and its allies are trying to run the show to their detriment and to undermine their way of life. They do not like it. They will resist by political means and by force when circumstances allow. In short, they will practice strategy. From time to time they will cooperate with each other in this endeavor, even if they have deeply conflicting interests of their own. And even within the West, how can we be sure that everyone will remain within the fold? The grooves of history run very deep and the pressures of politics and power are relentless. If the United States is to defend and advance a liberal world order, it will have to apply its power, including military power, and not merely its good will, to the task. Military power, in turn, must be guided by strategy and be focused on the outcomes of possible wars, not merely on its political and symbolic value.

As to the other set of criticisms of traditional strategy, we must acknowledge that developments since the fall of the Berlin Wall caution us against hubris or triumphalism. Even for a nation with the unprecedented relative power advantages possessed by the United States, it has been hard going. Yesterday's allies of convenience (China, Muslim rebels) have turned into today's adversaries, potential or real. Sometimes it is better to get out of the way of natural antagonisms, to let others exhaust themselves in futile conflicts. But resignation and passivity, which this perspective encourages, hardly seem like a recipe for success. If we cannot (and could not) control everything, surely we can control some essential things, or at least prevent hostile forces from doing so. Rood challenges us to apply strategic thought to decide what those things are. As to the idea of husbanding resources to meet truly critical challenges, Rood reminds us that this course is too often penny-wise and pound-foolish. When an existential threat does clearly emerge, it may be too late to react successfully. It is much better to anticipate threats and take precautionary action when the costs are lower—and not to fool ourselves with the illusion that the costs of defense in a hostile world will ever be low; or to allow fears of second-order consequences to rule the day. The price of defeat in the main is bound to be much greater.

Second, Rood challenged us with his argument that of all the instruments of political power, force is the effective (if not the final) arbiter of who rules among men. The contest for strategic advantage is not just a bloodless geopolitical chess game or intellectual abstraction, designed to score political points or gain leverage at the bargaining table. "There's going to be a war," Rood insisted. The contentious nature of international politics has not changed due to globalization, the existence of weapons of mass destruction, or our own recent difficult experience in Iraq and Afghanistan. The statesman and strategist must keep this fact—"there's going to be a war"—foremost in mind at all times. To fail to do so is to lose all hope of preventing a particular war from occurring and a likely recipe for defeat, or at least an excessively costly victory, if war does occur.

Here we run up against the argument that if we prepare for war, we will get war; and that we will miss opportunities for a peaceful settlement of international disputes. We should acknowledge that not every potential threat becomes a real one; not every crisis results in war; and every war must end. Blessed indeed are the peacemakers. Yet Rood's first order assumption—"there's going to be a war"—challenges us to clarify our thinking about real choices in the real world, such as the kind of war we might have to fight and the purposes for which it should be fought. Keeping this in mind when formulating policy is the best way to deter, or, if necessary, fight on our own terms.

Rood challenges us to be honest in this respect and not to assume that we will have our way in choosing the character of the wars that we may fight. As of this writing, the United States seems determined to avoid wars that involve nation-building activities (counterinsurgency), large-scale conventional operations on the Eurasian landmass, and wars involving nuclear weapons. This is understandable. We agree that hard thought must indeed be given to dealing with other types of military operations (for example, hybrid warfare, wars in the shadows, access-denial campaigns). But we must ask ourselves, are we ruling out the prospect of big conventional wars, or of nuclear weapons used against us, simply as a matter of political preference rather than as the result of hard strategic analysis? Others may not share that preference, and what were once areas of great American competitive military advantage may be lost, on the perhaps mistaken assumption that no one could dare take us on in those fields.

Third, Rood maintained that to understand truly the nature of international politics, and the reality that strategy is constantly at work in the world, one must appreciate the fact that nations will attempt to deceive each other about the fact, extent, nature, and purpose of their strategic preparations. He insisted on the principle that "nothing happens for no good reason." The clear and overt use of force, and obvious preparations for war, are only the tip of the iceberg. The strategic toolbox includes covert operations, propaganda, disinformation, "peaceful" economic investment, provocations, misdirection, and the like. Rood concluded that the West is particularly susceptible to deception because it believes that everyone else thinks and acts much as it does, and that there is a hard and fast line between "peace" and "war." Deception rapidly passes over into self-deception.

The authors recognize the counterargument that such analytical techniques, if overdone, can lead one into imagining connections among dots that do not actually exist, or imagining dots altogether. Conspiracy theories of one sort or another are rife in the Middle East, for instance, and this poisons the political climate there. Conspiracy theories play well in the movies, but real life is typically more mundane. People often make stupid mistakes, car crashes are usually just accidents, coincidences do occur.

That said, we cannot ignore anomalies that do not fit into the extant narrative about the direction of international politics. Why did the Soviets, the acknowledged masters of *maskirovka*, fail to take obvious precautions to conceal the deployment of missiles in Cuba? Did the Soviets fail to understand U.S. technical capabilities (despite the fact they were painfully aware of our U-2 photographic missions over Soviet territory)? Or was high state policy indeed at work? You won't know if you don't ask the question. Asking the question also gets one to the heart of the matter: in this case, the fact that, objectively speaking, the Soviets emerged from the crisis with the opportunity to consolidate their military position in the Caribbean-Cuban Salient.

Anomalies that suggest preparations for war should take on particular significance for the strategic analyst. They may reveal the political-military objectives of various powers and the means by which they intend to achieve them. In recent years, the United States and its allies have had a rough go of things in international politics. Rood challenges us to ask: What if our apparent loss of direction is not merely the result of uncontrollable historical forces, and the limits of our power and human foresight, but at least in part is due to the strategic purposes and actions of others? What if these purposes are long-standing, going back not only to 1991 but well before that? What if others are patiently accumulating the sort of strategic advantages that will put us at grave disadvantage in a war, or at least in a major political crisis, while attempting to conceal those preparations? Are objective conditions bringing about an alignment of hostile powers? These are the sort of questions we should be addressing, if only to find comfort in reasonable explanations, or if not, to regain the strategic initiative.

Fourth, Rood warned against the effects of the "democratic strategy deficit" — the propensity of democracies to downplay the likelihood of war; to believe that war will always be a matter of our choice; and to assume that we can have as much or as little of war as we choose. In the post-Iraq political climate, as in the aftermath of Vietnam, the default answer is likely to be the comforting belief that we will have little or no war in the future. This could lead to the neglect of strategy in peacetime and to the assumption that foreign policy need not take into account military factors.

History, however, strongly suggests that we will not forever enjoy the luxury of an easy choice for peace. When the strategic threat finally becomes clear, democracies have demonstrated that they can act forcefully and effectively. Rood challenges us to identify those actions that will minimize our strategic weaknesses during periods of democratic malaise and that will serve as the foundation for strategic recovery when the opportunity presents itself. Part of this process is to recognize the fact that democracies do exhibit certain traits in international politics that must be accommodated by statecraft. For example, it is difficult to sustain support for prolonged regional conflicts if those conflicts cannot be linked directly to threats to U.S. security. By the same token, we should recognize that totalitarians (and authoritarians) have their strategic deficits as well, different perhaps from those of the democracies, to be sure, but no less real. Hitler overreached, the Soviets (arguably) missed their moment, Saddam Hussein underestimated his enemies. We ought to be studying and exploiting those weaknesses, even as we seek to remedy our own.

Fifth, Rood argued that international politics are characterized by certain persistent patterns of great power interactions and their associated wars, as the great powers seek to organize the world to their liking or to keep others from doing so. Great powers exhibit these well-defined patterns of behavior despite apparent changes in political regimes. Certain "problems" in international politics have persisted for decades and centuries, often turning on the unification and division of nations. Identifying and understanding these problems permits the student of strategy to understand better what is going on in the world. Rood contended that the great problems of international relations should be studied closely because they vitally affect American security. They provide essential strategic indicators about the intentions and strategies of those powers capable of organizing the territory and resources of Eurasia.

Rood's categorization of the problems of international politics may seem outdated to those concerned with the very real contemporary threats posed by international terrorism, cybersecurity, transnational crime, and the like. Many of these threats seem to lack a geographic base and transcend the nation-state; they are everywhere and nowhere. Yet we would observe that those who pose such threats, if they are to follow the human imperative to organize and control their environment, must eventually link themselves with, or establish for themselves, political regimes that occupy a certain territory and have certain interests. As such, those who offer these new-age threats will enter into the realm of international politics and will affect, and be affected by, long-standing great power interests and conflicts.

Rood's roster of enduring problems of international politics challenges us to identify critical indicators that illuminate how the new threats may interact with the old problems. If Germany remains substantially demilitarized, how will it (and democratic Europe) cope with the violence and warfare that laps increasingly at its borders? Will the reunification of China—and perhaps efforts to create a greater China—bring about a new alignment of powers in Asia? Could Russia follow a trajectory similar to that of post–World War I Germany and seek to regain its place in the sun—or one similar to the Ottoman Empire in its terminal decline, with vultures circling over its remains? Who will attempt to fill the strategic vacuum that the United States seems to be leaving in the Middle East—and will our exit be "assisted" by those with even greater ambitions? How will the traditional great powers respond to the establishment of radical centers of power there? Will Russia, China, or radical elements become involved more heavily in the Caribbean-Cuban Salient? Above all, we must not ignore what Rood thought to be the most important indicator of a fundamental shift in the balance of power, the possible development of a real strategic partnership between Moscow and Beijing.

Sixth, in the context of his analysis of the Soviet threat, Rood offered a concise articulation of a transcendent American grand strategy. The most important American strategic objective, he explained, is, as it has always been, the prevention of direct attack upon the United States. If there is to be a war, Americans will want to fight it abroad. Rood concluded that U.S. influence ought to be exerted abroad so that strategic threats to the United States may be contained or canceled without recourse to full-scale or general war. The corollary, according to Rood, is that if you want to avoid fighting a big war, be prepared to fight a lot of little ones. To execute this strategy, the United States must have bases abroad from which to conduct military operations. Wars with Eurasian powers almost invariably require America to have allies in Eurasia if the war is to come out successfully.

By contrast, according to many experts in the field of international relations, there is no longer any need for massive military bases on the continent of Eurasia from which to fight a general or major regional war, and little need to worry about the military security of the Western Hemisphere. They claim that the existential threat posed by nuclear weapons ensures that prolonged continental-scale wars by great powers are no longer possible, and assume that there are no Hitlers or Stalins around who harbor grandiose ideological ambitions. Even for those who acknowledge that the world is still a violent and difficult place, there is a belief that, to the extent that any military facilities outside the United States are necessary, they should be designed primarily to serve political purposes and to support limited counterterrorism operations. For the most part, however, the current wisdom has it that the United States should deploy its military assets at home, or at sea and over the horizon, where they will not irritate the locals or unduly threaten great powers like Russia and China. According to this viewpoint, modern technology obviates the need for boots and airplanes based on the ground, and thus the United States does not need so many boots and airplanes.

Rood challenges this comfortable assumption about America's geopolitical security. The central fact remains: if a hostile power or group of powers is able to dominate the territory and resources of Eurasia, by whatever means, it will overshadow the resources of the United States and be in a position to control the global economy and threaten militarily the Western Hemisphere. Western allies on the continent of Asia can resist such an attempt only with substantial American support, and it is yet to be proven that remote, off-shore, high-technology, non-nuclear means will be sufficient to that purpose. Nuclear threats by the United States raise all the same problems of credibility and strategic and operational purpose that they did during the Cold War, especially if the initial aggression (or threatened aggression) is local and incremental. To base one's security on the assumption that a general threat to Eurasian security — one that must be met in place by an in-place, countervailing military alliance — can never occur again, is to say that history has indeed ended.

There are certainly good reasons to be cautious about where and how the United States may want to intervene militarily, especially in order to preserve or create access to military bases on the mainland of Eurasia. But such bases, from time to time, will be required, often to meet unexpected contingencies, some of them perhaps deep inside the continent. Before 9/11, who would have imagined that the United States would find itself at war in Afghanistan? If the United States does not "own" such bases it must obtain the consent of the locals, or of other great powers, to use their facilities — which means that it must have or acquire allies. That will only be possible if the United States retains a reputation for military competence and political reliability, something difficult to achieve if we are far over the horizon or have fewer boots and airplanes (and ships). Rood challenges us to think through the priority locations of those bases in Eurasia — the lodgments — that we simply cannot afford to abandon. Still more, he would advocate that we periodically undergo a "stress test" that examines our ability to meet a serious military challenge outside the canonical regional war scenarios.

To be sure, military power is not all that is required to assure stability and security in Eurasia. But we should take seriously Rood's persistent challenge — "What if there's a war? Who will win?" These may not be the only questions that public officials, military officers, scholars, and citizens should ask themselves, but they are certainly among the most important.

## NOTES

1. Harold W. Rood, "China's Strategical Geography and Its Consequences," in Vol. 1 of *China and International Security: History, Strategy, and 21st Century Policy*, ed. Donovan C. Chau and Thomas M. Kane (Santa Barbara, CA: Praeger, 2014), 1.

2. For such a nuanced perspective, see Walter A. McDougall, *Promised Land, Crusader State: The American Encounter with the World Since 1776* (New York: Houghton Mifflin, 1997); and Walter Russell Mead, *Special Providence: American Foreign Policy and How It Changed the World* (New York: Knopf, 2001).

# Appendix A

## In Memoriam: Harold W. Rood (1922–2011)

Harold W. (Bill) Rood was born in Seattle, Washington, on August 19, 1922, and grew up at the Mare Island Naval Yard in California. He entered the Army Enlisted Reserve Corps in September 1942 (called to active duty in March 1943), where he was trained as a coast artillery gunner. The army sent him to Stanford University to study engineering. He later served as a heavy machine gunner/radio operator in the Seventh Army, and in Patton's Third Army, in the European Theater of Operations.

After the war, Rood continued his undergraduate studies at Shrivenham American University, and Worcester College, Oxford, and obtained his BA from the University of California–Berkeley, in 1948. He did graduate work at the London School of Economics and at the University of California–Berkeley, where he was awarded both his MA in International Relations in 1952 (thesis on the role of the United States in the formation of the United Nations) and PhD in Political Science in 1960 (dissertation on American preparations for war, 1918–1940). His dissertation adviser was Paul Seabury, another gentleman-scholar with a wit very much like that of his student, and with a similar appreciation of the necessities of power. Rood helped put himself through graduate school by working as a Senior Laboratory Assistant in the Microbiology Section, Department of Bacteriology, at UC–Berkeley.

During this time of study, when the Korean War broke out, Rood applied successfully for a commission in the Army Reserve. He became an order of battle specialist and then a strategic intelligence analyst. He later served on the staff and faculty of the Sixth Army Intelligence School, Fort Ord and Fort MacArthur, California (1958–1964, 1968–1974). He became a member of a special army intelligence unit staffed by reservists, including for a time Edwin Meese, a close associate of then-California Governor Ronald Reagan. In 1969 he worked briefly on arms control and U.S. nuclear doctrine as a civilian in the Pentagon.

Rood was appointed to the government department faculty of Claremont Men's College (CMC) in 1962, just before the Cuban missile crisis, an event about which he later had much to say and write. In due course he was promoted to associate and full professor, and in 1982 he was named the first W. M. Keck Foundation Chair of International Strategic

Studies. He established himself as a favorite among the CMC undergrads while attracting a loyal following from the Claremont Graduate School (University). His roster of classes became campus staples, including Introduction to International Relations (a rite of passage for CMC students); Politics and Technology; Diplomacy and Military Power; and Constitutional Development in the West.

Rood won multiple Outstanding Teacher Awards at CMC, even though his views diverged from the antiwar and antimilitary conventions of the times. His article on the Vietnam War, "Distant Rampart," was the 1967 Gold Medal prize–winning essay in the U.S. Naval Institute *Proceedings*. He was prevailed upon to collect his thoughts in *Kingdoms of the Blind: How the Great Democracies Have Resumed the Follies that So Nearly Cost Them Their Life* (1980). During the 1960s and 1970s, he did classified and unclassified research for the Stanford Research Institute, a defense research contractor, in Menlo Park, California, where he lived with his wife, Juanita, and daughters Hilary and Elizabeth. He taught three days a week in Claremont, arriving on an early morning flight from San Francisco to Ontario on Monday, and departing for home on Wednesday evening. While in Claremont, he spent his time outside the classroom mentoring students who would later achieve considerable prominence in politics, government service, the military, the media, business, and the academy. But he also made time for those of lesser ambitions who nevertheless had a serious interest in strategy and in their country.

Rood retired from CMC in 2001, but he continued to lecture and write for the Claremont Institute and the *Claremont Review of Books*. He also continued to teach in the Defense and Strategic Studies Program established by William Van Cleave (his first PhD student at Claremont Graduate School), first at the University of Southern California and then at Missouri State University. A few weeks before his death in 2011, he told his former students and colleagues that he was writing about the strategic significance of the Philippines. They immediately began to take note of what was going on in the Western Pacific.

# Appendix B

## *Professor Harold W. Rood's Selected Reading List*

Adcock, Sir Frank. *The Greek and Macedonian Art of War*. Berkeley: University of California Press, 1957.

———. *The Roman Art of War under the Republic*. Rev. ed. Cambridge: Heffer, 1940.

Allen, J. W. *Germany and Europe*. 2nd ed. London: G. Bell & Sons Ltd., 1915. First published 1914.

Anderson, M. S. *The Eastern Question: 1774–1923, A Study in International Relations*. Houndmills, UK: Macmillan, 1991. First published 1966.

Angell, Norman. *The Great Illusion: A Study of the Relation of Military Power to National Advantage*. Auckland, NZ: Floating Press, 2014. First published 1909.

Baldwin, Ralph B. *The Deadly Fuze: The Secret Weapon of World War II*. San Rafael, CA: Presidio, 1980.

Barnett, Corelli. *The Sword Bearers: Supreme Command in the First World War*. London: Cassell, 2000. First published 1963.

Barraclough, Geoffrey. *The Origins of Modern Germany*. 3rd rev. ed. Oxford: Blackwell, 1988. First published 1946.

Baxter, J. P. III. *Scientists against Time*. Cambridge: MIT Press, 1968.

Bernhardi, Friedrich von. *Germany and the Next War*. Charleston, SC: Bibliobazaar, 2006. First published 1912.

Braisted, William Reynolds. *The United States Navy in the Pacific, 1897–1909*. Annapolis, MD: Naval Institute Press, 2008.

Browning, Reed. *The War of the Austrian Succession*. Palgrave Macmillan, 1995.

Bywater, Hector C. *Sea-Power in the Pacific: A Study of the American-Japanese Naval Problem*. Carlisle, MA: Applewood, 2002. First published 1921.

Caesar, Julius. *The Gallic War*. Translated by Carolyn Hammond. New York: Oxford University Press, 1999.

Cantrell, Robert. *Understanding Sun Tzu on the Art of War*. Arlington, VA: Center for Advantage, 2003.

Carter, Kit C., and Robert Mueller. *The Army Air Forces in World War II: Combat Chronology, 1941–1945*. Washington, DC: U.S. Government Printing Office (hereafter GPO), 1973.

Chandler, David. *The Campaigns of Napoleon*. New York: Scribner, 1973.

Charteris, John. *At G.H.Q.* London: Cassell, 1931.

Churchill, Winston S. *The River War*. NuVision Publications, 2007. First published 1899.

———. *The Second World War*. 6 vols. New York: Houghton Mifflin, 1948–1953.

———. *The World Crisis*. Rev. and abr. ed. New York: Free Press, 2005.

Clausewitz, Carl von. *On War*. Translated by Michael Eliot Howard and Peter Paret. Princeton, NJ: Princeton University Press, 1989. First published 1832.

Cole, David Henry. *Imperial Military Geography: General Characteristics of the Empire in Relation to Defence*. 12th ed. London: S. Praed, 1956. First published 1930.

Colville, H. E. *Official History of the Sudan Campaign: Compiled in the Intelligence Division of the War Office*. Uckfield, UK: Naval and Military Press Ltd., 2005. First published 1890.

Dalline, David J. *Russia and Postwar Europe*. 5th ed. New Haven, CT: Yale University Press, 1948. First published 1943.

Duff, Mountstuart E. Grant. *Studies in European Politics*. Whitefish, MT: Kessinger, 2007. First published 1866.

Elliott, James Gordon. *The Frontier 1839–1947: The Story of the North-West Frontier of India*. London: Cassell, 1968.

Ferguson, Bernard. *The Watery Maze*. London: Collins, 1961.

Fischer, Fritz. *From Kaiserreich to Third Reich: Elements of Continuity in German History, 1871–1945*. Translated by Rodger Fletcher. New York: Routledge, 1991. First published 1986.

———. *Germany's Aims in the First World War*. London: Chatto & Windus, 1967.

———. *War of Illusions: German Policies from 1911 to 1914*. Translated by Marian Jackson. London: Chatto & Windus, 1975.

———. *World Power or Decline: The Controversy Over Germany's Aims in the First World War*. Translated by Lancelot L. Farraar, Robert Kimber, and Rita Kimber. New York: Norton, 1974.

Fisher, David E. *A Race on the Edge of Time: Radar—The Decisive Weapon of World War II*. New York: Paragon House, 1989.

Forester, C. S. *Brown on Resolution*. Bath, UK: Chivers, 1999. First published 1929.

———. *The Good Shepherd*. Safety Harbor, FL: Simon, 2001. First published 1955.

Fraser-Tytler, William K. *Afghanistan: A Study of Political Developments in Central and Southern Asia*. 2nd ed. New York: Oxford University Press, 1958.

Freeman, Roger A., Alan Crouchman, and Vic Maslen. *The Mighty Eighth War Diary*. Osceola, WI: Motorbooks International, 1990.

Frost, Holloway Halstead. *The Conduct of an Overseas Naval Campaign*. Washington, DC: GPO, 1920.

Fuller, J. F. C. *Julius Caesar: Man, Soldier, and Tyrant*. New Brunswick, NJ: Rutgers University Press, 1965.

Fullerton, William M. *Problems of Power: A Study of International Politics from Sadowa to Kirk-Kilisse*. London: Hesperides, 2006. First published 1913.

Gathorne-Hardy, G. M. *A Short History of International Affairs, 1920 to 1939*. 4th rev. ed. London: Oxford University Press, 1964. First published 1934.

Gibbs, N. H. *Grand Strategy*. London: Her Majesty's Stationery Office, 1976.

Gilbert, Martin. *First World War Atlas*. 2nd ed. London: Weidenfeld & Nicolson, 1985. First published 1970.

———. *Prophet of Truth, 1922–1939*. Vol. 5 of *Winston S. Churchill*. Boston: Houghton Mifflin, 1977.

Graham, C. A. B. *The History of the Indian Mountain Artillery*. Aldershot, UK: Gale & Polden, 1957.

Grant, A. J., and Harold Temperley. *Europe in the Nineteenth and Twentieth Centuries*. 2 vols. London: Longman, 1986. First published 1932.

Great Britain Admiralty. *British Vessels Lost at Sea, 1914–1918*. Cambridge: Stephens, 1977.

———. *British Vessels Lost at Sea, 1939–1945*. Cambridge: Stephens, 1977.

Grey, Sir Edward. *Twenty-Five Years, 1892–1916*. London: Hodder & Stoughton, 1985. First published 1925.

Hale, Oron James. *The Great Illusion, 1900–1914*. New York: Harper & Row, 1971.

Hamill, Ian. *The Strategic Illusion: The Singapore Strategy and the Defence of Australia and New Zealand, 1919–1942*. Singapore: Singapore University Press, 1981.

Herodotus. *The Persian War*. Translated by William Shepherd. New York: Cambridge University Press, 1982.

Hopper, Bruce C. "Narkomindel and Comintern." *Foreign Affairs* 19 (1940): 737–50.

Hornblower, Simon. Vol. 1 and 2 of *A Commentary on Thucydides*. New York: Oxford University Press, 1996.

Horne, Alistair. *To Lose a Battle: France 1940*. Rev. ed. London: Penguin, 2007. First published 1969.

————. *The Price of Glory: Verdun 1916*. Rev. ed. London: Penguin, 1993. First published 1962.

Hoyt, Edwin P. *The Lonely Ships: The Life and Death of the U.S. Asiatic Fleet*. New York: Jove, 1989. First published 1976.

Jelavich, Barbara. *A Century of Russian Foreign Policy, 1814–1914*. New York: Lippincott, 1964.

————. *History of the Balkans*. 2 vols. Reprint, Cambridge: Cambridge University Press, 2006. First Published 1983.

Jelavich, Charles. *Tsarist Russia and Balkan Nationalism: Russian Influence in the Internal Affairs of Bulgaria and Serbia (1879–1886)*. Reprint, Westport, CT: Greenwood, 1978.

Johnson, Douglas Wilson. *Topography and Strategy in the War*. Washington: U.S. Marine Corps, 1989. First published 1917.

Jomini, Baron de. *The Art of War*. Translated by G. H. Mendell and W. P. Craighill. Gloucester, UK: Dodo, 2007. First published French 1836, English 1862.

Jones, R. V. *Most Secret War*. Ware, Hertfordshire: Wordsworth Editions, 1998.

Kato, Masuo. *The Lost War: A Japanese Reporter's Inside Story*. New York: Knopf, 1946.

Kerner, Robert. *The Urge to the Sea: The Course of Russian History*. Berkeley: University of California Press, 1971. First published 1942.

Kirby, S. Woodburn. *Singapore: The Chain of Disaster*. New York: Macmillan, 1971.

Langer, William L. *The Diplomacy of Imperialism*. 2nd ed. New York: Knopf, 1968. First published 1935.

————. *European Alliances and Alignments 1871–1890*. Reprint, Westport, CT: Greenwood, 1977. First published 1931.

Langer, William L., and S. Everett Gleason. *The Undeclared War 1940–1941*. Gloucester, MA: P. Smith, 1968. First published 1953.

Lewin, Ronald. *Ultra Goes to War: The Secret Story*. London: Penguin, 2001. First published 1978.

Liddell-Hart, B. H. *The History of the Second World War*. London: Pan, 2014. First published 1970.

————. *The Real War: 1914–1918*. Norwalk, CT: Easton, 1994. First published 1930.

Lipsom, E. *Europe in the Nineteenth and Twentieth Centuries*. 8th rev. ed. London: A&C Black, 1960. First published 1948.

Luttwak, Edward. *The Grand Strategy of the Roman Empire: From the First Century A.D. to the Third*. Baltimore, MD: Johns Hopkins University Press, 1979.

Luvaas, Jay. *Frederick the Great on the Art of War*. New York: Da Capo, 1999.

MacCartney, C. A., and A. W. Palmer. *Independent Eastern Europe*. London: Pan Macmillan, 1962.

Mackinder, Halford. *Britain and the British Seas*. Whitefish, MT: Kessinger, 2007. First published 1902.

————. *Democratic Ideals and Reality*. Westport, CT: Greenwood, 1981. First published 1919.

Mackintosh, John Malcolm. *Juggernaut: A History of the Soviet Armed Forces*. New York: Macmillan, 1967.

Mahan, Alfred Thayer. *The Influence of Sea Power upon the French Revolution and Empire, 1793–1812*. Whitefish, MT: Kessinger, 2007. First published 1892.

————. *The Influence of Sea Power upon History, 1660–1783*. Charleston, SC: Bibliobazaar, 2007. First published 1890.

————. *The Interest of America in Sea Power, Present and Future*. Charleston, SC: Bibliobazaar, 2007. First published 1897.

————. *Lessons of the War with Spain*. North Stratford, NH: Ayer, 1970. First published 1899.

————. *The Life of Nelson: The Embodiment of the Sea Power of Great Britain*. Whitefish, MT: Kessinger, 2007. First published 1897.

————. *The Major Operations of the Navies in the War of American Independence*. IndyPublish.com, 2007. First published 1913.

————. *Naval Administration and Warfare: Some General Principles, with Other Essays.* Boston: Little, Brown, 1908.

————. *Naval Strategy: Compared and Contrasted with the Principles and Practice of Military Operations on Land.* Washington, DC: U.S. Marine Corps, 1991. First published 1911.

————. *The Problem of Asia and Its Effect upon International Policies.* New Brunswick, NJ: Transaction, 2003. First published 1900.

————. *Sea Power in its Relations to the War of 1812.* Whitefish, MT: Kessinger, 2006. First published 1905.

Malone, Patrick M. *The Skulking Way of War: Technology and Tactics among the New England Indians.* Lanham, MD: Madison, 2000.

Marder, Arthur. *From Dreadnought to Scapa Flow.* 5 vols. Annapolis, MD: Naval Institute Press, 2013–2014. First published 1961–1970.

Marriott, J. A. R. *The Eastern Question: An Historical Study in European Diplomacy.* 4th ed. Oxford: Clarendon, 1969. First published 1917.

Marriott, J. A. R., and C. Grant Robertson. *The Evolution of Prussia: The Making of an Empire.* Hardpress.net, 2013. First published 1917.

Matsuo, Kinoaki. *How Japan Plans to Win: The Three-Power Alliance and the United States Japanese War.* London: Harrap, 1942. First published 1940 in Tokyo.

Maxwell, Neville. *India's China War.* London: Pan, 1999. First published 1967.

Middlebrook, Martin, and Chris Everitt. *The Bomber Command War Diaries: An Operations Reference Book 1939–1945.* Osceola, WI: Motorbooks International, 1996.

Millar, George. *The Bruneval Raid: Stealing Hitler's Radar.* 2nd ed. London: Cassell, 2004. First published 1974.

Monsarrat, Nicholas. *The Cruel Sea.* Reprint, London: Penguin, 2009. First published 1951.

Morgan, J. H. *Assize of Arms: The Disarmament of Germany and Her Rearmament (1919–1939).* New York: Oxford University Press, 1946.

Morris, Donald R. *The Washing of the Spears.* New York: Da Capo, 1998.

Moulton, J. L. *Warfare in Three Dimensions.* Athens: Ohio University Press, 1968.

Murray, Williamson. *Strategy for Defeat: The Luftwaffe 1933–1945.* Honolulu, HI: University Press of the Pacific, 2002.

Naumann, Friedrich. *Central Europe (Mittel-Europa).* Westport, CT: Greenwood, 1971. First published 1917.

Nicolson, Harold. *The Congress of Vienna: A Study in Allied Unity, 1812–1822.* 13th ed. New York: Viking, 1969. First published 1946.

Ogg, David. *Europe in the 17th Century.* 8th ed. New York: Collier, 1965. First published 1925.

Oman, Charles. *The History of the Art of War in the Middle Ages.* Rev. ed. Ithaca: Cornell University Press, 1960.

Peckham, Howard H. *The Colonial Wars, 1689–1762.* Chicago: University of Chicago Press, 1965.

Prange, Gordon. *At Dawn We Slept: The Untold Story of Pearl Harbor.* London: Penguin, 2001. First published 1981.

Price, Anthony. *Other Paths to Glory.* London: Orion, 2002. First published 1974.

Rodgers, W. L. *Greek and Roman Naval Warfare: A Study of Strategy, Tactics, and Ship Design from Salamis (480 B.C.) to Actium (31 B.C.).* Norwalk, CT: Easton, 1991. First published 1937.

Rohwer, Jürgen. *Axis Submarine Successes of World War Two: German, Italian and Japanese Submarine Successes in World War II, 1939–1945.* Rev. ed. Annapolis, MD: Naval Institute Press, 1999.

Rohwer, Jürgen, and Gerhard Hümmelchen. *The Chronology of the War at Sea, 1939–1945.* 3rd ed. London: Chatham, 2005. First published 1974.

Rohwer, Jürgen, Judy Soloway Kay, and I. N. Venkov. *Allied Submarine Attacks of World War Two: European Theatre of Operations 1939–1945.* Annapolis, MD: Naval Institute Press, 1997.

Ross, Stephen T. *European Diplomatic History, 1789–1815: France Against Europe.* Malabar, FL: Krieger, 1986. First published 1969.

Rostow, W. W. *Pre-Invasion Bombing Strategy: General Eisenhower's Decision of March 25.* Austin: University of Texas Press, 1981.

Ryan, Cornelius. *A Bridge Too Far.* London: Hodder, 2007. First published 1974.

———. *The Longest Day.* Hauppauge, NY: Barron's, 2014. First published 1959.

Saul, Norman E. *Russia and the Mediterranean, 1797–1807.* Chicago: University of Chicago Press, 1970.

Schevill, Ferdinand. *A History of the Balkans: From the Earliest Times to the Present Day.* New York: Dorset, 1991. First published 1922.

Schwartz, Seymour I. *The French and Indian War, 1754–1763: The Imperial Struggle for North America.* New York: Book Sales, 2000.

Seton-Watson, Hugh. *Eastern Europe between the Wars.* Boulder: Westview, 1986. First published 1945.

Seton-Watson, R. W. *Disraeli, Gladstone and the Eastern Question.* 2nd ed. London: Routledge, 2004. First published 1935.

———. *Sarajevo: A Study in the Origins of the Great War.* Reprint, New York: H. Fertig, 1973. First published 1926.

Sidorenko, A. A. *The Offensive: A Soviet View.* Honolulu, HI: University Press of the Pacific, 2001. First published in English 1970.

Sontag, Raymond J. "The Democracies and the Dictators since 1933." *Journal of the American Philosophical Society* 98, no. 5 (1954): 313–17.

Spears, Edward. *Assignment to Catastrophe.* London: Reprint Society, 1964. First published 1954.

———. *Liaison 1914: A Narrative of the Great Retreat.* London: Weidenfeld Military, 1999. First published 1930.

———. *Prelude to Victory.* London: J. Cape, 1939.

Spykman, Nicholas J. *America's Strategy in World Politics: The United States and the Balance of Power.* New Brunswick, NJ: Transaction, 2007. First published 1942.

———. *The Geography of the Peace.* Edited by Helen R. Nicholl. Reprint, Hamden, CT: Archon, 1969. First published 1944.

Still, William N. *American Sea Power in the Old World.* Westport, CT: Greenwood, 1980.

Stillwell, Paul. *Air Raid: Pearl Harbor! Recollections of a Day of Infamy.* Annapolis, MD: Naval Institute Press, 1981.

Sun Pin. *Military Methods.* Translated by Ralph D. Sawyer. Boulder: Westview, 1995. First published 4th century BC.

Sun Tzu. *The Art of War.* Edited by James H. Ford and Shawn Conners. Translated by Lionel Giles. El Paso Norte Press, 2005. First published 6th century BC.

Taylor, A. J. P. *Struggle for the Mastery of Europe.* Oxford: Clarendon, 2007. First published 1942.

Terraine, John. *Douglas Haig: The Educated Soldier.* London: Hutchinson, 1963.

———. *Ordeal of Victory.* Philadelphia: Lippincott, 1963.

———. *The U-Boat Wars, 1916–1945.* New York: Holt, 1990.

———. *To Win a War: 1918 The Year of Victory.* London: Cassell, 2003.

Thucydides. *History of the Peloponnesian War.* Rev. ed. Edited by M. I. Finley. Translated by Rex Warner. Boston: Penguin, 1954.

Topitsch, Ernst. *Stalin's War: A Radical New Theory of the Origins of the Second World War.* New York: Palgrave Macmillan, 1987.

Trotsky, Leon. *Military Writings.* Atlanta, GA: Pathfinder, 1971. First published 1924.

United States Joint Army-Navy Board. *Joint Overseas Expeditions.* Washington, DC: GPO, 1933.

United States President's Air Policy Commission. *Survival in the Air Age: A Report of the President's Air Policy Commission.* Washington, DC: GPO, 1948.

Watt, Richard. *Bitter Glory: Poland and its Fate, 1918–1939.* New York: Hippocrene, 1998. First published 1979.

Wheeler-Bennett, J. W. *Brest-Litovsk: The Forgotten Peace, March 1918*. New York: Norton, 1971. First published 1939.

———. *Hindenburg: The Wooden Titan*. London: Macmillan, 1967. First published 1936.

———. *Munich: Prologue to Tragedy*. 3rd ed. New York: Viking, 1968. First published 1948.

———. *The Nemesis of Power: The German Army in Politics, 1918–1945*. 2nd ed. New York: Palgrave Macmillan, 2005. First published 1953.

Wheeler-Bennett, J. W., and Anthony Nicholls. *The Semblance of Peace: The Political Settlement after the Second World War*. New York: Norton, 1974.

Whittaker, C. R. *Frontiers of the Roman Empire: A Social and Economic Study*. Baltimore: Johns Hopkins University Press, 1997.

Wilmont, Chester. *The Struggle for Europe*. Ware, UK: Wordsworth Editions, 1997. First published 1952.

Wilson, Trevor. *The Myriad Faces of War*. Faber & Faber, 2010. First published 1986.

Winslow, W. G. *The Fleet the Gods Forgot: The United States Asiatic Fleet in World War II*. Annapolis, MD: Naval Institute Press, 1994. First published 1982.

Wohlstetter, Roberta. *Pearl Harbor: Warning and Decision*. Stanford, CA: Stanford University Press, 1962.

Wolff, Robert Lee. *The Balkans in Our Times*. Rev. ed. Cambridge, MA: Harvard University Press, 1974. First published 1967.

Woytak, Richard. *On the Border of War and Peace: Polish Intelligence and Diplomacy in 1937–1939 and the Origins of the Ultra Secret*. New York: Columbia University Press, 1979.

Xenophon. *The Persian Expedition*. Rev. ed. Translated by Rex Warner. New York: Penguin, 1950.

Ziemke, Earl F. *From Stalingrad to Berlin: The German Defeat in the East*. Barnsley, UK: Pen & Sword, 2014. First published 1968.

# Appendix C

## *Win a Few, Lose a Few: World War II Remembered*

Harold W. Rood
*Claremont Review of Books,* Summer 1985. Reprinted by permission.
*Following named Enlisted Reservists are ordered to active duty. Will proceed from University of California, Berkeley, California, so as to report to Commanding Officer, Reception Center, Presidio of Monterey California:*
And there is my name followed by a serial number, 19133185. Thus began my first advanced course in the study of international relations, that game of politics, so entrancing, frustrating, and dangerous.

It was not, however, the introductory course; that had come from my father. He had served on the U.S.S. *Smith* (PG-17), a gunboat of the U.S. Naval Militia of the State of Louisiana, in the landing at Vera Cruz, Mexico, in 1914. When the United States entered World War I, he was on the U.S.S. *Oklahoma* which, together with the *Utah* and *Nevada*, formed a Special Detachment to the British Grand Fleet, escorting troop convoys to Brest, France, from the United States. In 1919, *Oklahoma* escorted President Wilson, who was on the liner *George Washington*, to France for the Peace Conference. My father drove the President to Paris to stay at the Crillon and on tours of the battlefields of France, and, when the Peace Conference was over, back to Brest where the *Oklahoma* escorted the President back to the United States.

Where I grew up on the navy yard at Mare Island, the armor plate and sixteen-inch guns of what was to have been the battleship *Montana* lay but a few blocks away from our house. Those great chunks of steel were the relics of the naval disarmament conference held in Washington in 1921 and 1922. That was the conference that promised to bring peace to the Pacific. *Montana*, along with its sisters, was scrapped to meet the requirements of the treaty concluded at Washington. Nearly completed, it was said that *Montana* cost more to break up than it would have cost to finish. Thus a first experience in what we would later come to call "Arms Control and Disarmament."

From time to time my father's shipmates from the war would come through the navy yard from the China Station or the Asiatic Fleet. Then there would be tales told of the days at war and accounts given of the troubled times in the Far East. When the U.S.S. *Panay* was sunk above Woosung in December 1937, the theater at the navy yard showed Norman Alley's film of the sinking. Alley was on the *Panay* when it was attacked and sunk by aircraft of the Imperial Japanese Navy. Thoughtful people seemed to understand, at the time, that the United States might become involved in the war that was going on in the Far East.

There was a copy of the first American edition of *Mein Kampf* in the house, and we listened to broadcasts from Berlin when correspondents like William L. Shirer gave accounts of the progress of the Nazis in Europe. My father would say, "Well, we shall have to go over there again and finish the job we should have finished in 1918."

The names of the ships of the Pacific Fleet were like household words to us: *California, Nevada, Oklahoma, Pennsylvania, Tennessee*—all part of the Battle Force. They used to come into San Francisco, where we would visit them while my father looked up old shipmates. *San Francisco* and *Chicago* were cruisers built at Mare Island, and we saw them launched. *Northampton* carried one of my father's best friends from the war, so there were always larks in the household when that ship came into port. Those ships were all part of the Scouting Force of the Pacific Fleet.

My schoolmates, who rode the bus with me to Vallejo, were sons and daughters of naval or marine officers. They had all lived at one time or another in places like Guantanamo, Colon, Cavite, Shanghai, or Peking. It was hardly possible, in the ordinary course of things, to escape having some impression about the nature of the world beyond the shores of California.

When it came time to take a job to earn money to go to college, I delivered mail to the ships of the Pacific Fleet when they stopped at Mare Island for an overhaul. Nearly every ship, in due course, would become notable for some action in the war. Ships that were built at Mare Island warranted special attention in their careers. Of the 52 submarines lost in World War II, five of them were built at Mare Island, so that one saw them launched and commissioned, and then watched them depart on war patrol. All five were lost in the Pacific.

The first serious book on European politics I ever had was *Failure of a Mission: Berlin, 1937–1941*, by Sir Neville Henderson, British Ambassador to Germany. It was given to me by a friend who served on the U.S.S. *Houston* when that ship was last in the United States. That was in 1940, when *Houston* was at Mare Island before going out to become flagship of the Asiatic Fleet. Its sinking off Java during an attack on Japanese troop transports meant the end of the U.S. Asiatic Fleet. The Japanese picked up nearly 400 survivors of the 1,000-man crew of the *Houston*. Some of them survived the Japanese prison camp.

The mail clerk from the U.S.S. *Kitty Hawk* gave us the first news of the attack on Pearl Harbor that Sunday morning. Some of the damaged ships came to Mare Island for repairs. Though we knew that my father's' old ship, *Oklahoma*, had been lost in the attack, the extent of the damage to the Pacific Fleet was not public knowledge, but the flow of wounded into the naval hospital at Mare Island and those who came into the yard on damaged ships told the story of devastation.

If the war in the Far East was close to home, the war in Europe was hardly less so, especially after the fall of France in 1940. Classmates from high school went to Canada to volunteer for the Royal Air Force. To those who were yet too unworldly to understand that the war in Europe was our war, too, the travelers to Canada were a curiosity.

The war in Europe would not become a personal matter until 1944 at Fort Benning, Georgia. In November, the 71st Division was alerted for overseas movement. The time of movement was a closely held secret, but you could tell when the movement to a Port of Embarkation was close. The Post dry cleaners stopped taking uniforms for cleaning from members of the division. As it turned out, that meant we should be moving out in less than a week.

So we proceeded from Fort Benning to Camp Kilmer, New Jersey, and then on to troopships at Brooklyn. The troopships joined a convoy off Sandy Hook and, under escort, crossed the Atlantic in about nine days. There were many calls to General Quarters aboard ship, much sanding on deck in life jackets as the escorting destroyers laid depth charges at every suspicious ping on their ASDICS. On February 5 we laid up off Southampton. The town was blacked out because England was still under air attack and attack from V-1s and V-2s. At dawn on February 6, we were escorted through the minefields off Le Havre to enter that harbor, full of sunken ships and the wreckage of war.

It was difficult to get off the ships which, having passed through the German submarine menace, now seemed safe havens compared with unfamiliar France. It did make one wonder whether the act of volunteering to enter upon what had by this time come to be seen as a dangerous enterprise, was really the thing to have done. All of those people working overtime in defense plants at home, able to sleep with their careful wives, earning good salaries, seemed to represent the essence of probity and discretion. But then, one reflected, there were folks with the mule-pack artillery in Burma or getting their feet wet in landings on Japanese-held islands in the Pacific who might conceivably be worse off than we who were about to enter combat in France.

Somewhere between Grémonville and Yvetot, not far from Rouen in Normandy, the division unpacked equipment, picked up more from as far away as Antwerp, and prepared to move out to the fighting. It was all pretty routine, living in tents in the cold French countryside. One knew it was to become more serious, however, when, one day, a month after landing in France, they began to issue real, live ammunition. One had had live ammunition before, to fire on the range, to go on guard duty, and to shoot at towed targets. Those times, however, every round had to be accounted for and unexpended rounds carefully returned. This time, we were issued boxes of .50 caliber ammunition for the heavy machine guns. Every fifth round was a tracer, with two incendiary rounds and two armored-piercing rounds in between. Then there were rounds for the bazookas to be used in defense against tanks, grenades (high-explosive, smoke, and white-phosphorus), ammunition for the carbines, and a full, basic load for each of the 1055mm howitzers. Nobody had to sign for anything. *Then* you knew it was serious. When the multiplex forms and the paperwork ceased to make their appearance, it was evident that a new dimension of the real world was about to be entered.

Even the first sergeant, whom we affectionately called "Wrinklehead" and other names more anatomically descriptive, when his back was turned, became quite friendly. He had the sense of humor of a copperhead with heat rash but had now become quite somber. No doubt it was the rumor that drifted down from the 14th Infantry. Some rifleman up there, upon being issued bandoleers of ammunition for his M-1 rifle, had expressed his evident distaste for a particularly odious first lieutenant by firing eight quick rounds through the officer's tent. It was said that the officer was then sent home on a slow freighter without escort. Only just, as it seemed at the time. Riflemen were worth their weight in rubies. First lieutenants were a dime a dozen—particularly odious ones.

Then there was the long night-time drive across France, passing through the outskirts of a darkened Paris, to an obscure village called Montbronn, to support the 100th Division in its attack on Bitche.

Most of us found it all quite interesting and, at times, more exciting than absolutely necessary to those who had by then become inclined toward a more sedentary life. Fighting through the fortifications of the German Westwall, driving to the Rhine at Speyer, then crossing the Rhine at Oppenheim with the Third Army seemed a piece of cake. We were held up for a day at Offenbach, outside Frankfurt, while 1,100 bomber aircraft hit Frankfurt to soften the defenses for the assault. Then it was on to Fulda and south to Regensburg where there was a battle, to Bayreuth, and finally into Austria. The war ended there when the division met the Red Army outside Linz.

Every day there was something to catch the attention of serious students of history: great cities in ruins and villages held by the SS, and by children and old men enlisted in local defense units. Allied bombers and fighters lay crashed in the fields along the route of advance; before us was scattered the wreckage of a retreating German Army that had but a short time before been master of Europe. Thousands upon thousands of prisoners of war were marched to the rear together with equal numbers of displaced persons, some liberated from the Germans and others fleeing westward to escape the Red Army.

Going through the woods, outside Fulda, I met a young woman with a small child. She asked about her husband, whom she said was a prisoner of war in the United States. What could one say, in halting German? He would come home soon because *"Der Krieg was aus. Alles ist kaput."*

The division overran three or four concentration camps. Here was evidence of a horror dissolving all sympathy for a beaten people: pitiful, starved figures so emaciated that their gender could hardly be distinguished, dead and dying by the hundreds. Those yet on their feet begged cigarettes and food. We gave them all we had and blankets and overcoats to protect their chilled frames from the raw winds of April. So some were saved, and some died from eating the food we had given them, which was too rich and too much of a shock for their starved systems. The least reflective of us could wonder at the terrible barbarism that had for six years ravaged Europe. The unforgettable signs were those dreadful concentration camp uniforms hanging like shrouds on the bodies of the dead and near dead. If the war had not made much sense before, it did now.

Somewhere near Steyr in Austria, the war ended in Europe. But that did not finish the curriculum in international politics. The division began its role in the Army of Occupation.

Those who cared to volunteer to go to the Pacific could do so. It was easy to volunteer. Having been through one war and surviving, a second war seemed less fearful than the first had been. Volunteers might expect a promotion and therefore a raise from 54 dollars a month plus the extra 10 dollars for being overseas in a combat zone (if one were a private first class). The real reason was that those who volunteered might expect to get ten days leave at home before they went to the Far East for the invasion. That was not to be sneered at. But it was not an unhappy day when news came of the atom bombs on Hiroshima and Nagasaki, ending the war against Japan. It did not require a high school education to understand that if one made it through one war alive and whole, the statistical chances of surviving an invasion of Japan were probably about zip.

The Army of Occupation did constabulary work. It manned roadblocks looking for war criminals and members of the SS who had evaded Allied authorities; conducted early-morning and late-night searches of hamlets, villages, and towns, looking for caches of arms laid up for some future resistance; helped restore public services and civil government; processed prisoners of war; and cared for thousands upon thousands of displaced persons.

The displaced persons included people who had been slave-laborers all over Europe, impressed for work in German factories and on German farms. There were thousands of Germans who had fled their homes under Allied bombing or who had fled from the advancing Red Army: parents looking for children, families seeking relatives, wives looking for husbands. Few had anything but the clothes on their backs and maybe a battered briefcase or handbag with a meager handful of precious possessions. Those precious possessions were seldom heirlooms—such things had had to be sold to buy food—but rather were keepsakes, pictures of loved ones, and letters from family members long gone.

It was a simple problem to repatriate the French, the Dutch, the Belgians, Norwegians, and Danes. They would be welcomed home, and home they would go. Those who belonged in the Russian zone of occupation—Poland, Hungary, and such places to the East—were less fortunate. Through an agreement among the Allies, those who came from the Russian zone and Eastern Europe were to be returned to Russian control. It was the only way that Allied prisoners of war and others from the West who had been overrun by the Red Army would be returned to Western control. The exchange was appropriately called "Operation Keelhaul."

Truckload after truckload of displaced persons from the East were taken to the border between East and West. They were not welcomed home. Some were marched eastward in long columns under the machine guns of Red Army soldiers. Many were taken behind some building or over some hill and executed out of hand. You could hear the machine-gun fire.

There was a young girl, maybe 18 or 19 years old, who sat huddled with her companions in the back of one of our six-by-six artillery trucks. Pitifully, she tried to catch the eye of her soldier-escorts, displaying her charms as if flirtatiously. It was not flirting, it was an appeal for help, for she knew, as did her companions, what return to Russian control meant. The young American soldiers did not know. How could one believe that the gallant Red Army, our brothers-in-arms, who had helped to rid Europe of the Nazi barbarians, could be no less barbaric, treating helpless refugees like enemies. That poor girl, trying so hopelessly to barter her body for survival to young men too innocent to grasp the significance of her gesture and ignorant of what lay ahead for those they had been given to safeguard on the journey east.

Forty years passes on: We have kept the peace in Europe at whatever cost. The barbarian Empire to the East has prospered and grown. France is revived and restored. Poland, where the war started, is still a prisoner. Czechoslovakia, sold out in 1938, left to the Russians in 1948, dances to an Eastern tune. Germany is divided, the East as much a captive of totalitarianism as it ever was under the Nazis, and West Germany a hostage to Western good behavior. And the British—they who fought on alone while the United States got half ready—their country is sad, dispirited, impotent, and dejected.

Forty years on. They said in that other war that the world could not exist half slave and half free. Yet here it is—still half slave and half free. All those reasons for the destruction of the Nazis—slave labor, concentration camps, anti-Semitism, totalitarianism, unprovoked war against a helpless people—are no longer reason enough for cold anger. That which was spawned under the broken cross of Nazism passes unnoticed when sprouting beneath the Hammer and Sickle. So here is the world, forty years on, more slave than free. And those who are free feign sleep to avoid that which must be faced. But there is no sleep for those who would stay free when the forces of barbarism are on the move.

If international politics teaches anything, it is that the strong do what they will, and the weak can but submit. But it is only the strong who can afford to be kind and only the strong who can protect the weak.

It is forty years since the ending of that great war when we all knew the justice of our cause. Should one now say that the cause is lost, or do those who cherish freedom dare defend it wherever it is threatened, to restore it where it has been lost?

Has the price of freedom now become too high, so that we shall, piece by piece, bit by bit, surrender that which forty years ago seemed precious beyond life itself?

# Bibliography

## The Writings of Harold W. Rood

Rood, Harold W. "AVOT—Harold W. Rood on the War in Iraq." Claremont Institute. October 2007. http://www.claremont.org/projects/pageid.2501/default.asp.

———. "China's Strategical Geography and Its Consequences." In Vol. 1 of *China and International Security: History, Strategy, and 21st Century Policy,* edited by Donovan C. Chau and Thomas M. Kane, 1–17. Santa Barbara, CA: Praeger, 2014.

———. "China's Strategy: Past, Present and Future." Unpublished manuscript, last modified 2011. Print.

———. "Commentary on Books and Other Works Useful in the Study of International Relations." *Classics of Strategy and Diplomacy.* Ashbrook Center. Accessed November 12, 2012. http://www.classicsofstrategy.com/strategyanddiplomacy/rood.pdf.

———. "The Constitution and National Defense." Claremont, CA: Public Research, Syndicated, January 1987.

———. "Courage Alone Is Not Enough Today." Claremont, CA: Public Research, Syndicated, 1980.

———. "Cuba: Payment Deferred." *National Review,* November 27, 1981.

———. "Distant Rampart." U.S. Naval Institute *Proceedings* 93 (March 1967): 30–37.

———. "Early Warning, Part I." *Grand Strategy: Countercurrents,* December 1, 1982.

———. "Early Warning, Part II." *Grand Strategy: Countercurrents,* February 1, 1983.

———. "Early Warning, Part III." *Grand Strategy: Countercurrents,* March 15, 1983.

———. "Early Warning, Part IV." *Grand Strategy: Countercurrents,* June 15, 1983.

———. "The 'Eastern Question' and Beyond." *Global Affairs* 3 (Spring 1988): 196–203.

———. "The Eastern Question: 'Peace in Our Times.'" Unpublished manuscript, last modified 1989. Print.

———. "Economy of Force." Unpublished manuscript. Print.

———. "Forty Years On: A Soldier Reflects." Claremont, CA: Public Research, Syndicated, October 30, 1985.

———. "A Free Society in an Unfree World: Peace, Justice and Defense." Unpublished manuscript. Print.

———. "Grenada: The Strategic Dimension." *Claremont Review of Books* 2, no. 4 (Winter 1983). Accessed July 18, 2014. http://claremontinstitute.org/index.php?act=crbArticle&id=1452#.U8bdQLEUp2A.

———. "Handwritten Notes on Gorbachev and Reform." Unpublished manuscript, last modified 1988. Print.

———. "The Increasing Soviet Presence in the Pacific." Claremont Institute, 1988.

———. *Kingdoms of the Blind: How the Great Democracies Have Resumed the Follies that So Nearly Cost Them Their Life.* Durham, NC: Carolina Academic Press, 1980.

———. "The Long View: Democracy and Strategy in Iraq." *Claremont Review of Books* 3, no. 4 (Fall 2003). Accessed July 18, 2014. http://www.claremont.org/article/the-long-view-democracy-and-strategy-in-iraq/#.VAsGtfldUpg.

———. "'Masters of the Narrow See': The British Isles in the Defense of the West." *Grand Strategy: Countercurrents,* October 1, 1981.

———. "Military Operations Against Cuba." *Claremont Quarterly* 9 (Winter 1963): 5–18.

————. "The Naiveté of George Kennan." *Claremont Review of Books* 4, no. 3 (Fall 1985). Accessed July 18, 2014. http://claremontinstitute.org/index.php?act=crbArticle&id=1556#.U8beZ7EUp2A.

————. "Naked to our Enemies." Claremont, CA: Public Research, Syndicated, 1980.

————. "Norway: Bastion of the North." *Grand Strategy: Countercurrents*, March 1, 1982.

————. "Political, Not Military: The Flaws of Western Deterrence." *Grand Strategy: Countercurrents*, December 1, 1981.

————. Remarks at the CEI Conference, Claremont, CA, April 20, 1979.

————. "The Sinews of Peace and the River of Time." Unpublished manuscript, last modified May 19, 1992. Print.

————. "Southeast Asia." Unpublished manuscript. Print.

————. "Soviet Strategy and the Defense of the West." *Global Affairs* 2 (Summer 1987): 1–19.

————. "The Strategy of Freedom." *Grand Strategy: Countercurrents*, July 1, 1981.

————. "Strategy out of Silence: American Military Policy and the Preparations for War, 1919–1940." PhD diss., University of California, 1960.

————. "Toward a Defense of the West: Spain." *Grand Strategy: Countercurrents*, August 1, 1981.

————. "The War for Iraq." Claremont Institute. April 2003. http://www.claremont.org/publications/pubid.285/pub_detail.asp.

————. "Why Fight in Vietnam." *Infantry Magazine*, November–December 1967.

Van Cleave, William R., and Harold W. Rood. "Spread of Nuclear Weapons." *Military Review* 46 (December 1966): 3–10.

————. "A Technological Comparison of Two Potential Nuclear Powers: India and Japan." *Asian Survey* 7 (July 1967): 482–89.

# Index

# About the Authors

**Dr. J. D. Crouch II** was a student of Professor Harold W. Rood in the early 1980s while pursuing a Master's and PhD at the University of Southern California. He taught at Missouri State University in the 1990s after Professor Rood returned from there to California. His career in government included positions as adviser to the U.S. Delegation on Nuclear and Space Arms Talks with the former Soviet Union in the mid-1980s, military legislative assistant to the late Senator Malcolm Wallop in the late 1980s, principal deputy assistant secretary of defense for international security policy in the early 1990s, assistant secretary of defense for international security policy in 2001–2003, U.S. ambassador to Romania in 2004–2005, and assistant to the president and deputy national security adviser from 2005–2007. He remains active on several government advisory boards and is a senior adviser at the Center for Strategic and International Studies in Washington, D.C.

**Dr. Patrick J. Garrity** is a research faculty associate with the Miller Center of Public Affairs at the University of Virginia. He holds the PhD in government from the Claremont Graduate School, where he studied with Professor Harold W. Rood. He has been a senior policy analyst (technical staff member) at the Los Alamos National Laboratory; a research fellow at the Center for Strategic and International Studies (CSIS); and a visiting fellow at the Johns Hopkins University School of Advanced International Studies (SAIS). He taught at the Catholic University of America and the Naval Postgraduate School. He is the author of *In Search of Monsters to Destroy? American Foreign Policy, Revolution, and Regime Change, 1776–1900*; the coauthor of *A Sacred Union of Citizens: George Washington's Farewell Address and the American Character*; and coeditor of the forthcoming digital edition, *The Nixon White House Recordings: SALT, February–May 1971*.